Conversions

A Philosophic Memoir

My fellow-phil.
student at PSU!
Too damn smart...

Conversions

A Philosophic Memoir

Abigail L. Rosenthal

Temple University Press, *Philadelphia*

Temple University Press, Philadelphia 19122
Copyright © 1994 by Temple University. All rights reserved
Published 1994
Printed in the United States of America

Library of Congress Cataloging-in-Publication Data

Rosenthal, Abigail L.
    Conversions : a philosophic memoir / Abigail L. Rosenthal.
      p.   cm.
    Includes bibliographical references.
    ISBN 1-56639-219-5. — ISBN 1-56639-220-9 (pbk.)
    1. Rosenthal, Abigail L. 2. History—
Philosophy.   3. Philosophers—New York (N.Y.)—
Biography. I. Title.
B945.R5274A3   1994
191—dc20   93-44719
[B]

To Léo Bronstein
1902–1976

Contents

Preface ix

Part 1 The Realm of Essences

Chapter One	Beginningwise	3
Chapter Two	Paris without End	23
Chapter Three	Green Age	37
Chapter Four	Purity and Impurity	47
Chapter Five	The Sense of the Argument	57
Chapter Six	Shoreline	65
Chapter Seven	*La Méthode éternelle*	77

Part 2 Analytic

Chapter Eight	Of the Impossible Position of the Jews	99
Chapter Nine	Of Silence in General	107
Chapter Ten	*¡Venceremos!*	117
Chapter Eleven	Of Women and Philosophy	131

Part 3 Another Paradigm

Chapter Twelve	By the Narrow Way	149
Chapter Thirteen	A Competitive Conversation	157
Chapter Fourteen	A Conversion	173
Chapter Fifteen	Thought Reform	179
Chapter Sixteen	Framed	195
Chapter Seventeen	Policía Internacional	217
Chapter Eighteen	Beginning Again	239
Epilogue		263
Notes		267

Preface

A recent exhibit at the New York Public Library at Forty-second Street, "400 Years of Native-American Portraits," included a painting on muslin that was titled "Picture history: Scenes from the life of a Sioux chief." The date given for the muslin was 1880, and the wall plaque explained it as follows:

> The picture histories of the Plains Indians were accurate portrayals of actual individuals and actual events. "The picture is the rope that ties memory solidly to the stake of truth," according to one Sioux historian. Individuals were identified, not by their facial features as in the European tradition, but rather by details such as shield paintings, war bonnets, and hair arrangement, which were specific to each warrior and never exactly duplicated.

The "picture history" from which this "philosophic memoir" is drawn was first set down on paper by me in the first year after the events with which this narrative concludes. That draft was finished in the fall of 1968. It was the most detailed, the most fully furnished with vivid images of scenes that I still remembered clearly. So *it* was "the rope" that tied memory "to the stake of truth." But other versions followed, in 1974, 1978, and 1982.

With each version, I was trying to discover more about the reasons these things had happened and the reasons I had lived them as I had. Each new interpretation that I came to, successively, that guided a specific draft, allowed heretofore lost recollections to float up to the surface of awareness once again—sometimes a smell, sometimes a word—and with them a whole riddle of experience unlocked. But the whole thing did not hang together. I could not see the *why* of it, from first to last.

I set it aside, therefore, in 1982, to begin work in earnest on the philosophic work that appeared in 1987 under the title, *A Good Look at Evil*, which was published by Temple University Press, with the invaluable help and encouragement of Jane Cullen, who was senior acquisitions editor at Temple. The next major project, put in my path as it were, was the preparing for publication of my father's posthumous book, *The Consolations of Philosophy: Hobbes's Secret; Spinoza's Way*, which was published, also with warm help and support from Jane Cullen, her expert colleagues, and David Bartlett, the director of Temple University Press, in 1989.

About a year after that book's publication, I felt sufficiently "in form" philosophically to confront those manuscript drafts once again, to try once and for all to find the thread of coherent, lived argument that ran through them. This time I reread each of the four main earlier drafts as I went along. Through the years, while I'd been typing each earlier version, I had talked with the people who were still alive, accessible to me, and who had shared some part of the story with me, checking their recollections against mine. I continued to do that. And, for the first time, I also brought myself to face the *correspondence* that pertained to what had once been an official dossier on me, going through all the letters, from me and about me, that had been in my father's files, and all the cables and the postcards. What I knew of the diplomatic side I had learned from my parents, the late Henry M. Rosenthal and the late Rachelle Rosenthal, when the story was over, in 1967. But the whole of what they told me then is borne out in the correspondence that I have been going through in recent months.

There was an issue of privacy. With regard to others, apart from family, who played a part in this story, I have changed their names and what I judged to be nonessential but identifying details for those people whom I believe to be still alive. The names of the dead I have left unchanged. The decision to drop the pseudonym I had used in the earlier drafts was a painful one. What I had found by experience, however, was that I could not recover the truth of the story—as I meant to do this time *without fail*—if I disguised so central a piece of it as the name of the storyteller.

This is a narrative about the influence of ideas on the narrator.

As such, with some shifts of emphasis, it is still an illustrative case of the "good story" that was defined and explained in *A Good Look at Evil*.[1] However, whereas in the earlier book, "history" was mentioned briefly as a kind of regulative ideal of the concept of story but did not otherwise play a great role there, here what is claimed is that the individual story itself is only made *fully intelligible* if it is seen as a localization of "world history." Nevertheless, the earlier concept of individual story as lived argument is maintained in this book.

So that guiding purpose—to show the argumentative thread—was what governed the selection process as I culled from these earlier drafts and other evidences. Where a certain kind of event repeated itself many times over, I have given only one or two instances. That applies above all to the events of Part 3, with all of which there was no need to bludgeon the reader. (However, if the narrative makes clear that something happened *only* once, then *that* is true, and to be believed.) In a few cases, for economy's sake and for the sake of showing how the ideas *combined to have their influence on me*, I have compressed into a single conversation what was strung out over two or more. But I have not knowingly changed what people said to me, or what I said to them, substantively. Where third-party conversations were reported to me, I have recorded them exactly as reported. And the fact that these are third-party reports is indicated in the text. Also, in the conversations that I was a party to, turns of phrase are as exact as I can make them, mostly relying on the 1968 draft for details.

Other things have been left out, of course: animal functions; the little grudges that lodge in the system; the low-level hysterics of daily life. All that *happens*. One could write a book about it. It happens, plenty. But, over the long pull, as one looks back on one's life (when one believes one is gravely ill, for example, as I have done now and again), those little convexities flatten out. The aerial view does not detect them. They are not the main event. They are the minor distresses of corporeal life.

But what about the "projections"? What about the "displacements"? What about the fact that I was perhaps associated from time to time with very angry people because I either "could not" or would not live my own anger directly? Well, yes. What about all that? Doesn't that take away from "the honesty" of this report, however sincerely the honesty is intended?

What is anger? Benedict de Spinoza had a lot of reasons to be angry, and I therefore borrow my answer from him, with all due respect.[2] Anger arises in the frustration of purposes, intimately held.

If (following the recommendations of Spinoza) one's chief concern is, all the same, to *pursue* those initial purposes, making them as realistic (in Spinoza's exalted sense of the word) as they can be, then one has not got that much *time* for one's anger. So, it may well be that one becomes curious about it (the anger) and watches its unfoldment *in others* with some sort of dazed or dizzying fascination.

Nevertheless, the more interesting questions—released by that curiosity—have to do with *why* those others were angry, after all. What long-term purposes that they had were frustrated and lived on, dissolved, in their anger? That is the more interesting question. In that question, the human face, human discourse, and the common bond are to be rediscovered.

The rest (about anger) belongs in the museum—where we collect and store the gargoyle faces that line the route we so laboriously climb up, the route of human history. Mere anger, raw, divorced from its intentionality, is not that interesting. The same goes, oddly enough, for mere lust that is served up raw, divorced from *its* intentionalities. *Pace* Nietzsche. I at least must refuse these invites to hell, however warmly they are pressed on us.

So much for the truthfulness of this memoir of my twenties, and its accuracy in the face of its emotions. And now just a brief statement on the score of its philosophical thoughtfulness.

Thought is truly thought when it acts. Act is truly act when it thinks. Governing idea and agency are inextricably bound up with one another in a life. This book, which is a true story, as true as I can get it to be, as true as I can remember and tell, is also an account of this thoroughgoing merger of life and thought. What here may be "philosophical," in the sense of exhibiting rigor, is just this microscopic responsiveness to each other of the thought and the life, and the corrigibility—in the space of one's own time—of these lived hypotheses.

The moment has arrived to thank certain people. The nature of this project made me reluctant to draw on the advice of colleagues and friends who did not know the story, at least until I was most of the way through the writing of it for the last time. The list of those I can name, who helped, is therefore a relatively short one. The real people, some of them nameless here perforce, who helped me *at the end of the events* narrated here have my great gratitude and will always have it.

My father and mother, my sister Lucy Rosenthal, and a few other people who were appropriately qualified and knew the story—such as Elsa Grossman, the late Léo Bronstein, and, later, John Bacon—read one or more of the earlier drafts and gave me their helpful reactions, some of which (in the case of my parents) I have recorded in the space of this narrative. To all these people, present and absent, my thanks are due.

Among the other things that Léo said to me, affectionately, was this: "All your life you have searched for *purity*. And you found it, finally, in the one thing one can find on earth that is absolutely pure: *evil*."

Without evil, its correlative, good, and the struggle to maintain one's moral identity over time, there is no story, in my opinion. There is no "history," in the sense that will be articulated here. There is no romance, in the sense that this story is one.

To those of my students at Brooklyn College who labored with me through an elective course in the philosophy of history in the spring of 1992, where some of the views of history set down here were first adumbrated, a tribute is due and now happily given. I am also much obliged to the Board of Trustees of the City University of New York, to Brooklyn College, and to my colleagues in the Department of Philosophy there, for granting me the two term-long sabbatical leaves that made it possible for me to complete this book at this time.

I feel very fortunate that Peggy Brooks has remained a supportive friend to this project through the years. With Cristina Aldana Duckett, and with my philosophical colleagues Mary Bittner Wiseman and Edith Wyschogrod, some of the problems that I was fielding as I went down the homestretch were aired and put in perspective in those splendid conversations that we had. For their support and friendship, I am most thankful.

Acknowledgments are also due to Claude Choquet, for kindly correcting my rusty French, and to Manuela Soares and her overseas family, for graciously doing the same for my still-rustier Portuguese.

The owners, the staff, and the regulars at Food Liberation—John Sr., John, Peter, Ward, J. T., Terry, Douglas, et al.—provided spirited and tactful company when I would stop in at odd hours, for lunch or an afternoon break. To all of them too, a salute.

Sandy Deak's sterling professionalism as word processor–typist was indispensable. Joan Vidal as production editor and Roberta Hughey as copy editor played vital, highly constructive parts in the production of this book. I am indebted to all those at Temple University Press who have been concerned with this project. And to Jane Cullen, for once again extending to me her wise and supportive editorial guidance all the way through, I am most happy to be able to express my gratitude at this time.

Part 1

The Realm of Essences

Chapter One

Beginningwise

When I was a young girl, my chief aim in life was to become a famous saint, a great lover, or both. Not right away, of course, but when at length I would be grown up.

What above all I did *not* want was to settle into being the usual sort of grown-up, who never said exactly what he or she meant—it was impossible under the clothes and the posturing and the arbitrarily changing colors of the skin to tell what the person meant or whether he or she had ever really meant anything, and whose life seemed through and through a willed construct.

It wasn't that I held people like that in contempt. In one way I admired their abilities to patch together constructs that were so nearly consistent, so close to persuasive, that teetered on the brink of the genuine and were adorned with so many authentic elements, and then, after the initial burst of creative engineering, to remain so nicely and civilly confined within these shelters to which apparently they alone held the keys. But what attracted me about becoming a great lover or an outstanding saint was that I thought that neither of these things was an artifact. These things represented to me ways to become real.

My parents, and a few parental friends within their inner circle, were to me real. I was essentially their fascinated student, and being their child just gave me the chance to study with them longer—as I think about all that now.

A few years back, I wrote a philosophical article about my parents, and more especially about my mother, which piece was titled "The Filial Art." It was my tribute to the great art with which my mother practiced the calling of mother, and my attempt to work out in fairly educated terms what might be the reciprocal, daughterly art. I couldn't get it published in America, but *finally* I got it published in England.

Then, more recently, I have seen to the posthumous publication of my father's *Consolations of Philosophy: Hobbes's Secret; Spinoza's Way*, writing its biographical as well as accompanying philosophical introduction. Although most of the philosophical critics whose reviews I have read so far have been almost startlingly appreciative—both of him as an author more than ten years dead and not obviously a power in the profession and even of me as his faithful filial mediator—in the present-day profession of philosophy itself, we are not exactly celebrating efforts to live in *the historical mode*. By that I mean living with ceaseless attempts to see one's present thought, feeling, and action as the precise outcome of a long but clarified past, woven of persons and ideas—and speakable. Yet these writer-editor efforts of mine fully to express my sense of filial piety have been such attempts, to live in the historical mode. And to complete the course of my studies with my parents.

In the sharpest and steepest contrast imaginable, as if one were visualizing a vertical line of jagged cliffs juxtaposed against the horizontal sweep of ocean waves, the emphasis in more fashionably current philosophical writing would still be rather on the fault lines, the places where you *couldn't* see the connections, the junctures where, for one reason or another, the original thread of meaning was being dropped.

For example, in the English-speaking world, the attention of philosophers has of late been focused on the question of "personal identity"—how it is that I know I'm me. The usual claim nowadays is that I *don't* know, not really, and—face to face with the hazards of neuron misfirings, memory blackouts, surgical severings of the corpus collosum, evolutionary maladaptations, and incoherently conditioned role playing—"personal identity" tends to dissolve, under analysis, into mere floating islands of experience. Analogies with the chinoiseries of Buddhist antimetaphysics have been from time to time openly acknowledged by these tough-minded analytic philosophers, whose commitment to the latter-day microparticle materialism of the West remains otherwise staunch. Put these two, great, cultural floating islands together (the episodic in Buddhism and in current Western "personal identity theory"), as some people do these days, and you have the kind of pseudo-Buddhist koan that doesn't get you anywhere: the sound of one bare foot tapping—on a rock it can't find.

So the theme and rhythm of quite a lot of current philosophical writing is still the episodic. On the Continent, that sort of thing used to be called "the absurd." But even to call something "absurd," one must *follow* it for a while. Which is why the absurd is passé too.[1] Not too many people will give something undivided attention for long enough to find out whether it really *is* absurd or not. Perhaps a visitor from another era might think that there had not been enough devotion among us even for that much detective work to happen.

In the course of devotedly following Socrates around, Plato *discovered* personal identity. The real thing, I mean, not the current subdiscipline. What today we often look at instead, under the heading of "personal identity," is the discontinuous.

In decided contrast, both of my parents had this exceptional power to be "historical": to be themselves from the beginning, to remain so over time, and to become even more so by the end of their lives. It was as if they had internalized some invisible filament within the time process. What current philosophy would want to say about such a talent, I don't precisely know. I think that, for the most part, when it wears its professional guise, it is unaware that there is such a thing as a genius for that. Either it is unaware, or it is professionally undisturbed by the awareness.[2]

Actually, great people are a kind of mirror in which other people can see their many little faces crowded together in reflection. Apart from the very few friends of the inner circle, people in general looked in the great convex mirror of my parents and saw what they themselves brought to the mirror—what psychoanalysis purports to see, or cultural anthropology: biological and cultural detritus, in other words. They saw some sort of conscious vital force that made them uneasy and got various labels. Among the labels was "Jewish," or "something Jewish"—whatever they meant by that.

In the spring of 1979, when I was in the sixth year of a struggle to be reinstated with tenure at Brooklyn College of the City University of New York, I myself had an experience of "something Jewish."

I was walking from the studio apartment on the Upper East Side where I lived to what was then called the Board of Higher Education (now the Board of Trustees), where yet one more hearing on my case was to be held that morning. There was about a mile and a half to be trudged over, and I was carrying a heavy satchel, loaded with all the documents that pertained to that stage of my case.

It was a late spring day and rather warm, even that early in the morning. I was quite weary. I felt so alone. My father had died two years before. My mother would begin to die that summer, as perhaps I already sensed. The people I would soon be seeing, from the side of my adversaries, I knew and had seen many times before.

For me they had become cartoon figures, like the ones in Daumier's cartoons about the law: greenish or reddish, insulated from innocence, smiling their secrets of the bureaucracy at one another, talking over their padded shoulders and behind their cupped hands, all safely salaried by the city. I had no job contract for that fall. The building, which I also knew, the Board, had the smell of countless old, official miseries on its heavy concrete shanks.

Finally, I was headed down the last block, the one that goes from York Avenue to the East River, on Eightieth Street. (The Board is sometimes referred to, simply, as "Eightieth Street.") As I remember it there was a concrete overhang, just before the door of the Board. The long block I was walking slanted downhill, toward the concrete overhang at the far end of the block, and the river.

Suddenly I perceived that there were figures behind me, a whole series of them, one behind the other, connected to one another apparently, and the nearest one connected almost umbilically to me. They were vibrating at a faster rate than we do (at that same moment I became aware that we human beings "vibrate" too), and they seemed to be about a foot or more off the ground, on a kind of path of their own, made—like them—of finer stuff, something like the "yellow brick road" in *The Wizard of Oz*. This path of theirs wound its way above the concrete sidewalk I traversed now as if it had always been there: an additional world behind the visible one.

I was not able to see these figures as clearly as one sees real people or, for that matter, hallucinations. Nor were they as faded and porous as daydream figures. They had a specificity—there were details—that I could not have put in a daydream. In clarity, they were somewhere between real and daydream figures. I was afraid to turn and look at them as they stretched out behind me, lest they fade altogether.

As to what they looked like, they had silvery shimmering garments. One could not see their feet. They were bearded, but *not* with the white, "Old Testament," patriarchal beards that one sees in Protestant children's Sunday school book illustrations—and which had been part of my Jewish iconography too, since my grandfather had looked like that. My grandfather (the one who was a Talmudic scholar) had been tall and muscular, white bearded and heroic, like God in the Sistine Chapel, and that's what I would have expected the archaic Jewish appearance to be. But these figures had black, tight-curled, "Assyrian" beards. So they did not look as I expected.

Nonetheless, they were connected to me by the most warm and intimate of liens. I could not tell if they were rabbinic ancestors or something else. They did not have much individuation. But they knew *me* very well. And their line stretched back and back to their point of absolute origins: Ur of the Chaldees. They went as far back in time as it is possible for anything Jewish to go. They went all the way back to the beginning: straight and direct.

Now their path wound on ahead of me till its left and right edges met together in a point, the way parallel lines appear to meet at the horizon. Only this point was not at the horizon, since their path came to closure just under the concrete overhang that presaged the Board of Higher Education.

They were saying something to me, which I could hear distinctly, though it was not audible to the ear: You have been on a pilgrimage. You have been on a long pilgrimage, they said. And it is over.

Just as the parallel lines of the path that they walked had curved together and met right at the door of the BHE, so it was over, now. Nothing could be clearer.

The concept of "pilgrimage" is not Jewish as such. But it was not unfamiliar to me. In my heart of hearts, I had long felt that it must have been the secret of this case. Whatever people cared to say about it, it had been a fight for justice, I felt, in a small but real historical context. And the fight's true witnesses could not have been the bystanders with the reductive descriptions ("self-destructive," "naïve," "foolhardy," and so on). So they must have been *these* figures, who had been above the battle, but near it, the whole time. I didn't look at them, even sidewise, any more. Afraid to lose them, I looked on ahead, and they faded as I came up to the dark entrance of the building.

While it is certainly possible to read this as a projection, thrown upon the screen of my senses by nearly intolerable sorrow, fatigue, and despair—and anyone is free to do that who likes—I myself did not decide to doubt my vision. That is, whatever the undertow of thought and emotion jouncing around in me, I did not doubt it on the practical level.

Perhaps I was all out of ideas by that time. Or I didn't have any better ideas. In any event, I *acted* as if it were all over. At the hearing, I didn't intervene over the small points, of advantage or disadvantage to me, that were being contested. I did not fight for myself any more. By and large I just sat there, absent, slumped, cherishing this small warm light of certainty in my heart.

Afterward, in midsummer, when an official from the Professional Staff Congress (the union) telephoned the summer home in Maine where I was visiting my mother, with the good/bad news that I was to be sent back to the college—but for yet another corrosive year of harassment miscalled "evaluation"—my fear and frustration found their voices in the sobbing protest, "They lied to me! The rabbis lied to me! It's *not* over." But when, about a year later, in the summer of 1980, another union official rang the phone in Maine again, this time with the amazing message that I was being granted tenure "retroactive to 1979," I understood instantly. It *was* over. It *had been* over, ever since the day "they" had said so. "They" had changed the past.

Some time after these events, I was describing this vision to a very old friend. My friend was a painter who had been imprinted in childhood with the folklore of certain lost, Eastern European, Jewish villages. When I'd sufficiently sketched for her (verbally) the picture of these rabbis, or ancestors, her eyes half filled with tears. "Angels," she said softly. "They were angels."

"But I thought angels were blond and had wings."

"Not Jewish angels," she shook her head, with a wry half smile.

The Jewish angel is the angel of history. The Jewish province is the province of history. The Jewish concept is the concept of history.[3] That is the reason those angels were so strikingly on target about the *time frame* of that part of my pilgrimage.

This book is what one would call a philosophic memoir and so forms a part of a personal history. The genre presupposes some concept of world history, of which an autobiographical work would be illustrative on the local or first-person level. Saint Augustine wrote the first such complete autobiography, *The Confessions*, which starts at the beginnings of his personal memory and ends with his account of his life's purpose achieved.

Augustine's *Confessions* is not just a slice of adult experience, such as someone might write who had advised a succession of presidents, or conducted a series of battles, or perhaps led a succession of forays into the literary caves, the bars and the dens, as a raconteur-scribbler. What Saint Augustine wrote was, as he believed, the *full* story of himself. Such an effort can only be made to work against the backdrop of "world history," the full story of humankind itself, which Augustine had of course also attempted to sketch out, in his *City of God.*

World history precedes personal history in the logical sense that the whole is always prior to its parts. That is to say, where there is any understanding to speak of, the parts are understood through the whole—not the whole through the parts. But also, in the experience of living, one does not get to see how the circle of one's life reaches closure merely by adding part to part, seriatim. (So much, on the negative side, our friends in personal-identity theory have in fact rediscovered. The floating islands *don't* a continent make. The continents *don't* a globe make. About that, they are quite right, only neglecting to note that one has to start with the globe. Otherwise, one doesn't know where the islands are, or which island one is talking about.)

But test this. Try starting the other way, just with memory and without a world-historical framework. Go back to the beginning. Leave all the "general concepts" out of it. Try. Can you even remember who or what you were at the beginnings of empirical memory? Who can recover memory pure? I remember how it *felt* to be me, but always the memory is blurred by the jarring admixture of welcome and disapproval with which I was being herded through the early fence posts of experience. There was always a bit of surprise about the welcoming and also about the disapproving. I felt I was neither the one welcomed nor the one disapproved of, really. The welcomers and disapprovers saw in me much more determinateness than I felt was there. I was simply that passage through that field of experience.

The "fence posts" through which I was being herded were the words, the gestures, the decor, the behavioral practices and codes of conduct, and the theoretical links that said: You are moving from here to there, or from there to here. And (wittingly or not), your trajectory has signaled your intent and fixed the outcomes in certain ways. And people have been doing this, facing in one direction or another, for a long time. We know what these other people are. We know where they are. They are all part of a bigger picture, of the biggest picture, of the animated, set-to-music, great machine painting of world history.

Yes. That is everybody's childhood—even the childhood of the personal-identity theorists—who neglect to recall how they too were historically schooled, but in the highly stylized practice of *dis*-connection (which has its own theories of history), and by whom they were so schooled, and with what penalties of ridicule and rough handling attached. "Dis-connect certain designated patches of experience, one from the other, or else we will dis-connect you, small patch, from the rest of us." So went the instructions, implicit and explicit, and they were not delivered just once.

If one is born, as it happens, a Jew, one ought to try to understand what is called "world history," for one is being situated within that thing daily in childhood—by word and gesture, by welcome, by admonition, by decor and encoded conduct, and, in many cases, by explicit hypothesis. The Jew's historical understanding does not precisely follow the lines of the Augustinian hypothesis. It is the older, the original one of its type, of which Saint Augustine wrote the most influential revision. Augustine did not work directly from the original Jewish understanding of history either, but from Paul's, who had written "the version for export."[4]

The Jewish concept is of course biblical. It includes, among other components, briefly the following: a short span of total historical time, with an absolute beginning and a last chapter, and a single pair of human ancestors who in some important respects resemble their Creator. Note: We are not talking about whether there is any reason under heaven to *believe* this narrative, nor even about whether there is a God. Here we address only the question of what the biblical concept of history *is*.

This concept forms a contagious part of the Western psyche as such. People who have believed in nothing have yet appeared to believe in something—evidently derived from the biblical concept—which they have called "history." When the French existentialist-phenomenologist Maurice Merleau-Ponty recalls a young friend who was later to die heroically in the French Resistance saying, after the Hitler-Stalin pact of 1939, "Je n'ai pas de philosophie de l'histoire," he is recollecting a cry of cultural despair that reverberates down the tunnel of time, as we know time in the West.[5] And, in the West, we experience time partly the way the Bible represents it.

As has been said, the time to be reckoned with is quite short in the Bible. In the rabbinic view, only 5,755 years have elapsed (as of A.D. or C.E. 1994) since the creation. The rabbis simply continued to count in the generation-linked-to-generation fashion worked out in Genesis. The point is that the human imagination can wrap itself around such a time in its entirety. It is epic time, of course, but this is one single, vast, unitary epic. The whole world, with all its ethnic and economic and natural-disaster and border-dispute subplots, is included in the unbroken epic. When, at last, the earth, which "is the Lord's," comes to be "filled with the knowledge of God," the epic will have been concluded, and we will all get leave to go home—whatever "home" is. We'll just give a prize to the bard and get out—wherever "out" turns out to be. S'finished, we'll be able to say. For it *will* all be finished, one bright day, on the biblical view. (Whatever has to be finished, will be. Whatever doesn't have to be finished, won't be.)

It is quite otherwise with the times of the world-ages of India or of the pre-Socratics—say, Anaximander or Democritus—or for that matter of the contemporary cosmologist, which are limitless. There is nothing in the human imagination that can frame such times as that. Framed *by* such times, all that we mortals can say or do in our short lives will seem to be taking place on a narrow strip of stage, artificially rigged with lights and briefly swept bare, behind which great, red, dark-mouthed boundlessness will still hang like a curtain.

But history in the biblical sense of the term is a movement from its absolute beginning to an end that purports to resolve on a higher level the problems implicitly present at the beginning. This last-page "resolution" can be interpreted mystically, as the Kabbalists do, or eschatologically, as traditional Judaism and Christianity have done (things may not get better in the interim, but the messiah will arrive to set them right at the end). Or it can be resolved into wholly secular terms, as presumably Merleau-Ponty and his "young friend" had done. Then it turns into the theme of secular progress, by violent or peaceful means, toward a time of universal enlightenment and beneficence. Or all three interpretations can have play together. But without it, without this universal narrative with an absolute beginning and a better end, the "young friend," who had a real name but is perhaps also ourselves, despairs. Despairs and loses hold of personal identity, precisely *because* he or she cannot attach that to the longer story. And then, after the despair, the young friend can, if we like, make—out of all those successive, differently ranked losses—a new fashion. The fashion of the episodic.[6]

Only the biblical God could start and stop time itself (or everything that counts for us about time), irreversibly, at once, and at will. This, more even than His freedom from sex and death, is probably the meaning of His exalted, much-vaunted "transcendence." To this kind of God-limited time, add the way in which the Book of Genesis traces all human origins to a single pair, created—as the book famously says—"in the image" of God.

What sort of role or responsibility the parental man/woman will have as this mirror or reflection of God is not as yet clear. But it must obviously be large enough to satisfy all who are concerned. It must therefore be something profoundly dramatic, in the way of a role. To do justice to the demands of such a story, one ought at least to try to imagine oneself as its bard, and in that way come to see what sort of song *must* be sung on this theme.

The theme, as we recall, will be this: Here at the beginning is one human race, without internal strata, class divisions, or fissures of any kind. From it an epic will spin itself out that—whatever it may contain that is too much or too little—will still be *short enough to be remembered* by all who are concerned. And all will have to be concerned, one way or the other, since all are herein attested to have a common ancestor, patrimony, and inborn tendency to try to be the mirror of God. (I'd be concerned about the meaning of such an *attestation*, even were I thoroughly convinced that there was no God.)

Such a theme would be quite taxing to work out—and of course fashionable despair will have no funds from which to pay such a tax—but what *was* the tax? How was it to be reckoned? Who paid it, and when, and why?

Here is where Judaism and Christianity differed. It was not over *who* the messiah was.[7] The schism between Judaism and Christianity is over *what* the messiah is, and so more fundamentally over what the saving principle of history is. Thus it is a real difference over the meaning of history. To see what this difference amounts to, let us return to "the beginning."

Something must have happened to set the biblical epic in motion. Something purportedly solemn and terrible. Let us call it "the first disobedience." Why? Why did he do it? Why did Adam sin? And (this was the even-more-solemn question), why did God create him with that fatal flaw and then punish him so terribly? These are the human questions to which the messiah's advent is supposed to be God's answer.

These human questions are so terribly boring, however, that one can only conclude that they must be the wrong questions. No matter what kind of a religionist, or lapsed or former religionist, one is, this can't be a good job of question formulation. If God exists, He isn't boring. Even if He doesn't exist, our misguided hope in Him couldn't be so stupid and boring as that. This is sheer obfuscation. Let us try to see through it, to a clearer view of the biblical epic.

The Fall is to "history" as cosmogony is to cosmology. The "very beginning" is something that, by definition, we were not present at and cannot observe. Any hypothesis about it would therefore have to be an extrapolation from what data we do have to an inferred best explanation.

The data we have on this subject are collected for us into the whole connected human narrative so far as it goes: the biblical epic itself, after the Fall. Once we see clearly what is there, in the narrative after the Fall, we can work backward, to the question of origins, or causes. Very well. What *is* there?

We find people, after all. They suffer, more often than not. They fight, for various reasons. They win, sometimes. They don't win, at other times. They are liable to get sick. Sooner or later, they die

or are removed from the scene. They have lifelong intimate relations, and these are almost inseparable from their lifelong human
struggle for preeminence or dominance. Most of these people have
many worries, and they have to work hard. They aren't classical
Greeks. For one thing, they prefer to keep all their clothes on, and
for another they don't have a lot of time to spend in the gym. They
are not trying to be beautiful as such or merely to strike the right
balance between forces of nature. They do not seek glory as such or
mere immortal renown. Their optic is long-term, large scale, and
not primarily aesthetic. Their work, their actions on the map, are
both productive and consequential in moral terms. These actions
will make a big difference, for good or evil.

The hypothesis of the Fall is that these very people who could so
act and suffer, and who could realize that their actions made a big
difference, were (by hypothesis) supposed to have emerged from a
place and condition in which they didn't suffer, their actions (being
all to the good) made no moral difference to speak of, and they
couldn't have seen what difference they would have made (which
is what having no "knowledge of good and evil" means) anyway.
And, we are given to understand by the storyteller, this counterhistorical condition was the "better" one, the one from which we have
all, unhappily, "fallen."

But all this is mere storyteller's convention! He pretends to descend from an even better land, and to tell of an even better state.
It is a kind of letter of recommendation, self-sealed. Nevertheless,
as we all know, the historical condition is the one where the storyteller finds himself, finds his audience, and—on any reasonable
grounds—*it* is the condition he will have to prefer. Can the singer
wish that he had no score, the dancer no stage, or the players no
rapt audience? Even if such wishes were being voiced (and the "we
are shut out from the Gates of Eden" story does give them voice),
they would only form one more part of the history-making performance. "History" is the right place to be, its indispensability being
conferred on it by the very narrator who "tells" the place of history
into existence.

So the question is not, What really happened before anything
else did? It is also not, What are the counterhistorical conditions
that predated scriptural "history"? The question is, rather, In what
situation did the teller find himself, that made his telling of world
history possible? If we can determine what *the story-telling conditions* were, then the other question, the one about what really
did happen beginningwise, *breisheet*, at the very beginning, will at
least have its proper frame of reference.

The Jewish thought, going as it does from "beginning" to "end,"
is often described as excessively "linear" and "judgmental." Of late,
it has been found the frequent subject of unflattering comparison
with the "organic" and "global" and "intuitive" approaches of those
who would urge on us a return to the cyclical view of time, to eternal archetypes, to the myth world, the hero and his hero quest, and
so on. Yes, so, Jewish thinking is linear and judgmental, and many
think that a fault.

The storyteller seems to tell his story in a literal straight line,
from a supposedly literal "very beginning" to a supposedly literal
"very end." Why does the storyteller do that? Whence his obsession
with linearity? So many other narrators from other cultures appear
to have done without it, or used it only provisionally, before bringing an "episode," linearly described, to its inconclusive close. Why
has the biblical storyteller nailed himself to that line?

The point about linearity is that it is inseparable from what
we call justice. When you come before a tribunal, the question the
judge or jury will ask you is, What happened? And what happened
next? What happened, if you please, after that? Also, may it please
the court, just what happened *before* the first thing that you've
told the court? "Who drew first?" as we say. Who started it? And so
on, linearly. The questions have this preoccupation with time because justice is, at least preliminarily, the effort to reconstruct what
happened. And what happened always happened in time, sequen-
tially, which is where the fairness or unfairness of it all has to be
established.

Who set it up? Who dunnit? And we who ask also ask while
the sand runs through the glass, or while the clock ticks, or while
this court is in session. Our questions too observe a sequence and
situate themselves within the same time frame as your answers.

It is before the bar of justice, in some sort of lawful society,
that one *can* take testimony, compare witnesses, and reconstruct
what happened in an orderly sequence. God Himself must respect
the evidence so gathered, to a certain extent. He can "change the
past," or what we call the past, in some measure. But there are
limits, even for Him. What's done is done and therefore lies open to
evaluation.

It may be objected that in Genesis, the book of the "very beginning," God is given room—He is given the whole desert—in which
to deal directly with outstanding individuals, who seem relatively
unfettered by the constraints of a lawful society, and who have yet
drawn His especially strong preference and favor. It is as if God
can see them clear, precisely because they don't live in cities and

don't have to report to courts of law. In fact, from these glitteringly singular encounters in Genesis, it seems rather a comedown for God that later He will be reduced to dealing with a motley mass, from which there will emerge (but only from time to time) other outstanding individuals. So the objection would run, to this thesis about lawful society.

What happened, then? How did God shift from the level of the individual to the level of the mass, and was it some sort of come-down—whether on His part or the part of the storyteller? Or did things happen the other way around? Did the other books of the Pentateuch precede Genesis, at least "logically"?

I think that, yes, they must have happened the other way around. It was not that God, having first had meaningful contacts with outstanding individuals, then decided rather disappointingly in Exodus to try to do the same thing with a nation and just had to take what He could get. Rather, the fact is (because people are in large measure social and historical products) that there are no such Adam-and-Eve-like, Cain-and-Abel-like, Abraham-and-Lot-like individuals, standing on an empty desert, silhouetted against the windy sky. Genesis was therefore not written at the very be-ginning. Something else had to have been written and remem-bered first.

Things must rather have transpired in this way. A group of people, a particular culture, animated (as the book says) by a single visionary leader, decided so to constitute itself as to become a nation made up of outstanding individuals. *That decision* was itself consti-tutive of "the beginning," since it was the pivotal point from which the lines of memory could be traced back to a speculative "very beginning," and forward to an anticipated "very end."[8]

What does it mean, in this context, to decide to constitute one-self as such a nation? How does anyone set about to make such a decision?

At the very least, the parties must mutually agree—with God underwriting the contract—to try to be "absolutely" fair.[9] If you want to try it some time, you will see that *in any real context*, such as the context of people living in families, for instance, it gets to be rather a tricky business. What does "absolutely" fair mean? Now factor in disputes over land and water and strategic high ground in tight places, and the business gets trickier. Now assume that the people who have made this decision already had a culture and weren't about to get rid of it, and assume it was one of those an-cient cultures in which all of the little chores of life had their ritual component. These rituals will now all have to be reconsecrated, as integral components of the covenant. It will get even thicker, and trickier, now on the ground.

Here we are. It's no longer a "classroom example." It's not even a "clean" situation. It's too late for such cleanliness. The house is already furnished. The sands are already occupied. For a theory of justice that would prefer to be founded on what John Rawls calls an "original position"—a position in a thought experiment wherein everyone's life commitments and interests have been cleanly bracketed so as to be left out of account—this prior tenancy by real interests is merely unfortunate. But what is the point of a search for absolute justice that, by pretending to transcend the real situations on the ground, acquires a distance from them that is merely aesthetic? In the real world, there is no such position as Rawls's "original" one.[10] Nowhere can we find the time for such a position. Nowhere can we find the place for it.

So any people that wanted to decide to be "absolutely" fair would *not* start with a clean slate. They would already have some commitments, necessarily, and some habits of their own, and some interests to defend. If they lacked all these, they would not belong to the order of space and time and the senses—the historical order. But they *did* belong to the common order. We have even excavated their household articles.

Nevertheless—and despite all this furniture of prior commitments—a transcendent standpoint would also be needed here. If the decision to be absolutely fair is to be ushered into the historical world, that joint decision (the covenant) must hold not only amongst and between the people who are willing to make it, but also between them as a whole and a "God transcendent of time."

By "transcendent God" is meant first of all an atemporal standpoint, but one that bears immediately on a certain kind of conduct in time. By the terms of this agreement the covenanters are lifted out of time, out of nature itself, and then put back into both under new conditions.

For that, real power is required.

What kind of power? First of all, the covenanters must be preserved from entropy. For the purposes of such a covenant, they are no longer to be considered mere grains on the shifting dunes of endless time, nor mere reflections of the beautiful and divine faces of nature. Nature turns up many faces, after all. And the winds erase whatever is written on the dunes of time. So all the rich vagaries of paganism (even philosophical paganism) cannot give to this agreement its guarantee, for the overriding reason that *this agreement is an absolute*, but one that has a role to play in the empirical world.

The gods cannot quarrel about it, as they quarrel about everything else, in paganism. The divine too must submit to it, must help to enforce it when nothing else will do so, and must underwrite it at all times. For this one needs something more than Plato's forms, or Aristotle's Unmoved Mover, or even the hegemony of dharma. One needs an agreement, a covenant, a promise—something on which one can, as it were, shake hands. In other words, one needs the wills to do it—the wills from the finite side and the Will from the infinite side.[11] That is required by the nature of the enterprise, even if there turned out to be no such thing as a divine will.

From that contractual point where the two kinds of wills have met—the point where and when the pagan flow of things has been stopped absolutely—we get the "imaginable time" of Jewish Scripture. It is the contract that renders time finite, short, and wholly imaginable. Before the bar of "absolute" justice that this contract alone dreams up, the empirical questions can be framed: What happened first? What happened next? And after that? And then?[12] This is the kind of time that *fits* in a universal epic. It travels from that contractual point backward to the first day, and forward to the last day. The latter will involve universal human *redemption from unfairness*—all other kinds of redemption offering ecstasies that risk partial irrelevance to the human situation. (This point is not being advanced against ecstasy. But one has to be Jewish *too*.)

Then and only then, that is, after the covenant, could this people have "remembered" its outstanding forebears and gone back to write its Book of Genesis. They (the figures in Genesis) are its foreground and background, its culture of memory. They start the lineage that made its achievement of shared civil life into a transmitted thing, partaking of the force of biology and tradition both, rather than something that was merely stuck, arbitrarily and conventionally, to the contractual point.

The memories of the outstanding individuals in Genesis are not "made up." They are emotional necessities. And they are the heart's core of any history. But they also follow, as emotional necessities, from these present a priori conditions: that we all have a transcendent sense of justice and that we are all actors in a global drama. In their link-by-link linearity, these progenitors also follow from an empirical fact, traceable ultimately to the same a priori conditions: that we who read this, like they who wrote it, all live in settings that may require us one day to give evidence in courts of law.

What the covenant between God and Israel does is render these universal conditions of absolute justice empirical. It forces them to show up at ground level, without their usual highly aestheticized distance from the real world.

The concept of history is thus a by-product of the act of cove-

nant.[13] People are incessantly in revolt against the concept, because
of the strains that it puts on them, and incessantly projecting their
revolt backwards against the original, empirical, real-life covenanters. (That almost goes without saying.)

It may well be that what we call world history—this dream of
a complete epic—is always partly an *imaginary* by-product of the
act of covenant. But then again, in Scripture, it is so "truly" imagined! In the spare tales of Genesis, which are largely about the
tricky business of fairness in family relations, the whole, many-
layered history of the covenant is compressed. And the covenant
(as we know from searching ourselves) is real enough, since its defining concept is absolute justice. Since childhood, we have all been
troubled with such a concept. It is innate, most probably. And in
such a concept, there is always trouble brewing—trouble enough
for many stories.

Those who have tried to deal with it know that the concept of
absolute justice is not found coherent or transparent in the philosophical literature on the subject. Even if it could be made so on
the theoretical plane, on the plane of applications it would always
find itself interthreaded with habits of thought and of conduct that
would never quite fit all the requirements of any actual, unfold-
ing situation. Even with a will to absolute justice, even with the
best will in the world, in real life there would always be this unfittedness, this lag, which would find its way into positive law, and
which would then be read as unfairness by any particular persons
or groups affected. And this unfittedness of social habits to the
momentary situation is especially noticeable when whole societies
deal with other societies, or with their own subgroups. But even
between man and God there is this discoverable lack of fit, this disparity—of power, of ability to take the long view, and of safety. God
is safe, after all. God has insurance. But man is not safe.

The best that the concept of justice can be, the most it can be,
is an occasion for good-faith argument. For dialectic. Judaism is
therefore still a dialectical operation. Training in it is still training
in argument, and the arguments ("remembered" as they can be
only in the time-stopping context of covenant) go back to the very
beginning. For example:

> And Cain said unto the Lord, My punishment is more than I
> can bear.   (Gen. 4:13)

God, we recall, *listened.* He considered the reasons Cain put forward. And, evidently, He decided that they were good reasons. Ac-

cordingly, He transformed the stigma of Cain into an insignia of protection.

After that unsettling beginning, the arguments—weaving their way in and around the chain of the narrative—simply continued.

> And Abraham drew near and said, Wilt thou also destroy the righteous with the wicked?   (Gen. 18:23)

As is well known, God and Abraham would go back and forth on this one, but mostly the affair was going to be concluded on Abraham's terms. God would come down considerably from His original, awkwardly distant, mighty, and infinitely outsized perspective. The point here is that they *both* were in possession of that "knowledge of good and evil" about which the storyteller pretended such high dudgeon and distaste in the beginning. Each had a different perspective on what he knew. And both perspectives were necessary, if the story was to be a good story.

Whatever escapist regrets one might feel about having this mutual knowledge of good and evil, it is evident in the text that, after Adam and Eve "fell," they or their descendants began this long conversation with God, bits and fragments of which we find there recorded. And, from the first, the conversation has turned into an *argument*—about justice in history.

(Naturally, it was otherwise with them before they "fell." Then, the story tells us, what they did was this "imaging" or "mirroring" of God, as per the formula of their creation, and what it came down to was perhaps just the way they looked, and walked, and felt, being alive. They were, so the storyteller implies, in a "state of grace," where everything is clear and more or less at rest. That can happen, and therefore it can be "remembered." It is the realm of essences. It is an excellent thing, even an ecstatic thing, to have happen to anybody. But it is *not* preemptively the only thing desirable for human beings who are aware of God in the human situation.)

At the point where the real human narrative begins, whatever was prefigured in the Edenic "imaging" or "mirroring" activity becomes the joint effort, by God and man, empirically to bring about justice in universal history. Because of the inherent obscurities and difficulties of that project, it also became this argument about what that providential design would have to mean.

That said, we come now to the differing constructions that Judaism and Christianity have put on the meaning of history. From the Jewish perspective, that argument about universal justice would lack all interest, pith, and point if everyone, after the Fall, were simply to be *defined* as guilty. Job is on the "Jewish" side of this dispute, when he maintains that he is not subject to fair reproach on empirical grounds and also not willing to have his deeper innocence redefined as guilt by well-intentioned theologians.

> My righteousness I hold fast, and will not let it go: my heart
> shall not reproach me so long as I live.   (Job 28:6)

While God does not give all the right of the matter away to Job, He certainly gives it to him more than to those hypocritically pious friends who do not trust God enough even to address Him in argument. The trouble with Job's theologian-comforters is that they will not stoop to notice the central fact of history viewed as a struggle for absolute justice: *One can suffer, being innocent.*

This Christians must implicitly deny, at least insofar as any human being must be viewed by Christians as a sinner by definition. Without that Pauline doctrine—on which Augustine in turn founded his philosophy of history—the death of Jesus would need a different, or at least a somewhat more subtle, explanation. As matters now stand, the doctrine of Original Sin still explains that death as required if God Himself was to have the legal warrant to admit into His own presence such sinners by definition as Job or Abraham. The death of Jesus becomes therefore the expiation for man's otherwise unfortunate and relatively graceless presence in history. On that view, one would have little incentive, or only a negative one, for remembering one's own personal history, since *it too* would have to be thought *somewhat* unfortunate, and *relatively* graceless.

The gist of the contrasting Jewish view is that "history" is the right place to be and is the very place from within which to invoke the presence of God. This arena summons God, as it summons us all, to argue together. There is nothing wrong with either Job or Abraham. Nothing wrong, that is, that can't be worked out in that argument. And so one has all the incentive in the world to remember the history of the whole world—and one's place in it.

That one can suffer, being innocent, the religions that came out of India must also deny, on levels gross or subtle, insofar as for India almost all suffering—divine incarnations excepted—is the consequence of bad or mistaken action under the doctrine of karma. Only Judaism has noticed and affirmed this point, without any "pagan" dividing or dispersing of the being, the power, and the moral authority of God: One can suffer, being innocent. But on any other view, there is no *philosophie de l'histoire*. The human epic, which was meant to inspire us to act justly in a convergently common cause, would be instead about nothing much. It would be merely episodic, even if the episodes were wonderfully aesthetic, or greatly uplifting to the mind and heart in other ways. After the uplift, the mind would fall back again.

The longer argument, between God and humankind, is then necessarily about justice and injustice. There is nothing else worth fighting about. If there were nothing at all worth fighting about, life would be dull. There would be no story. Infinite Love itself requires some other state than its own opacity and stasis.

It's not that, in the absence of an issue of justice, there cannot still be a fight, on the frozen tundra for instance, and a saga about that fight that is notably well sung. But really, was that fight worthwhile? Was it *quite* fair? Is there a human being, no matter how strong or blond, who can completely blank out on that question? Yet, having asked it, one is immediately at an absolute beginning point. And the rest, sooner or later, will have to follow.

Now some people maintain that the God of Jewish Scripture is a fearsome God, because there are these—sometimes rather heated—arguments. But that's not the right way of conceiving it. It takes the greatest trust, the greatest degree of intimacy, to argue with someone about justice and injustice, in all simplicity and candor. The person I was closest to in this life was my mother. And she was the only one to whom I could say, lightly and freely, that she'd been horribly unfair. For I knew that she thought I was a nice person, no matter what I said.

These arguments are a song of love.

This is almost all that has to be said in the way of macrohistorical prologue. There are just these further things to say. The events of this personal and, possibly, philosophical memoir form a part of the human epic, the latter being a quest for absolute justice in history. The nuclear event of the epic is the covenant between God and Israel, from which contractual point the whole of our creation and the final redemption of us all can be at least surveyed.

Perhaps some other point would have afforded the same view or does so now. It is not the only mountain. But it is the only mountain of its kind. To that covenant, other peoples and creeds have in the course of time attached themselves, usually paying it the tithe of misrepresentation and ingratitude. When the messiah comes (or comes back, or is merely imagined to have arrived, as the case may be), all that will have to be straightened out.

Chapter Two.

Paris without End

In the year when this memoir begins, I was twenty-one and on a Fulbright grant to study the concept of man in aesthetic experience. In Paris, appropriately enough.

I was looking for the Absolute. All my life I have looked for the Absolute, and that first year of my grown-up life was not an exception. But since the medium of the Jewish search is ordinarily the historical context in which one finds oneself, the first responsibility that I felt in those days was to penetrate to the very heart of Paris—to know it so thoroughly that its place in my search would be forever established and exhausted. I would never need to know it more or better. I would know it, and all that it meant.

Was all that "conscious"? Yes, it was, in a flickering sort of way. But that kind of question currently carries with it a freightload of presuppositions about the stuff stored in what our contemporaries like to call the *un*conscious. Turning those presuppositions over every which way, they all come down, finally, to this one: that the unconscious is devoid of conscience. That it lacks intrinsic moral shape. This "unconscious" neither knows nor cares about what every child and every old person the world over knows: that in this world you reap what you sow. Everybody knows this. Only the so-called unconscious doesn't know it.

This "unconscious" is widely supposed to be incorrigible. Its only ambition would be to freeload off the groaning banquet table of the world. No memory traces of failure, anticipations of mortality, or whatever, are believed to slow it down. No disillusionment with regard to the inexhaustible appetites it is imagined to contain. No awareness of the multitudinous devices by which we cheat ourselves in exactly the same coin that we have cheated others. And this very "unconscious" is supposed also to have the sangfroid to be simultaneously overseeing the whole situation and assigning to consciousness the rationales, the masks, and the other concealing/revealing devices that will hide the "unconscious" in its careening phoenix flight across the world! On this reading, the "unconscious" is constantly interrupting its delusive pagan revels in its Arcady to get on the other line and give shrewd, tight-lipped, superconscious instructions to consciousness, its double agent in the real world.

This is not mere theory. It's also an alibi. And not such a great one, if one wanted to inspect its infrastructure bit by bit.[1] But under that theory, or alibi, the whole medley of complex, idealistic, half-articulated beliefs and tendencies with which I actually set out in life, at the opening page of my young adulthood, would quickly reduce to a few doubtful rationalizations for the gigantesque opportunism of my fathomless unconscious.

The spectre of the unconscious as filled to the bursting brim with dark, swirling, unmentionable propensities and equally hidden but astounding stratagems of concealment has been borne along a stream of romantic and postromantic intellectual influence.[2] And there are some probable older influences that, since they would be religious in nature, would be harder to document in their effect on nineteenth-century secular thinkers. However, what Freud's dark romanticism seems to have effectively revived was the "hyper-Augustinian" or theologically pessimistic approach to human nature—the approach that the secular thinkers of the American and European Enlightenment had tried so hard to modify.[3]

At this writing, Freud's empirical claims are failing to check out in any systematic way.[4] Nevertheless, his ongoing influence in the culture works as a discouragement to those who may want to tell their life stories truly and coherently. If one wants to tell one's own story, one has to try to remember it. And, having remembered it, one does well also to try to insert it into what has been described and recommended in Chapter One, "Beginningwise," as "history" per se. But insofar as one credits Freud's theory of the dramatically named "Oedipus complex," historical consciousness itself will be that much less accessible.

The reason is plain enough. If, as the Freudian claim implies, one's affection for the parent of the opposite sex "unconsciously" threatens to mutate into incest, then the only way one could avoid defiling the parent-child relation would be to distance oneself from it. Filial piety would then be most fittingly expressed by filial *im-piety*. Nor could one ever willingly retrace the series of personal memories going back to one's origins with eyes open. Decency would mandate averted eyes. And no one in that eyes-averted position could possibly reconstruct his or her personal history accurately. You'd have to pay someone to tell you what you allegedly "remember." One's past would therefore become the domain of the experts. It would not be one's own.

In sum, an alleged syndrome (the Oedipus complex) whose onset in personal life no one can remember is still widely allowed to becloud the real personal history that everyone can remember. That is, everyone can remember personal history in some degree, unless so paralyzed by anticipatory self-disgust that he or she no longer has the heart to try to remember.

In this respect, the so-called Oedipus complex plays a disempowering role similar to that of the Augustinian doctrine of Original Sin. Both hypotheses give an account of a "father/son relation" in which an offense against the father is supposed to have occurred before the onset of personal memory. So both make it more difficult than it would otherwise be to accept one's historical existence.

Let me try to explain what's involved in the doctrine of Original Sin, by means of a simple analogy. In place of God, Adam, and progeny, picture a human father and son. Now picture the father telling his son, "You can play with all the toys in my house, except one. Just don't spin that shiny, new, striped, spinning *top*." And let's suppose that the father, by some science-fiction device, has managed to implant in his son *an inclination to trespass*—against the perceived limits. Not one that is irresistible. But it's there, the inclination. So the father leaves; the boy spins the top; the father comes home and finds out what has happened. Then what?

If my analogy holds, between this story and the Pauline-Augustinian story of Original Sin, then what the father does is retreat to the attic! "That's it, kid," he says, as he goes up the stair. "*Never* will you see me again. We won't eat together. We won't speak together. I'm leaving you to your mischief. I'll provide you with the means to scrape by. But otherwise, you're on your own. And don't break any *more* rules, while I'm in the attic."

Some time passes. We can suppose that the conduct of our boy has had its ups and downs, but that on the whole it's been inglorious. After all, the worst thing you can do to another person, when he displeases you, is to freeze him out. Yet that's what this father has done, and done the first time that his son broke the rules, and done although he had a hand in forming his body and character. Had they remained on speaking terms, the son could have pointed out how, seen in the light of all that, the punishment was disproportionate. But *this father* will not come back down the stair to hold the argument. So there is the son in quarantine, and it's so disproportionate that any social worker would be appalled and might well recommend that the child be removed from that big empty house and placed in some foster home.

Finally one day the father reappears at the foot of the stair. "Son," he says, "you are so guilty that nothing you could possibly do would make up for it. If you staked yourself out on an anthill, it would not atone. You are just guilty. Guilty indelibly. So, I'm going to *help* you. What I'm going to do for you is take off this leather strap and beat *myself* until the blood runs down and I'm half dead. Understand clearly what I'm doing now: *I* don't deserve it. *You* are the one who deserves it. But you are *not good enough* to get it! So I'm going to do it and get it, as a stand-in for you. And, *on those terms*, I will consider that you have atoned—for spinning the top—and I'll forgive you. Fair and square. But if you aren't duly grateful, or if you fail to recognize this as true fatherly love and forgiveness, then I'll go back up the stair once again."

The son has been handed a script with a part for him in it. But he can't act this part. Because nobody could. It's intolerable. What will he do now, since the show must go on? What he'll have to do is divide up the script, passing the bad lines to other actors and keeping the better part for himself. Is there an older brother in the house? There is? Excellent. Let *him* take the rap for the flagellation, and the younger brother can just read those closing lines about "love" and "forgiveness." And about being "nonjudgmental." I should say so! If I found myself in a script like this one, I would suspend judgment till the last curtain call.

Meanwhile, there is still the older brother, thank God. Let *him* be the one to ascribe to the father unbreakable rules that are too hard to keep, with no guidance if one wanted to learn them, and no mercy if one made a mistake. Never mind that *these aren't the older brother's views* of his father. Never mind that *that hasn't been his relation* with his father. Let's *not* ask him for his input. This is an emergency, after all. Sauve qui peut. Whoever can should save himself.

Under the hyper-Augustinian doctrine of Original Sin, historical motivation traces back to something very bad that we will not be able to remember. Only the authorized theologian can reliably "remember" it on our behalf. Likewise, under the Freudian hypothesis of a universal Oedipus complex, historical motivation traces back to something so bad that we will have made ourselves "unconscious" of it, both personally and collectively. Only the authorized psychoanalyst will be able to "remember" it for us. It's too bad to be directly remembered.

What I think people are really suggesting, therefore, when they ask, How much of what was going on in your story was "unconscious"? is, *By the way, weren't you really a sinner?*

The answer is yes. In part. That's what I was. Nor is it that discreditable. It's only human. It wasn't Original Sin, in the Augustinian sense. It wasn't the Oedipus complex. Nevertheless, not every motive that I had was pure, nor every thought precise and unclouded. The word "unconscious" is the pretend scientific and secular code word for sin. And those were the motives of which I was unaware (though not, in Freud's technical sense, "unconscious"), at least until their consequences had made themselves fully felt in my life of that time.

But one way I know that the intentional object of my persistent search was a high one, or the highest one, was that each misstep along the way seemed then and still seems to me to have been necessary. Also, there is the fact that a steep price would be exacted for every misstep. When you journey (as you hope) toward the Absolute, you pay as you go.

There was a fellow Fulbright scholar named John Armstrong on shipboard with me, who remarked, as we leaned together over the choppy brow of the Atlantic, "Wouldn't it be funny if this weren't a real ship, but a ghost ship, full of dead people who still think they're alive?" One year later he was dead on the road to Khartoum. Nancy Sendler, the girl John had loved that year, would be killed in a highway accident just after the story ended that is told in this memoir. And the part of me that had begun sobbing in anticipation at the pier, thinking, This is going to change everything, was entirely right. So, in a certain sense, it *was* a ghost ship. We all begin our stories with such poor and insufficient ideas, whose insufficiencies will finish us off one way or the other, in time. But that *is* the historical condition.

There were various sorts of people who were part of the Fulbright group going over with me. Some had a kind of sun-burnished, slightly sodden hopefulness, compounded mostly of youth and weather. Many, perhaps a majority, played that theme of youth and hope backwards, by voicing their "honest" second thoughts about the voyage. "Why the hell are we going to France this year?" they would say to each other, nodding.

I think that those questions arose out of the project of cashing in on the erotic powers of youth as soon and as advantageously as possible. For example, it seemed that a fair percentage of the Fulbright women I was to know were already affianced. If they were in love with, or even alive to, their absent fiancés, it was undetectable. Their voices were impassively even and soft, and they were affianced, it often turned out, to ministers. They appeared to do quite a lot of knitting. It was 1958; many young women knitted, then. They were concerned with emotional consolidation. Perhaps the concern had arisen in the first place defensively. Yet, judging from all the controversial subjects that they *never* touched on, what was being held in trust for them could not have been anything much larger or more inclusive than just that: security. Position in the world.

Love? Even love has to have a little scope. Children? Even children have to live toward the future, to live in the universal narrative concerning justice and mercy—to live in history. So emotional consolidation must have been the principle on the interest of which they were then planning to live. Perhaps, as things have turned out, they have the principle still and in equal measure. But, the situation of women being what it was in those days, that too is doubtful.

Another portion of the grant holders I knew, let us say 30 percent, got their library cards and plunged into the dark recesses of the Bibliothèque Nationale, there to advance a daily furlong on a research project that was well integrated with an academic career they had already mapped thoroughly. They did not have to "know" any mysterious essence at the veiled heart of Paris. They certainly didn't believe in figuring out the answer to the question of how to be the image and likeness of God by struggling for mercy and justice in universal history, nor did they believe in any other equivalent, remote high thing that they told *me* about. (On the face of it, they were therefore *un*like the fiancées of divinity school students, who did at least appear to believe in the god in the bank.) They believed in good scholarship. And it was not remote. For this group, there would not be any difficulty, at the proper time, about finding a suitable mate. Virginity would not be an issue. Nothing would be "an issue," that I could see. And they really did know a lot about "psychology."

There must have been a large group, size indeterminate, about which I knew nothing at all. Instinct, natural tastes and affections, all must have put us, from the first, out of range for each other.

And what, by the way, about us all was *America*? It was a kind of empty space of possibility, in France. So, if it wanted to help make us visible, France had gallantly to provide us with its setting, just then, the one it has provided to the whole world at different times. Before the ship docked at Le Havre, sinking and rising in my narrow upper berth, I would have this persistent dream during the nights. I dreamed I had arrived in Paris, France, found it uncomfortably small, not particularly foreign, traversable in a brief fraction of an hour, and holding no secrets: open, obvious, and disappointing. At the time, it was my worst fear. Anyone American who entered my circle of friends that year would have had to share, or at least to understand, that fear. To walk into one's youth, as I then planned to do, was to walk into one's history, and it had to be, at the very least, real. The empty, wide-open spaces that we inhabited and represented had first of all to be enclosed.

Happily, the French countryside, as I saw it for the first time from the train window, was beautifully and intricately foreign. It unfurled in geometrically compartmentalized shades of sky blue, pale daylight, and rigidly edged farm fields into one rough-textured vision—under which the train was rolling and rolling on its little round French wheels—as if attuning this vivid *paysage* to a medley of distantly familiar French folk songs.

The city of Paris overwhelmed me. Breathtaking were the sharp-angled, brief views of its flower-laden, awning-shadowed alleyways under its strangely delicate northern sun. The bus was turning us Fulbrights into the Cité Universitaire on the edge of town. So the damp streets, hung over with perfume, were only glimpsed, and the glimpses wrenched away, as we rolled into that absolutely faceless, mammoth housing development for foreign students.

But what solemn beauty that brief ride had disclosed! What a promise, and what a sober challenge its narrow side streets had lain down: to allow such a city to take one's measure. To live at the measure of such a city (as one of my mother's French friends had put it to me one time without even a whisper of self-consciousness): la plus belle ville du monde.

In general, the American effort, among the young people who would turn out to be my friends, would be to maintain integrity. It was a Protestant and post-Enlightenment sort of integrity, as it seems from here. Behind it, never spoken of except by dim, joking "Freudian" allusion, was our countrymen's sense of sin. In the front window, it had in view the rights of humanity, viewed in a charitably hazy and generic way—divested of that unforgiving, Parisian, cosmetic attention to the carnal details that converted American existence in that city into a project of ironic and half-doomed resistance. Of this resistance project, John Armstrong was—whenever anyone gave him the time—the natural leader.

John was Scottish, a first-generation American, and—my guess from here would be—a lapsed Presbyterian (though in those days I couldn't tell one Christian denomination from the other, and I never asked him). But the lapse, from whatever denomination, would have set in somewhere along the route of an Ivy League acculturation.

John was an odd boy. His *face* kept changing. Sometimes, he would duck behind an auburn handlebar mustache, which was not too common a piece of facial equipment in those days and made you not connect the earlier with the later slides of him, when he'd let his bland all-American face show, smiling, serious, and a little too white for comfort. He was subdued but jolly, a little clownish in the New England version of good style (just enough and not too much), and, when he finally would show up in full view, both practiced and courageous in the business of drawing the line. There were all kinds of little short-changing expatriate practices at which John deliberately drew the line, from buying at the PX where only the U.S. military was entitled to enjoy all the discounts, to overextending our vacations, to spending any single day in Paris without bringing to completion some self-assigned proper scholarly task.

"Whatever you *do* in this life will be your marker," he said to me one time. "It will be your epitaph, your boundary stone. Every act, no matter how small, tells what you were, and that's all anyone will be able to commemorate."

We had been sitting at a café deep in Montparnasse, and we were sitting by ourselves for once, the conversation between us rolling on, and leaving its tracks behind us in the deep sands of recollection. The café where we had stopped, John told me now, had once been frequented by Hemingway and all that famous crowd. And, he admonished me, it had *not* become a better place to be on that account. Nor was our present conversation magnified in any way by the long grey shadows of those celebrated predecessors.

The second admonition did not happen to be one of which I was in want. I thought we were sufficiently interesting in ourselves. At least, we were to me.

When someone who was a serious Christian by upbringing or ancestry ceases to be one, what tends to follow him out of the trackless past will be the lingering belief in his expulsion from Eden— from grace, that is—and the need (if he is a decent sort) to redeem what he will feel must be a *dire* condition. The classical virtues will partly do the work here, and John had them. I didn't think that *I* was in that condition, the dire one, but I always listened to John Armstrong. He was so boyish, though a little older than we, that it was pleasant to take his moral imprint—among others, always among others.

"Abigail, you may *say* you believe in immortality, but you have no way of backing that up. The fact is"—and he looked my way as if calling the class to order—"that this present life is all you have. And you really know it."

With an admonitory forefinger, John thus addressed his massed, unseen, otherwise leaderless legions. "The Greeks, Homer, understood how things work. Up in the sky, there are these gods who seem to be racing around in their great stage machines, but they don't really exist. The only part that's real is those men, playing for the only stakes there are. The characters in Homer all know it. And *that's* what they have to tell us."

I thought about that. (Perhaps he had read Nietzsche's *Birth of Tragedy*, but I hadn't, then.) I was in Paris, after all, to study the concept of man in aesthetic experience. But the reason I *had* to do that was that I'd always had trouble disputing an image. Except with another image. Which left it that nobody won, but (as I fondly thought) nobody lost either. We all stayed in the game. "John," I submitted with unpretending banality, "when you die, and get inside the pearly gates, and find out there's a whole next life going on—how will you feel? *Very* mad?"

A breath that he let out shone like a desert mirage in front of us both for a suspended few seconds. "Yeah," he gasped, laughing at himself at last. "I guess I would be."

The American young men I knew on Fulbright grants seemed to regard their female compatriots with a good-natured esteem that came near to being disembodied. What we all shared was our apparent common humanity, our reasonableness, and the fun of squandering long male and female afternoons in relaxed conversation. We did not suffer from the British sense of caste and class, nor from the frenetic eroticism of a Paris that looked to us to be incessantly afire. So the fellow feelings of expatriation could collect, as we talked, into a tall, sheltering, Yankee umbrella over Paris.

At that time, I did not try to situate my American men friends too closely, in the sociological sense. That might have inadvertently lodged them at some rung on the life ladder of heartless competitiveness where, once or twice, I would see them in after years and scarcely know them anymore. It was enough in those days to say we were "not French." It was clear that they were companions but not confidants. Their clean voices were not too distinguishable, as they rang, thoughtful, friendly, gallant, and never too close, all those resounding warning bells of home.

Though they were certainly honorable and had other talents besides, the rest of the young men I knew were not so outspoken in their rectitude as was John Armstrong. And they did not make their educated sense of life's dark side quite so articulate either. So I would like to imagine that he spoke for them all, on their more epic side, though not for me or my women friends, quite.

The women friends and I had a different problem, which did not seem so central to the human epic as the problem John Armstrong had sketched, of the importance of rectitude in the face of life's brevity and hope's futility. What our problem was will perhaps become clearer once the Parisian setting has been sketched.

The French "existentialism" and the French "Marxism" into which intellectuals of the period were finding their way represented their assessment of the Second World War's aftermath on the plane of ideas. But social Paris was in turn tremendously influenced by the plane of ideas. It danced attendance on whoever occupied that plateau. Costume and all the erotic rhythms were played out in accordance with the ideas.

Since I took the search for the Highest to be perforce conducted on the historical front, no detail of the strange world that fanned out before me could be merely a matter for indifference, ironic or stoical resistance, or carving up for career purposes. Rather, every detail was a clue to something that people were doing and thinking, people who belonged with me to the human epic. Even if I did not then use just that language, that was approximately what I thought and felt.

What were these people up to? What did they think? Was it right; was it wrong; and would it help the epic? Or perhaps the situation here was more complex—certainly more complex than the fiancées of the divinity students or even than John Armstrong thought—and the mentality of Paris was appropriate on its own terms but not obviously helpful to the epic. Whatever the truth was, I had to find it out.

In the metro, along the Seine's banks, in the crowded alleys of the Latin Quarter, lovers walked. I did not know what they were. I had never seen anything remotely like them. I imagined that they were, as we said then in America, "going steady."

A few weeks rolled by, under the bridges that spanned the River Seine, and someone, Nancy Sendler I think it was, told me that they were all *sleeping together.* I was both very surprised and indignant. Spontaneously. Was that the mysterious training ground where they had learned that strange, rhythmically interlocked walking dance that they were inflicting on me? Good grief. Where was air? Where was chastity? Where was a transcendent standpoint?

The girls were large eyed and just incredibly un-American. A girl here, as it seemed, was not embarrassed to look into a bearded male face adoringly, then to turn away pouting like a stubborn doe, then to giggle spontaneously when brushed by a bristled kiss on the cheek, or slowly to lean a shapely thigh forward for her lover just as slowly to squeeze, with both of them balancing on a single metro strap from which height they would exchange languorously slow, fathomless smiles before turning blankly from each other's gaze to stare, over their shoulders, at all the other people who were also there, quiescent in the metro. So they made time and space for this, on the social map.

What ideas were being acted out here? What I then surmised (and I am not now possessed of better information) was that the quintessential French story on this subject had been Tristan and Iseult's. Their fatal passion, justified on its own terms by the magic philtre they had drunk by accident, had cut like a "stroke of lightning" (as the French termed it) through the weave of medieval obligations, so that everything gave way before it. There had even been a separate god of lovers for that medieval pair, who had exercised protection independent of the authorized Creator. It seemed that true lovers who were French would be gnostics by vocation, which is to say inverters of the social and the metaphysical order.

I did not think it sufficiently explained the gnostic part to recall that marriages in those far-off days had typically been arranged for the couple, so that—understandably—erotic imagination had to have play outside established norms. So had Jewish marriages been (arranged), and yet at least some of these (Jewish legend went) were foreordained by the Creator too and therefore could yield fulfillment for the husband and wife, even while they stayed *inside* the Jewish metanarrative. In fact, since the Creation, what God had been doing (the Jewish tradition sweetly maintained) was *making* such marriages—between partners in history, people whose life arguments were so intertwined as to have become fused.

What I therefore supposed was that, in this Catholic country, passionate love had to be a law unto itself, because man the sinner was just not considered sufficiently lovable if approached in his merely historical context.[5] So what the "stroke of lightning" had to

do was cut through the history in order to cut out its own kingdom of one kind or another—but always a sealed fortress within
the world's larger kingdom.

Once one has conceived love as involving this disengagement
and then (with the onset of modernity) has got the supernatural
elements lifted out of it, it becomes mere erotic biochemistry, as
in Stendhal, or, as in Sartre, self-deception. Wholly aestheticized,
self-encased, self-confirming, sure of itself, and—since it has nothing to do with the river of time—sure of its self-terminating, self-
exhausting character as well.

The prototypes, Tristan and Iseult, had died and thus preserved
in amber their moment. Their modern successors, more confined
to the natural order, simply took for granted that they would outlive their moment. The French popular songs of the day were full
of regrets for the singer's years of erotic eligibility—lost and, by
definition, irrecoverable.

Among my women friends, all this was the subject of endless
mutual conversation. We didn't, of course, agree with this French
idea of love: self-enclosed, outside of time, but threatened at every
moment by time and change. But we could not be unaffected by it.
For the fact was that we none of us had any margin, as women. It
was not a question of "status," as the newly minted feminists would
begin to describe the thing a few years hence. It was a question of
room—room to retreat in, to retreat and turn again and beat some
other path.

For what we relied on was what the Marxists might have called
a "substructure" of youth and worthiness for romance, supporting us and all our professed values. But the substructure could be
undermined at any moment, and indeed, moment by moment, it
would be growing more precarious. When and as that happened,
we'd have become abstract. That was the worst thing that could
happen to a woman: to become a professor of values not attached
to anything concrete that was in fact valued. So the erotic details
of life that the French forced upon our notice were, inevitably, extremely preoccupying. Such arms, or others that we could invent,
would be what we would have to muster to defend against the in-
vading army—of time and age and an overprolonged virginity—
that threatened any day now to occupy our part of the country and
to render us abstract.

The Anglo-American moral philosophers have reminded their
readers that something can be intrinsically worthy without being
in fact desired. And colleagues of mine have expressed incredulity
that I, who could (much later) survive a seven-year professional

grievance without feeling especially diminished by it, could not live through this youthful moment of erotic precariousness without feeling excruciatingly endangered. But in 1958, when women had no margin as women, I just could not see my way around this female predicament. Nor do I happen personally to know any women of that era who could, although no doubt they existed.

Is a woman who is not and has never been considered desirable as a woman just as much a woman as if she had been desired? Well, yes, if she has some other mode of feminine self-presentation: motherhood, for instance. But, among other things that it does, motherhood publicizes the fact that somebody *has* desired her, as a woman. And if she has no other such mode? Well, then, no; *we* didn't think so. We didn't think that she was just as much a woman. And out-of-wedlock motherhood was very nearly a fate worse than death for us. So, in the event of motherhood, the desirer, the man, had to be not only attracted but retained at one's side in the character of a husband.

It seemed to me then that one "transcended" the female predicament at one's peril, because transcending it could leave one shorn of the erotic value that alone allowed one to escape being found ridiculous.

But why wasn't transcendence an option? Surely the fiancées of those divinity students thought that it was. In their minds, they were knitting beige woolen angels' wings, to wear up in heaven, when they had safely soared over this vale of secular unbelief. Surely they were not without some sort of uplifting religious conviction. Perhaps their external narrowness was just the protective padding that they knitted tightly around those convictions. In any case, that sort of retreat was not open to me.

History, in my eyes, was not just the vale of secular unbelief and exile from Eden. On the contrary. It was the right place to be, the best place for God and me to hold our argument. And if I became ridiculous too soon, I couldn't be a real player on the historical stage. One had to try to be a player, in the everyman play I conceived myself to be in. There are no nuns in the Jewish narrative.

What about the life of the mind? I was, after all, also embarked on that life. Could I not transcend the female predicament by withdrawing upward into the life of the mind? Aren't the ideas, as Plato said, eternal, transcending time and space and all the conditions of empirical embodiment?

Although I loved the life of the mind, it was not for me a self-sufficient objective. What I was interested in primarily was the truth about life, not the exercise of the mental faculties. And for me the truth about life was to be worked out between human beings and the historical God in the setting I have said. In those days it puzzled me that people said they would feel fulfilled if they had written their book. I could not imagine that the purposes of one's *life* could be summed up in the writing of a book!

So the loss of femininity, the loss of womanly value, was an intense preoccupation with us. We discussed preventive measures, containment measures, concealment and cosmetic measures tirelessly. The big question for us was how to endow our feminine existence with ineradicable value . . . and how to endow our values with feminine existence.

Chapter Three

Green Age

It was a leaf-blown Saturday afternoon in November. I had come up the rue de Vaugirard at noon to the Luxembourg Gardens, facing which was the Jewish student restaurant. Since, on the assumption of a religious need, that restaurant let anyone who paid for a ticket eat there, it became a place for friends to meet whose student cards had assigned them to separate restaurants, and the solution for those who weren't now or never had been "students," but who still needed a cheap meal. Those were the days of the Algerian struggle for independence from France, and in consequence a good number of Arab students ate there too, whenever the Foyer Musulman was closed, its entire staff having been placed under arrest.

CLOSED

said the sign on the door of the Foyer Israelite.

"They are never open on Saturdays," said the bearded, unfamiliar voice beside me, in English. It was a dark-clad foreign student, not French, and surely not American. He was thin, a little taller than me. I did not notice how he looked, particularly.

"Oh, of course. It's the Jewish restaurant! I should have known that."

"Well, for my part, I'm going to another," he remarked, in French.

"Fine, I shall go with you," I rejoined, in the same language. "The ones I have tickets for are all closed."

"You can always eat at the Beaux Arts. They let anybody in. You only have to show that you have a card for *some* student restaurant."

We moved around in a kind of do-si-do on the sidewalk. Vaguely I noticed that I did not feel crowded, although, with people usually, I did. We had started walking.

"How is the food there?"

"Bad, but about like the others."

"Oh." We were pacing along at a fast clip, keeping a rough step. "What nationality are you?" I asked curiously.

"Grrreeek."

"Are you really?" I'd never met a modern Greek, though I felt I had met many ancient ones. "No, really? How marvelous. I was just studying a little Greek. How simply *splendid* to be Greek. And what city are you from in Greece?"

"Ahhthens," he pronounced for me.

"Oh really." It was olive and gold, in my young philosopher's imagination—a place of mystery and light at the end of the tunnel formed by this history-encumbered, sharp grey presentness of Paris.

"You sound like Montesquieu's 'Comment peut-on être persan?'" he said dryly. But he couldn't help being a little pleased. "Whhaht are you stud-y-ing?" he inquired in English.

"La philo," I said shyly, thinking, oh dear, this will sink me.

"Ha-hah! So am I," he exclaimed, in somewhat stilted but evident delight this time.

Into what female company, I wondered, was he accommodating me in his mind? De Beauvoir? Héloise? Or perhaps someone else he knew, more accessible and less celebrated? Many things were acceptable here, in a certain milieu at least, that were still viewed as anomalous in the States.

"It's a good thing you came by, or else I would have gone hungry this afternoon. But never mind. I would've done it for the good Lord's sake."

"And what a peculiar sublimation that would have been!" he articulated at once.

I laughed. The Parisians whom I'd met so far did not use those Freudian terms, although they understood them.

"Are you Jeweeesh?"

"Yes."

"You have a very Jewish face."

I had once read an ethnographic essay on the Greeks. There it was explained that Greeks were very puritanic. The thoughts of these people never went below one's eyes. He was steering us unerringly through winding side streets, nearly aborted alleys, and seemingly doorless doorways until we came up to the Foyer des Beaux Arts. There was the usual crush of self-preoccupied, sternly red-mouthed, bearded young Frenchmen, dark hair billowing and dancing to frame their white faces and necks. Like memory itself, French students in those days never wore anything bright. In their dark suits, they seemed to continue to show the aftereffects of nineteenth-century realism, in the style of Courbet or, if they wore more informal dark sweaters and pants, then they'd shifted in time as far forward as postimpressionism and the style of Manet. Since the monitors *were* lax on the pass rules, they simply took our tickets, and we elbowed through the penumbra.

Seated at one of the crowded long tables, over the plates clattering and decorously aggressive demands for the bread and the salt from every quarter, we chattered. He had been to Israel with a close Israeli friend, he said. In fact, he had tried to sign up during the Sinai campaign of 1956, but they had not accepted him.

In the Paris of students, in those days, being Jewish seemed to give one somewhat more importance than being a blandly uncomplicated American did. Americans had to answer for segregation. For wealth. For escaping the bombs and the invader. Jews had only to accept, without of course overdoing it, the prestige of having been—as a group—singled out for outstanding victimization by the still-unforgotten German Occupation. Mind, the prestige was not moral. It was fleshly. One *was* a certain condensate of historical suffering and endurance. Essence is what has been, as Hegel has said. The "essences" that people acknowledged here were primarily aesthetic. The word "aesthetic" comes from the Greek, *aisthetikos*, meaning roughly, "pertaining to perception." So it was aesthetically important to be reckoned an essence incarnate. It started one off socially, giving one at least the presumption of shape.

"What connection do you trace in your mind between Hellenic culture and the culture of Israel?" I asked him. I wasn't an expert at small talk. Besides, I genuinely wanted to know. Why did I want to know? I was pretty aestheticized myself. On the other hand, perhaps the question was not a mere piece of posturing, but a deep one, still being turned over and over within the astral precincts of Western philosophy. And perhaps I had asked it because I wanted the answer—not about how his thinking processes went, but about the connection itself, between Athens and Jerusalem.

He made some not-lame rejoinder, though what it was has slipped from my memory now.

He had liked Israel a good deal, he was saying now at the Beaux

Arts. I was impressed with his wholeheartedness. I'd read that the modern Greeks were highly ethnocentric. It felt very easy to me to be so judicious in taking the measure of his historical form, since I felt so balanced and stabilized within my own.

We turned now to the question of my ostensible Fulbright project in Paris. Had I met a certain philosopher of art at the Sorbonne?

Yes, I had. It was one of a number of such meetings that others, more preprofessional than I, might have coveted, but that I found forced and embarrassing, and that my advisor from the Commission Franco-Americaine was then, to my chagrin, arranging. I explained this.

What did I think of him?

"You know"—I swept my hands in a V shape upwards with all the airy pseudodecisiveness of youth—"he is Catholic."

Two German students seated across from us burst out laughing.

"For my part," I continued decisively, "I think that Christianity is mostly a phenomenon of art, and that *art* is the meaning of 'the word made flesh.'"[1]

"Yes of course," the Greek student said emphatically.

"And how much of the classic, the ancient Greece is still preserved in that country today?" I wanted naïvely to know.

"It is preserved through the culture of Byzantium. It is a Byzantine classicism."

So glass- and gold-inlaid mosaics were lighting up the inside of a mere dark, closeted dome. And outside, there was still the sky—now more remote. Poor Greece. My head was full of thoughts, that day. I didn't think about him, particularly.

We walked back together down one of the broad avenues of the Latin Quarter. The last few brown leaves clung to the November branches, while our leisurely path lay empty under the strong fall sunlight. It seemed an unusual day.

I was asking him about a Greek film I had seen. Was it true in real life, as in the film, that when you are a Greek girl from such a village, and you are seen speaking alone to a man, "the very walls of the village will turn against you"?

He laughed. "When I was a boy, and fleeing the communists, I was given shelter by a peasant. The same man who hid me had earlier killed his sister with a knife because she had a lover."

"Did this man feel no remorse?"

"No. He thought he had done well."

"Did she not leave even the thinnest shadow over his days?"

"Well, when I pointed out to him that precisely in *another milieu* what his sister had done would have been taken as quite normal, so as to show him how unnecessary was what he did—when he understood that, afterwards he was quite sorry." Placid and nonjudgmental when describing the limitations of the peasant's outlook, he was now fiercely disapproving as he gave his quick contrasting sketch of that "other milieu" of the libertine upper classes. So unhealthy, he opined.

"So the film that I saw was not so realistic?"

"What film is? American westerns do not show the reality of America, do they?"

"I suppose not. But then again, perhaps in their way they do show *something*"—and amending that reservation as he looked his scepticism—"of the American unconscious at least."

He nodded sharply.

I had read very little Freud, and, like most girls of the fifties, I was aware that the language of Freud tended to put you in rather a less flattering light than you wanted to be in. But if you aimed to talk to people and to move on their platform, you had to find a common vocabulary. N'est-ce pas? And here, in Paris, the ability to make these sociological and Freudian comparisons seemed a rarity. It bespoke an "advanced" mentality.

We had come to a halt before the door of his building. "You live *here*?" I said in English. "How lucky you are."

"Through a friend," he grinned dryly. "In Paris, it's always through a friend."

I smiled through the cold. It was time to go.

"I would like to sketch you some time."

Ah. "Okay. But fully clothed, you mean," I added, having myself sketched from life at the Art Students League in New York City.

"Yes, of course. The face only." He shook his head with decisive disapproval, apparently as puritanic as the rural Greeks I'd read about. They looked only at the face. A woman was her face. Then again, this man was not rural.

"You have an extraordinary face." He was looking at me pointedly and speaking English. "Very Jewish." Pause. Then rapidly, "And very beautiful . . . if I may *say* so."

We exchanged names and the other information.

I was looking down, frozen in modestly exquisite acceptance of the first delivered compliment of that kind that I felt I *deserved*.

One day, some weeks later, I was walking next to the curved wall of the Luxembourg Gardens with Harper,* a woman friend, southern, who had a Fulbright grant in Paris to study sculpture. As

*Not her real name.

we two young women neared the corner of the rue de Vaugirard, a too thin, pale-cheeked figure was in front of me, reaching out to shake my hand, and saying that he had not had the means of telephoning me before now, having lost my address.

I didn't recognize him. Throughout our first conversation, I had adopted what seemed to me to be the local custom of communicating verbally and through the pores, sight unseen. Now I was embarrassed. In prepackaged American terms, I certainly couldn't situate him. His clothing was dark and nondescript and would probably always hang too loose. He had the look of someone who'd been hungry or ill at some time in his earlier years. His eyes were archaic. They had depth, and the eyelids had great precision. It was a Byzantine classicism, in them.

There seemed to be a drama under way, and I did not think it would be fair to the rest of the cast and the producers to back out now and ask them to get the understudy—though it occurred to me that might be prudent. So we set a time for me to sit for him.

The apartment of his married sister, where he took me that first time, was a large, nearly unfurnished room, except for a "kitchen" that was curtained off and—this was the attraction of the place for him—a phonograph, which proved not to work, on the bare wooden floor. But for young married people's quarters in Paris at that time, it was not bad at all. A Frenchwoman of a certain age, dressed with elegant simplicity, had been there when we first entered the place.

I had the impression that she was the mother of his sister's husband, his sister's *belle-mère*. At any rate, he had escorted the two of us through parts of his sketchbook, with its lead-pencil studies of successive nude French girls, all of whom he seemed to *know*. Overprecise, was my quick estimate of the sketches. They were drawn with the hard lead of someone who grips reality too tightly and does not trust himself to admit the spaces. I had sketched from the life too, but never from someone I knew personally!

The Frenchwoman said, upper-class laughter pirouetting in the round tones of her voice, "The poor one. She must be *cold*." In this social ingathering of femininity, present and absent, dressed and undressed, Pheidias* was at ease and bantering. I merely eyed these cool pages of pensive girls doubtfully, while exchanging portions of civilities with the Frenchwoman, who in her turn had taken tactful, rapid leave.

After briefly looking about the place, I took the seat that he offered: some few faded cushions on the floor. "How shall I sit?"

*Not his real name.

"Comfortably," he said sweetly. "When you are comfortable, you are graceful."

At any rate, when one was comfortable, one could hold the pose for a long time, as I knew, since I was not unaccustomed to posing for friends. Fully clothed, of course. At my insistence, he had rushed up a cup of coffee before we began, in response to my claim to be starving. He moved now in rapid, staccato segments around me with the kitchen stuff, stiff and short on breath. "I do not know why I am so nervous tonight."

Yes, well, perhaps I do know, I thought. At length, he assumed his place across the floor from me, dark, cross-legged, and in dead earnest. After a silence broken only by the pencil's scratching, he asked, "What sports do you like?"

(Discus throwing, Harper later told me that I could have said.) "I like all sports," I answered instead truthfully, "but I'm not good at any. Mostly I like being alone in nature, walking in the rain, watching the birds that take shelter under the leaves when it rains, and watching the early flowers that just fall so willingly—without any arrière pensée."

"Have you read any books on psychology?" he broke in.

"Everybody has read some books on psychology."

"Tch, tch." He shook his head disapprovingly. "If you had read any psychology, you would recognize that these are substitutes for sexual needs. You would know yourself better."

"Have all your feelings about nature been replaced by feelings about sex?" I asked him curiously.

"Not all." He had been disappointed by his first sexual experience, he told me, as he went on with the sketching, black, white, up and down.

Very few well mannered American men of that time would have described *any* experience of theirs as a "first sexual experience," and none would have confessed to a girl that he was "disappointed" by it. What a strange, sensually overfurnished world he lived in, I thought, despite these bare floors.

"But every time I deed eet, I was disappointed," Pheidias said artlessly, with a candid severity.

We spoke English and French interchangeably. In French, we were still using the *vous* form. Too bad English was no longer furnished with it. I liked personal relations to have these receding and ascending stages, because even back then I thought that real life should have a story line.

Goodness, but the plot was thickening rather fast, even for me. He was, as it turned out, a communist! How had that come about?

The route may seem to us now rather roundabout. It began
—as Merleau-Ponty had described the situation about ten years
earlier—with taking stock of the Second World War's aftermath.[2]
In the course of the war, a certain kind of mind-set had been nullified, and communism was imported, perhaps as a placeholder. The
set of prewar intellectuals—at least those described by Merleau-
Ponty—had believed that the same values could be attributed to all
thinking human beings, across national, racial, and religious lines.
Theirs had been the world of the Enlightenment, the bright world,
geared toward the future and progress, on which ideal the American Republic also had been founded. In fact, in his description,
those youthful friends of his sounded somewhat like we Americans
still were, in our own eyes at least, right then (in 1958).

It was a bit hard to picture, since we Americans really did seem
to ourselves then to come from a virgin country; whereas what
pressed down upon us most in Europe was the brute heaviness
of history, making streets narrow, crooked, and dark with time,
hacking faces—often separated by just a few cobbled streets and
a sentried bridge—into one national script and character, rather
than another. Could intellectual Europeans ever have been quite
so innocent of prejudice, so generous, and so inclined as Merleau-
Ponty recollected to treat each person just as an end in himself,
and not as a means? Well, Merleau-Ponty's privileged college set,
Normaliens all, had perhaps been like that. Anyway, so his formula
went as to life here before the Occupation.

What happened next, Merleau-Ponty recalled, was not just that
France had been invaded. The private mind of the individual was
invaded too. One found that, even if one tried to retreat into literature or into one's musings on universal human themes, the outside
world read these as "the reveries of captives." And even if one tried
not to compromise with the invader, there were so many small and
large daily routines in which one's cooperation was extorted that
resistance itself became at best partial. Unless and until one had
got oneself killed, that is. Short of that, everyone was compromised
in different degrees.

In the course of this experience, what one discovered was that
one didn't inhabit the realm of universals. One never had. What
one inhabited was a socially constructed space, an artifact, in other
words. Which had just been demolished and replaced in large measure by a different artifact. Values, then, were not universal but
"contingent" and were therefore (the existentialists were quick to
draw this inference) "absurd" in the sense of ultimately groundless.

One wasn't, then, a person of intrinsic worth. This was Merleau-Ponty's discovery. One was a captive Frenchman, or a captive Jew, in that case. The point was that one's very privacy was now discovered to have been the product of a dialogue internalized. Not only had one not been free alone, one couldn't even be *alone*, alone. The terms for solitude had been set within the larger social dialogue and always would be. (In fact, the problem of realizing universal worth in these contingent settings seemed rather like the problem that my women friends and I now had, of safeguarding our feminine worth in its contingent setting. If it was not going to be recognized by others in a timely and decisive way, how could we hold on to it for long? Nobody is that strongminded . . . as we too were sensing anxiously, in our ways and trying not to feel.) In sum, to go back to the argument of Merleau-Ponty, the prewar belief in the universality of Enlightenment values was now seen, in the postwar light, to have been an illusion.

To take this argument toward its Marxist conclusion, as Merleau-Ponty did next, one makes the following moves: Eternal and universal values should have some sort of metaphysical foundation, equally eternal and universal. Since, in the absence of a certain contingent political structure, values heretofore denominated universal had turned out insignificant, it may be concluded that there are *not* the requisite metaphysical supports for universal values. It follows that any speech that invokes universal values is false and must be giving masked expression to some baser, ulterior motives. The ulterior motives would be likely to have to do with unfair exercises of human power. We will now take the gamble of believing that all these unfair exercises proceed from an economic substructure that we can change. If we don't make that wager, then for us "il n'y a pas de philosophie de l'histoire." And if we do take the wager, then we must set aside all recourse to these merely "formal" values until the day when we will have secured a Marxist economic basis for reinstalling them as truly universal.

At any rate, the war and the depression that preceded it had seemed to promote a dark view of human nature. And the images evoked by that dark view were more forceful certainly than the arguments.[3]

"Don't you find that the communists have mauvaise foi?" I was asking Pheidias now hastily, in French.

"What do you mean by 'bad faith'?" he smiled crookedly, in English.

"That . . . they are very cynical."

"There are communists who serve out their careers in obscure provincial posts in France, sacrificing their lives for an ideal that they themselves will never live to enjoy. Do you call this 'cynicism'?"

"They seem to me to be involved with death," I said absolutely. "That's what I think of their materialism. That it's a preoccupation with death."

"I know what will happen to me when I die," Pheidias said disapprovingly. "I will rot."

"Oh, I will *too*. And the worms will eat me, and the grass will grow over it, and the birds will build their nests from it, and everybody will be happy except me!" I laughed, and he laughed too and shook his head, as if the objects of his disapproval were dissolving, slightly, into light.

As we left his sister's place to look for a restaurant that did an evening trade for hungry and poor students, I asked him why he'd never joined the Communist Party.

"Because," he replied, not unintelligently, "I don't like trouble."

"You sure talk a lot of trouble."

"Wh-what?"

"That's a country expression. I said that you *talk* a lot of trouble."

"Oh. Ha-ha!" He laughed appreciatively.

I felt I was doing quite well, as we walked into the night streets side by side. I remember his having to run all the way up the four flights of stairs to retrieve one of those French books on aesthetics, with the pages not yet cut, that I was always ferrying around with me and had left by the door in his sister's apartment. "How nice you are," I said sincerely, as he ran up to me, fresh, slim, and tireless. He said nothing, but his face was absorbent of every light and shadow in the breathless evening.

Chapter Four

Purity and Impurity

"Tu viens chez moi?"

"Oui."

Oh, why didn't I look for someone more suitable, or—since all Paris probably didn't hold anyone like that—simply take up my knitting instruments till I got sent home again?

More suitable? Whom would you suggest . . . for a person of my sort?

It was a black evening, and Pheidias and I had issued out of a café together into the snowy street. "How beautiful Paris is in the snow," I sighed, and he said nothing. "Let's walk," we agreed, and padded through the soft, pillowed snow underfoot, till we rejoined the quais, above their glittering night river. The conversation had gone back to communism, and we were still arguing about it. Something is going to have to give soon between us, I thought, or we will start to lose tension. Not that we will bore each other, exactly, but we might well sail past our peak. So we passed rhythmically together through the soft night.

Pheidias was showing me, in leisurely fashion, the seventeenth-century stone house where his sister's *belle-mère*, the lady whom we had met, lived with her husband. Pheidias too was from a top-of-the-line Greek family, as he'd mentioned, but disinherited now by his fiercely anticommunist father.

"If communism comes here," I asked, looking up solicitously at the lofty, lighted windows, "what will become of people like your sister's in-laws here?"

"I don't know," he returned composedly. "Perhaps they will have to share the house with a few other families, perhaps not."

We turned to walk silently back again. "Of course, you *know* that under communism only the means of production is shared, not consumer goods, don't you?" He gave me a sharp look.

"Yes," I answered doubtfully.

"Tch tch." He—rightly enough—didn't believe me. Not any more than I believed him.

"Will you come to my room?"

"Yes."

It was a long climb up the dark, winding stair to his *chambre de bonne* above one of the ancient streets of the Latin Quarter, but, in the ascent, the sense of excitement mounted with us. Apart from a night table and a desk, he had only a bed. We sat on it, the lamplight flickering over us and over the scarlet, tapestried wall coverings of his low-slanted room. (His decorative concept had borrowed nothing from the Bauhaus, but it suited me, in its intrinsic ornateness.) An intricate iron grille outside overhung the streets below, joining us to a chorus of large-windowed balconies and low-angled roofs, under the pillowed sky.

We had talked long enough, and I wanted to repair to the "bathroom." But there was no such American thing, as it turned out. He walked me grimly down the hall to a dark cubicle with a wooden door and a seatless bowl. It was tough, this particular cultural adjustment. On my way back, the timed hall light flickered out, banking the hall in its unforgiving black darkness. Not knowing where the switch was, I was not able to take a single step forward or back. Finally, he opened the door, and a panel of light fell on the corridor.

"Thank goodness," I said. "I was lost, completely." Sympathetic, he hurried me back to the lamplight. "Do you have a towel?" I asked. "And soap?"—determined to play out this American purification rite to the bitter end. Accordingly, he walked me back to the faucet on the stairwell, where I washed and dried my hands under his unsmiling supervision. It felt to me as if I must love him.

"I'm in love with Pheidias," I said to Harper on another day, later during that week. "And I want to have an 'affair' with him. But I *don't* want to marry him."

"Oh, dear," sing-songed Harper, tapping her shoe anxiously and protectively on the grey pavement. "If you don't want to marry him"—she shook her head rhythmically—"then you don't want to have an affair with him."

I was worn out. The traffic went by us, and I registered confusedly the vacant blaring of *klaxons*, the stop-and-go lights that were blinking, the muddled cacophony of vehicles delaying each other down the white middle of that stock-still Paris afternoon. The motions of restlessness went by me, and I thought, well of course I didn't mean by "affair" a real *affair*. But one had to say *something*. One couldn't just wait on the corner for the light to change, verbally too. And all these dull avenues lit up behind me.

"Tu viens chez moi?" You are coming to my place? he asked me gently, on another occasion, some days later. Generally, in the evenings, we would land at his place about nine, having met first at a café, and I would leave about 10:15, explaining that I had a cold. In the interval, his bed would be littered with my clean, white, ladylike handkerchiefs, which I would have pulled out of my handbag, one by one. "You have there a quantity," he would sniff, mockingly.

"Oui," now I muffled my smiling answer to his question in his shoulder. We paced the long streets slowly, leaning into each other like one stately, intertwined statue that was gliding on invisible tracks. This was the very dance step that had looked so mysterious to me in those first crowded days in Paris. It was easy, as I was discovering.

"Hallo, Abigail." It was Benjamin,* a boy whom I'd known in college. He was here for the fall season. Ubiquitous and unconcealedly superficial, he peered at us curiously where we had broken ranks in the white street light. "Where were you *going?*" he asked frankly.

"We were just walking . . . along," I offered, evasively. I was always glad to see Benjamin, but just now I would be gladder to see him off.

"Are you an American?" He peered deliberately up at Pheidias's raised, bearded chin.

Pheidias had not moved. "No," he unbent enough to say, in the frozen night air.

We all laughed, a little.

"Well," he giggled, as no invitation was proffered. "So long. See yuh."

"Bye, Ben," I said with casual cordiality.

"Who was that?" Pheidias asked severely, after a moment.

"Oh, he's a very nice friend from college," I explained—feeling protected from all such friends and their niceness by Pheidias's irrational wrath. We climbed the long, breathtaking staircase to his landing.

*Not his real name.

"Pauvre victime," he was crooning, as he lay back on the bed. "They are going to take from her her freedom, her rights, her house, her children"—all the things I had noted, at one time or another in our conversations, that communists triumphant were wont to take away from one.

I shook my head at him reprovingly. "It is true. You should not joke."

He wheeled about on the bed, with the swiftness of a wood sprite, looking at me upside down. "Your eyes are very pretty."

It was almost the first time he had said something—about eyes— that jibed with the ethnologist's report. "So are yours," I returned a bit awkwardly, grinning. But it was true. His were. "Do many people in your country have archaic eyes?"

He shook his head, egoistically, and sat up again, still moving with disturbing speed.

For the first time since I had started coming up to his room, I was leaning up against the wall, sitting across the narrow bed, with my feet off the ground.

He took a place close beside me now, against the same wall.

"J'ai peur de toi," I said automatically, and truthfully. I *was* scared. What, after all, was I doing here with this stranger?

That is the absolutely crucial question. And, by the time it occurs to one, one never has a long time to consider it. All the great questions in life arise in real time, and are settled in real time, when one is on an emergency footing. If one hasn't settled in one's mind what to do a long time previous to the occasion when the question arises, or carved the right habits into one's psychosomatic structure, one is not likely to do the most prudent thing.

"One would think, a child of twelve years," he murmured, next to my ear. "Pourquoi?" he said, as I made some resistance. And then, seriously, with a declaration: "I love you, in a certain fashion. And if I don't love you more, it's from fear . . . that you won't reciprocate."

"That's my case too, more or less."

"We have talked too much of politics, and not enough of love," he said reflectively, in the warm lamplight. He moved forward soundlessly now, and we kissed.

It was like our walk outside, a slow and mutual manipulation.

"It's more fun than eating," I said to him, somewhat surprised, when finally we drew back from each other.

He smiled sexily. "You know how to kiss very well," he observed, when we had tried it again.

That, I felt, was on a par with saying that one had a lot of class.

He moved furtively, with a slim hand swift as an otter, rolling it under my skirt.

"No! Wait a minute! Hey," I muttered rapidly in English, about to carry on with What kind of girl do you think I am? but even in 1959 that sounded a bit silly, so I just looked at him with a half grin, shaking my head.

"Pourquoi," said a soft voice in my ear. "Tu ne vas me dire que tu es vierge?"

"But of course! But what have you been *thinking*!"

He pondered this. "Usually, virgins don't feel anything."

"Well, in America," I said grandly and vaguely, "they do feel things."

"But I don't know any virgins of your age."

"Well," I fibbed, "I may be the only virgin that I know." I was pretending to him, and to myself, that we were discussing a commodity, when what was under discussion was the whole future course of my life.

He shook his head impatiently, as if roused abruptly from some utter unreality, and sent his hands back to their earlier workplace.

The un-American lie that had just passed my lips, and the slight shift of emphasis toward an unrefined view of this topic, had put me off balance. We were now, as it suddenly seemed, engaged in a *physical* struggle. If things once take that turn, a woman has lost some ground that is tactically crucial. I no longer knew exactly what *I* was doing. Whereas he did.

"You'll see, you'll see," he was repeating gently, looking at me insistently.

I stared at him.

"It's not wrong, it's not wrong, there is nothing wrong about it," he said simply, rhythmically, crooningly, shaking his head, looking at me.

Or, if it was, you couldn't prove it by Schopenhauer, Nietzsche, Darwin, Freud, and Marx. What it felt like was cold, extremely smooth, and quite impersonal. But it seemed that there was more closeted behind the partition of these opening sensations. Strange, undefined reactions were starting from *above* the places that his hand could reach. I had thought that there was a line at that frontier that you couldn't cross. Now it seemed we were suddenly *over* that line. "Stop!"

He stopped immediately. "You don't like it when I put my hand *inside*?" he asked me curiously, after a moment.

That depended on what you meant by *like*. "No," I said, obscurely but emphatically.

"That is curious." He looked down, thinking. "Usually, when a woman reacts as you have, that means that what she feels is pleasure."

Oh, I thought, shaking my head, baffled. I had not known that one was not supposed to react in that way.

"And another thing," his glance started up again. "Are you sure that you're really a virgin?"

Oppressed by his misunderstandings, I protested. Here I was going through something for the first time, and he was acting as if it was some shopworn thing. "Well, of course I am a virgin! I *told* you that I was a virgin!" I got up from the bed, a bit tardily for any overall purpose I had heretofore entertained. There wasn't a great deal of space in that room, but I went to the edge of whatever spaces it could be found still to hold.

He smiled argumentatively as I looked back over my shoulder. "I put my hand in as far as that."

The gods, Plato said, do not hold arguments the outcome of which turns on a measurement. I had never held such an argument either. "But, Pheidias, why would I lie to you?"

"Many girls lie about that." And there was the sly grin of some rather low-down worldly experience.

"Look, Pheidias," I tried to explain. "Really. America is a new country. We don't know *how* to lie there."

Yes. And, for my children, there are always the mountains. So said the poet once, about the Republic, the perishing Republic.

He was slightly amused, but unimpressed.

He was equally unimpressed about the convexities, which my hands described, of a western saddle.

Finally, I told him about Tampax, a New World invention that had yet to make its way across the Atlantic. He'd never heard of it, wanted to have the engineering principle of it explained, which required that I ruin a spare one for him, but with that he finally subsided. I think he was really convinced. That and my attitude. But mainly that. V'là le front populaire! Nothing to count as evidence that is not strictly material.

"At any rate, your husband will never believe you."

I smiled confidently—my husband would so believe me—not seeing what he was leading up to.

"Ecoute, Abigail," he said in French decisively. "I love you. I would marry you tomorrow, only I haven't got enough money."

At the mention of marriage, I breathed in relief, for in that sacred, incantational word I hoped and believed I could rediscover the boy I must have chosen, out of the loveless crowd. I could marry him, the lucky fellow. I wouldn't, of course. But I could.

"I believe that you are noble, that you are good, that you are intelligent, that you are pure" and so on and on, a soft litany. In French. "I see all the qualities in you."

Well, perhaps it *hadn't* been so wrong. Perhaps he had had the right to that liberty.

"And"—there was an almost imperceptible, diagonal gesture, taking in his whole body, that startled me—"I want to see you in the nude."

"Wh-what?" I shook my head. Shook it a few times. We all have our little fancies. There was no call for him to have felt ashamed of this one. I had read enough *about* Freud and company for me to know that. And a girl could even feel flattered to have occasioned such a small fancy, but . . .

His agile fingers were running down the front buttons of my green knitted sweater, snapping them.

"Hey! *Wait* a minute."

Hey, wait a minute. In those companionable and casual sounds of the voice lie all the difference between the nineteenth and the twentieth centuries, the difference between Artsybashev's Nietzschean "She surrendered to another's will," and our more colloquial "Well, I guess things got out of hand." When you come to think of it, it's not a *very* great difference.

"You *cannot* undress a woman," I explained to him gently, tactfully, elegantly and, as I thought, decisively, "unless she is first 'dressed' in her own consent."

He took this in. "That means you are ashamed" was his good materialist misreading of what I'd so carefully articulated.

I was starting to sense that my words had been drained of their power. But I hadn't even *known* that one could do that to words. Nor did I see clearly now who or what had opened the drain, so to speak.

He, meanwhile, was still at it, pulling the green sweater down and away over my wrists.

I called him by his full name. Arrestingly. His full name should have some power. I slapped him once across the face. Medium hard. (I didn't like to hurt people.) *That* at least should have some power.

We both grinned, in embarrassment.

I decided to get up, reasoning that this little bed had become a place that was fraught with risk.

He was behind me, arms under me. Somehow I was first contained in those arms and then carried back to the bed's flat surface. Stubbornly, persistently, I tried it again, kicking this time (but kicking only slightly, since I still didn't like to hurt people).

No modern girl who goes about the world unchaperoned (and

takes what I'd fondly believed were just *minimal* risks) can save her virtue today, unless she damn well doesn't mind hurting people. Or unless God saves it. A girl from an earthier culture than mine might carry a knife and be willing to use it, or threats and be willing to follow through on them. The feminist movement has tried to train women to fight dirty when they, quotes, have to. If any woman reading this has acquired that skill, more power to her. It's for sure I had not acquired it. Nor did I believe it was "feminine" even to think that way.

"I am going to rape you," he said inevitably, in French.

"If you do that, I will never forgive you," I replied. "Never."

"You are so beautiful when you are angry."

"Listen," I argued, "I, the real me, isn't here. I'm not *here*. You're supposed to love *me*."

He laughed outright.

In the battle of the gods and the giants,[1] it is the gods who can be more easily made to look ridiculous.

"You're laughing," I said bitterly, as we joined what communists have called, in other settings, *la lutte finale*. The final battle as regards clothing, at least.

"I'm laughing stupidly, senselessly," he said at once, in French, stopping. The clasp was loosened, and I hadn't realized that all you have to do is jerk a brassiere upward, and it loses its usefulness, for all that it is still locked under your arms. His face smoothed in what looked like a religious emotion.

I turned my head aside, unable to witness this *catastrophic* defeat. At a loss. "I have *never* been undressed in front of a man," I said to the wall. "Not even a doctor." It was paralyzing.

He shook his head. What kind of an upbringing had I had?

"Will you give me that?" he asked softly, having gone on to take all the rest without asking, and now fingering a chain and a green, stone pendant, as I kneeled on the bed, head averted, like a stone statue in the bright lamplight.

I bent my head slightly, and he laid the necklace on the night table below the bed. "What beauty," he said, with a kiss brushing my ear.

I shook my head. Now he knew it all. Besides, how would I get those clothes back on? They were under the bed—everywhere.

"I have never seen a woman like you," he repeated.

"Pourtant, there are better ones," I said in French, lying down comfortably alongside him.

"No," he shook his head with what looked like utter conviction.

Undeniably, I was beginning to feel a little happier in the nude.

The existential question, What is my body for others? was receiving a pleasant answer.

"Listen," Pheidias said. "Get under my sheets. You'll catch cold."

"No!" I protested anew. "This is some further twisted ruse. You just want to see me in your *bed*."

"Don't be ridiculous." He shook off the suggestion. "Listen," he said to me seriously, "right now, I don't *feel* any physical desire. And it's a good thing for you that I don't, or it would be," he used the menacing English idiom, "short shrift."

Short shrift, indeed! I thought indignantly.

"But I can't sit here when you are nude in front of me."

Well, whose idea was it? I thought—but now thought it safer not to say.

Doubtfully, I obeyed. I had not won on a single front tonight.

What I felt then, rightly or wrongly, was that—although psychologically and physiologically still a virgin—I had already stepped, almost accidentally and certainly without meaning to, into a vast and antique realm in which the parts for men and women were all prepared and laid out. It was an important piece of the museum landscape of history, and suddenly I was in it, and it had come alive for me. I did not know where it ended or where it had begun. I only knew that there were other gods here.

I wasn't free. There were parts of me, fragments broken off, that belonged in that earlier museum. I wasn't free to look up and see the chariots of fire coming. I wasn't free.

I sat up in bed. We were talking about whether or not he was trustworthy. I believe I pointed out that *communists* believe that the end justifies any means. He replied with apparent anger that he had not known that I saw him in such a bad light. I raised one warm rounded arm to his neck, the sheet falling below one breast at the same moment, and said, sweetly and—in the light of what had just occurred, incomprehensibly—"Do you not *see* that I have confidence in you?"

He plunged into a chaste hug as if I were a pillowed haven, instead of a mere girl made of flesh and angular bones, and then kissed me till I was out of breath.

Well! I'd better not try that too often, I thought.

Anyway, it was about time to look for my clothes. He was surprisingly helpful. There was a last metro at 12:15. My skirt had been torn in the fracas and, as I hooked it up, he promised to repair it for me. I scoffed. "I will never wear that skirt again."

"On the contrary. It's a most attractive skirt. You will wear it often."

As it turned out, I was right. He couldn't sew worth a damn. "When I told you that I couldn't sew, I knew how to sew better than *that*," I was to tell him, while he grinned helplessly, having done his lopsided best.

A jagged tear like that in the wool cannot be mended, except by what the English tailors call an "invisible weaver." (Or except by the Invisible Weaver on the plane behind the empirical one.)

Now he sat on the bed looking at me as I regained all my clothes, and I felt a sudden, liberating sense of the feminine power. I glided to his waiting knee, put up encircling arms, and kissed him searchingly.

"It seems like a dream to me," he muttered huskily, "that you embrace me voluntarily."

It was a dream. And it belonged to the dream. And so much for definitions of man through aesthetic experience.

He picked me up in his arms as he had done before, but rotating now as if we were *both* just innocent children, and then walked with his burden to the grill-worked balcony, where we looked out together over the soft city night and got ready, taking in this view, to leave his peaked chambre de bonne.

So we clattered down the six or seven flights of stairs, ran rapidly into the chill streets, and trotted to the Place St. Michel, a few blocks away. Pheidias's face was grim in the white streetlights. If we missed the train, he would not laugh, as an American boy might do, for lives sometimes hang on that, as Europeans had already learned. We kissed at the station, that being the signature on our adoption in the city where all lovers are the same, or *at least*—so a French song of that year went—where they are that for so long as they are lovers.

Chapter Five

The Sense of the Argument

My next days revolved like the transparent spokes of a giant waterwheel around the one question. Were there no other questions?

I went to join the writer Richard Wright at the back tables of the café, le Tournon, where he presided in his homey Black-American exile. To me, at that time, Wright was a celebrity, my first—maybe my last—celebrity, for no one else will strike me quite that way. He had acquired and fairly won his fame. And he *talked* to me, big, handsome, and expansive as he was, like a warm American hearth fire in the dank foreign cellar that was the Tournon! One time, he even read me some haiku poems that he'd been composing and seemed mildly struck by the precision with which I described back to him what he had achieved. He'd given me a less jovial, more puzzled and focused, considering look than usual, on that occasion.

We'd been introduced by my friend Anna,* a Czech girl who had been my father's student and knew Paris well. "This," Anna had said, "is my good friend Abigail Rosenthal, Fulbright scholar, and Abigail, this is—"

"Richard Wright," I had agreed.

His eyes seemed to wink jollity because I'd recognized him, and he'd answered, nodding, "You're American?"

Today, the writer was chatting as he often did with some young

---

*Not her real name.

people as I sat there, taken in, protected, and entertained, till he took note of a silence behind me. I spun round in my chair, aware that it was Pheidias, who looked like a bearded sentry of archaic time, clucking at my café idleness and joining me to him with one long, tentative, extended finger at the top button of my tweed coat. I looked up at him. In an undertone, we arranged to meet later. He was gone, and I seemed to brush bits of the wine-dark sea spray from my clouds of dark hair.

"Is that *him?*" said Wright, exaggerating the pronoun.

I nodded. In a tête-à-tête with Wright, a few days before, I'd mentioned that I had "met someone."

He laughed. "As if it weren't obvious. He's no good *at all.*"

"Why do you say that?"

He shook his head expansively. "Abigail, I've seen the American male, the French male, the African male, the Asian male—and I can tell you: That man is *the worst.* 'Ohww, Aah-bi-gail, plee-ee-se . . . I'll *die* without you.'"

It was a huge exaggeration. It was falsetto. Nevertheless, he must know something. I asked him to tell me more, but he refused at the time.

"Why does Richard Wright spend so much of his time in cafés, talking to young girls?" Pheidias said to me irritably that evening, when we met again. "The air there is not healthy. And, by the way, would you ask him for me why, if, as he says in *The God That Failed*, he became disillusioned with the Communist Party, he did not found a *real* Communist Party of his own, a new one?"

"Tell Pheidias that I think 'the Communist Party' is anything the men in the Kremlin say it is," said Wright to me shortly, when I asked him. For a fact, Pheidias was the only human being—man, woman, or child—that I ever saw Richard Wright cut dead at the Tournon.

On another day, in the chill afternoon, Pheidias and I strolled a circuitous half mile toward the Boulevard St. Michel, under the shadowy ramparts of buildings now familiar.

"Tu sais l'amour," he crooned, in the gentlest of Greek altos, "c'est éternel. Mais dans les conditions favorables."

Well, at least he wasn't saying he would die without me. A certain intelligence was at work. But was this all life was to confer, as my present allotment? This fragile, revocable tissue of feelings? "Pheidias," I frowned. "I have seen girls who began with one affair and then, when that one did not work out, with another, and then with a *third*."

"Yes," he nodded absolutely.

"They"—I was confining my objection to the aesthetics—"they wore a mask." But the *faces* that I had seen! The horrid, pale, matted faces, with crumpled hair and mouths set in the firm, bitter rhythms of alcohol and resignation. They were masks that told all, and that had nothing left to tell.

"Everyone wears a mask," he said soberly—and inaccurately. "You wore a mask too, when I saw you again after the first time we met. I believed . . . you were not pleased to see me."

"Of course . . ." I said half-involuntarily.

"What?"

"It is true that *their* case might not be mine."

"Of course, it is true," he spoke feelingly.

Whatever their case was like, I really had no argument. There was no way, in my own mind, that I could undo the implications of that recent evening in his room. No one else *could* be the first, now. And the very fact that I thought along these lines already was testimony to the success of the means he had used, which were classic: Take more than the object of your attentions would willingly have surrendered. Then leave *her* to make the further justificatory moves that will at least allow her to *place* what has happened in a plausible setting.

Besides, it had not been *just* a phase of seduction. It had been such a phase superimposed on something else, I felt, something larger and better. Something *like* love. (Perhaps all seduction has a trace of that character. I couldn't say.) I had no idea what to do. It seemed to me that what was between us was something to be pursued till it had been at least identified—backward in time to where it had veered away from us and forward in time to where we could capture it once again. And it was to be brought, as I hoped, to its own reduced-scale self-completion, on its own terms. Even a false, or a half-false, incident in one's life deserves to be given a chance to show its true meaning and character. Or, to put it more precisely, it was not the half-false *incident* that deserved to be given a chance: It was I, who had to be afforded the means to see what reality might have been lying behind it.

We didn't have assertiveness-training classes in those days. Had I been the fiancée of a minister, I would never have gone to Pheidias's room. Had I been trained by a nun, I would not have allowed to a stranger an "occasion of sin." I would have known that a new male acquaintance is by definition a predator, that all men are like that. My Czech friend Anna was no votary of virginity, trained as she was by the war and the refugee camps after 1948, but she would have broken Pheidias's window before she let him tear off

her clothes. Broken it with her bare fist. And there were also perhaps more pampered American women, secular graduate students
with a psychological turn of mind, but tough and practical, who
could have said, even in that time, "*Nobody* treats me like that.
We're through."

But I wasn't one of them. He had really surprised me. And now,
in my own mind, I was already halfway over a river nobody could
cross—and remain on the path that I still meant to walk. It was
quite afflicting. All that I had to lean on was my own search for some
better understanding, one that would leave us both, as I hoped,
ready to part but reconciled. It was a rather frail reed.

"Will you love me even if I want to remain a virgin?" I asked
him in French, standing by the shadow-inlaid metro station door.

His face was swept clean of any guile, and he looked somberly
at me. "I don't have the choice," he replied in French.

Northeastbound, one night later that week, across a network of
steel tracks, I spied Harper in her rich-American's fur coat, standing on the metro station platform opposite mine and waiting for
the westbound train. *Harper* would help me. "Call me," I yelled to
her across the tracks, calling her name.

"What?"

"Call me," I yelled again, as her westbound train came roaring in.

Pheidias moved across the narrow space of his room to his desk
to check my watch, which was lying face up. "Don't bother to get
up," he said coolly. "You will never make your train."

"What do you mean?" I got up to inspect the watch's face. "I can
make it."

"You cannot possibly make it in two minutes."

"I'll stay with Nancy," I suggested. Nancy Sendler lived in a
chilly, overlarge, uncompromisingly French room, with nearly
door-sized windows and massive wooden armoires, in the neighboring sixth arrondissement. The direct access that she had to the
lavatory and the exit was shared with the French *famille* that occupied the rest of the rooms of the apartment and paid its rent, as I surmised, from a part of the proceeds derived from my friend Nancy.

"You cannot disturb her at this hour."

That was probably true.

"I'll walk home."

His voice pitched higher. "It is dangerous." He paced the tiny
room like a lynx, while I sat half-dressed and bare shouldered on
the bed. "I advise you to make the best of it," he said, in reproach at

a gesture from me that suggested that I thought I was trapped. "I'll sleep on the floor."

Sent out while he changed, I used the contrivance at the murky back end of the hall. By now, I could find the *minuterie*. But when I returned, I found him already in bed, in his shorts, nude shoulders gleaming.

"I thought you were going to be over there, on the floor." I indicated the only bare corner of his cold, tiny room.

He grinned at me fastidiously.

So I shouldered in beside him, on that extremely narrow bed, clad in my underthings, and a sweater.

"Civilized people *remove* their street clothes when they sleep."

I slid out of the green sweater, thinking that the washing facilities here did not exactly reflect my understanding of the civilization of the 1950s.

We lay still together, talking a little. I had never *slept* with a man before. It was forbidden fruit, in a way, but maybe it had a certain innocence too. Like a slumber party? Gingerly, I unclasped my brassiere. He pulled it through my arms for me, assenting vigorously. After a little while, I shrugged off the other things that I wore, *seeking* now the lost comfort of the nude, as if any comfort were better than none.

He murmured approval, and I grinned and turned toward his arms, wanting to rest in them. But he had slipped off his shorts as well, leaving his much more untrustworthy *male* genitals exposed to the four winds under the blanket. I relaxed against him anyway, but more doubtfully now.

We moved restlessly, unsleeping in our narrow arena. Once, he came to climax against my belly (a native custom perhaps), with me lying beneath him in unsmiling discomfort. But I did not know on what grounds to refuse him that imperious "substitution."

Toward dawn, when I had thought this dangerously long night over and survived, he moved over me once again, working himself back to climax nearer the dividing line. "Why there?" I squirmed, shaking my head vigorously.

"Because elsewhere," he said, "it's disgusting."

The aestheticized world could not coexist with *that* word. "No!" I said nonetheless, as the organ in question pressed uncomfortably hard by the danger point.

"I will move away in time," he promised.

Still I resisted, shifting my legs sidewise.

He turned his eyes on me undividedly. *"Be a woman,"* he said, with a kind of stern, imploring contempt for me.

Now I hated him. But I had no further court of appeal. Motion denied. Henceforth I felt him taking charge over me. It took so long. I should not worry that it takes so long. He had given his word. His *word* must be good. But it seemed to be taking all the time that I had. Why was one pushed so, out of the secrecy of one's being? It was happening just as if one were being pushed into a trap. *Into the trap.* The rude mechanic trap.

"Why, it's nothing but a trick"—I sat up speaking dirt-hard American—"a dirty, filthy trick!"

"I'm sorry, Abigail," Pheidias was saying in halting English, at the same time, "that the first time we have done it, it had no significance . . ."

Oh, but it had. It had all the significance of the injustice between the sexes. Of the injustice that *makes up* the sexes. What could he have done? It was not his fault—it was as much my own, as the saying goes—but tears were pounding like breakers against unyielding cliffs for all the women who had ever been tricked and done in, in time, for it was my time, as a woman, to be.

I plunged around, intending to pillow my head on the hard narrow mattress, but he would not let go of me. He was pressing his lips to my wet-rivered, upturned face, hugging me in hungry importunity, and grieving himself.

I despised and hated him, but now for the first time also suddenly *feared* his power over me, for if he were to let me go, what really would become of me? Abandoned strumpets littered the beaches. Waves of time pounded them into cockleshells. Good God. I cried on inexhaustibly, begging him to let me cover my face, but afraid now to push him away.

Later that morning, after he had convinced me to sleep a little, he brought me a bit of bread from the *épicier*. It was brown and dry, with some honey smeared on it.

I bit into the bread but could not swallow it. "It sticks in my throat," I informed him.

"Are you so unhhhappy?" lugubriously in English he questioned me.

I nodded and sighed, large eyed. "Oh, yes."

On a good day, I would not have been able to swallow that bread either. It was too dry. But I gave him the bread to understand me by, since all of his frames of reference were material. He looked red eyed and florid. Whenever, later, he wanted to sob, color always came into his face. Otherwise, he would remain pale.

I got dressed slowly then, in yesterday's clothes. Now we spoke only English, its harsh, uncompromising outlines my reacquired language.

"Listen," said Pheidias to me. "You are no more a virgin. But not because of that. It is because you spent a whole night, with a man, without any clothes, in the same bed. That is why. *No* girl is a virgin after that."

He was trying to reason the thing out for me. I would not *always* be beached here. He drew an analogy between what I thought of virginity and the obsessions he'd had when he was eighteen over death and the alternatives of immortality or extinction. But later, when he got older, he said, he had thought about other, more *interesting*, subjects. So too it would prove in my case. "Besides"—he regarded me quizzically and added in French—"there is a spring by the sea where once a year the goddess Hera goes to bathe . . . and become virgin again."

Would to God.

All the rest of that overcast day he stayed with me, while these new, somber-hued shadows moved over my life. We walked through the streets together, I numbly astride the sensation of sexual penetration that, unaccountably, would not go away.

I entered the knowing, dark-green recesses of the Tournon with him, head down, humble under his arm, childish in the aftermath of that welter of tears, and there I had to stop him from running a hand of Greek ownership over one breast, in full view of the others. Everyone saw, though of course no one was looking.

Back under the electric streetlights in front of his house, at ten o'clock in the evening, I finally said that I would leave him and go for a walk alone. "And," I stabbed, "I will never see you again."

"You will see me again," he said absolutely, smiling briefly. And he set a date, two days ahead.

Dimly, I could already sense that for me it would be a long, hard, two days' wait.

"Go home now," he told me very seriously.

"No. I am going for a walk." I nodded willfully in the direction of the River Seine.

"All right," he granted permission. He was not going to oppose me on a stubborn thing, in spite of the darkness of the wild night and the lateness of the hour. "Goodbye"—he kissed me, like one who held, and would always hold now, my life strings in his hands.

I made my way headlong, under the criss-crossing, red-and-white blinking streetlights, to the far side of the river, where I found a perch halfway down the stone steps that descended from the quais framing Notre Dame.

The Seine was at flood tide that night, so it churned but a few feet from where I sat huddled—bearing up wooden planks, a stray rubber boot, and unnamed shapeless objects, chunks of black refuse, within its cold currents.

Alone for the first time in twenty-four hours, I crouched in the cold, stone shadows and tried hard to think. In Russian novels, the girls drowned themselves. So I stared down at this, my careening, inky river. All of the future that I used to have had halted above its black quakings. What was a girl supposed to *do*, now?

Experimentally, I leaned over the water and trailed its rapids through my fingers. On the instant, a nervous male voice at street level was asking me sharply, Was there anything wrong? *Mademoiselle?*

Very firm for once, I succeeded in packing the intruder off. *My* decision remained to be taken. It was mine.

Since all this had *happened* to me, I reflected vaguely, as if inhaling the black tide, I would do well to take it in as my destiny from now on, and embrace it in some way. What made that destiny seem so sad, then? It would be part of that destiny to learn philosophy, to sit in the cafés, to observe the parade on the thoroughfare outside. To be left alone. To be free, to set out in prolonged pursuit of a lost self-transparency. To leave him, after all, one day, taking back all these life strings. And never, for very long, to see my feminine feelings held up and made much of in the social continuity.

The waves heaved and sank and whirled coarsely away. I stared at them enviously. Would drowning here put me at one with such things?

I reflected. I would feel an icy chill, and the random battering of oncarried objects, and the lungs filling, but that would be all. Life's repleteness would not then fill me, would rather pass over me, and I would die—merely leave this strange world—uncaptivated.

I was beginning to feel the cold. Rubbing my numb ankles nervously, I got up.

Sometimes, life absolutely gets away from one. At such moments, some people call on Providence for help. Thinking myself utterly alone in this upreaching, I walked on, footsteps thick and slow, pursued by the senses of an argument that had appeared nearly to put an end to me, and had after all preserved me alive.

Chapter Six

Shoreline

Pheidias had been right, of course. For the two days that followed, I suffered one intrusive impulse: to fly to his door, plead for love without letup, and run up the white flag. The supercilious curiosity of my devoutly French, widowed landlady and her virginal daughter left only marginal marks on the welter of changed feelings through which I now made my uncertain way. Since returning to my room, I'd found no assumptions that were self-evident and framed no enduring resolutions, except one: to be honest, wholly honest, with myself. Without such self-transparency as I could muster, my historical quest would have lost its informing substance: its truth.

So far, I had almost not had to lie to anyone else, either. My landlady had asked where I'd been and had paused for the reply she expected—*with Harper*—knowing, as I did not, that Harper had already called to inquire anxiously after me. Catching the glint in her eye, however, I'd answered briefly, "Chez une amie." If I'd wanted to take this as having been translated from the English, it would not have been a lie. In English, *friend* can be male or female. But *une* is not *un*. So it *was* a lie, after all. My first sad lie. And traceable to the erotic precision of the French language.

On the second morning of these ruminations, Harper called. "I was out the day before yesterday, but I tried to get you all evening and all day. Your landlady said she couldn't tell me where you were!"

"Oh, I didn't get home till the following night." I had never lied to Harper in my life, and I wasn't about to start now.

"Abigail, if I didn't know you better, I'd say, what have you been *doing*?"

"And if you knew me better, you might say the same thing," I blurted illogically.

"Abigail!"

I rang her carved wooden doorbell a few hours later.

The heavy door opened, and we kissed softly on each cheek. As we came into her room, she was saying to me, "Why didn't you call me after you saw me that day in the metro? If you needed to see me, you ought to have come here. I was very *angry* at you for calling it fate, and letting me let you down!"

We stood facing each other.

"Now, what has happened?"

"Oh, Harper?" I sobbed helplessly, the question that was not one in my voice, and she embraced me, patting my back in long-spaced, long-fingered pats. "I'm not a virgin any more."

"Well, that's not so bad."

Never has anyone said anything to me more expressive of *genuine* friendship.

We sat down on a pair of ottomans, stockinged knees bumping against stockinged knees. My skirt, which was straight, rode up slightly, on account of the low angle of the ottoman.

"Yes, a lot of hands have been up its skirts lately, haven't they?" she crooned, nodding like a wise flamingo.

I had to laugh. It *was* funny.

"Of course you *know* that my fiancé and I went to bed together."

It was a small sun, no bigger than the hand of an honest man. But it was able to light my whole sky. "No," I shook down a few spare tears. "I didn't know." But still, I felt, perhaps that had been *love*. This was mere sensuality. Sensuality and rape. "But I'm not going to *marry* Pheidias." He had hurt me too much. How could I marry him? I had known that by the Seine. Rape was too low an activity. Being the bride of a rapist was stooping too low.

And she told me her whole, sad-comic, picaresque story.

I listened. So this is what it's like to be real, and to get your heart broke, like other girls. What she gave me, most directly, was that priceless sense of the feminine solidarity. "But, Harper, suppose I get pregnant?" Of course there'd been no precautions. I explained that it had been a rape, as indeed—by my somewhat blurry lights— it still seemed to me that it was.

"You'd have an abortion. If I'm still in France, I'd go with you to Sweden." Harper was to leave France in June for her wedding.

"But, Harper . . ." I looked down, and then into her eyes directly. "Isn't that a sin?"

She shook her head and looked at me with great kindness. *Southern* kindness. "There are *many* sins, dear."

I took this in. Maybe so. It was nice that she thought so. "Pheidias and I have a rendezvous at 4:30," I said nervously, after a moment. "I will have to leave soon."

"Then you will need to make use of my mirror." She looked on judiciously while I washed my eyes and then put on my two subtly pale shades, overlapping, of lipstick. "Remember too," she said, "that if Pheidias wants to marry you, that it's he who will be hurt. So you be gentle with him, and come to me for support."

"But what happens after you leave?"

"But let me help you while I'm here. And have faith in who will be around—in someone's being around, that is—to do it when I'm gone. Our whole lives we do that!" she said to me clearly, as I faced her briefly at last in the stairwell. "You didn't say to your parents when you were born, 'Don't take care of me—you'll die someday and then I'll be dependent on you.' And it's really the same thing!"

"Okay," I nodded.

It was sure okay with me in principle, and she had been unforgettably good that day, in fact. No woman friend could have been better. But it also needed an Invisible Weaver to repair the fault line in the self-weave that had just become evident to the touch, stretching from edge to edge of my being, in the hard loom of the world.

Pheidias was relieved to see me gentle and smiling, in the mood that I brought to him from Harper's room, and we embraced with this cool, reciprocal forgiveness. The long days began to fill up. We did not quite repeat the great experiment, but still, I had a lover. *Tiens.*

I walked along the rue de Tournon thinking of him. A gendarme on sentry duty remarked to his fellow gendarme, "Smile of love," and, involuntarily, my smile broadened.

I met Anna at le Tournon. "Where have you been?" she asked sharply.

"I've been with Pheidias this whole week," I said revealingly, "and partly I've let the whole world drop." A French girl at a table nearby eyed me collegially.

I met John Armstrong for breakfast, on one prematurely balmy winter morning. "And speaking of sex," he remarked to me for no special reason, looking out at the cool, hazy terrace of our café, "Abigail, what's *your* opinion of the big subject?"

Not too fast, I warned myself. Slow down. Be careful. He's an American. They can condemn. But one was also condemned for seeming overly puritanic. It was tricky. "I think . . . that it's one of the best things around . . . only," here I went on more rapidly, "some people make a racket of it."

He clucked his tongue, as if in private disapproval of something. "What I can't see," he said to me, "is the attitude that you find toward it in America."

"What attitude is that?" I asked him, eager to be filled in where I could be, knowing nothing about "sex" except what I had learned from Pheidias. And Pheidias had never even used that *word*.

"Oh," he sighed, from what sounded like the hollows of sufficient experience, "you know, the kind of pretty girl, popular in the fraternity, always making jokes about sex . . ."

What was funny, I wondered, about sex? And why was it sexy to *joke* about it? And what fraternity?

"And then, when you get her alone, and you start getting, well, uh, friendly, and everything seems to be going along . . . till, all of a sudden, you put your hand in the wrong place, and it's, 'Stop that! What kind of girl do you think I am?'" He wound up in a shocked false-contralto.

I chuckled. He didn't try to look at me nor I at him. One tended to feel so safe with American boys. They never seemed quite to know whether they were talking about one's very own story, or about some other girl's. Even if they had some intimations, the best of them were much too mannerly to inquire. "How do you think a relationship between a girl and a boy *ought* to develop?" I wanted to know.

"Well, bed is what you want. At least, it's what the guy wants. And meanwhile, the girl is, naturally, hoping to string along with everything but. So the relationship goes on, and some intimacy develops, and naturally that keeps changing from day to day, and all the changes add up, until . . . one day . . . she's in it."

I must have looked puzzled.

"The girl . . . is in it."

"I would have thought it was in her," I blundered, a blunder I will regret to my dying day. But then, I suppose he knew. And was just checking me out, as one person (devoid of redemption) to another.

"I mean"—he giggled politely, and then looked serious—"she's in the situation. And, *very often*, it's over her head."

In the novels that had heretofore formed my thinking on the subject, the chief thing "over her head" would be the nearest river. Or the afternoon train. I was curious to see what, as a young American man with a strict sense of honor, John would have done about a situation that was potentially over a girl's head. But maybe it was over his head too, for he kept me in the dark. The story about the pretty girl in the fraternity was left with no ending.

Since our ill-starred intercourse, Pheidias and I had gone back to arguing, and to that dumb joining of outsides that so irritated him—but not me. Not any more. Let it be as "disgusting" as you please. There were many sins, dear. Among them, aesthetic sins.

He suggested we try something that he called "*soixant-neuf*."

"What is that?"

"Pense aux nombres, six [6] et neuf [9]."

"Oh." I shook my head vehemently. "That's out of the question! Certainly not!"

Well, then, why not do the "normal" thing?

For one thing, I was not about to get reembroiled in that anguish over an awaited period that had made me feel dragged through the welfare rolls of experience.

Pheidias was in bed with a bad cold when I told him the good news. "Maybe you are sterile," was his sole comment.

"Small price to pay." I shook my head. "I would have killed it."

"I would have killed you," he replied, coldly and sincerely. More patiently, he went on to explain tenderly to this modern girl that woman is a vessel. She is not sufficient unto herself. She is a vessel for the transmission of life.

I felt so sheltered—sheltered from evasions and mere moral mediocrity—by these passionate excesses of his Aegean heart, and so ecstatic to be free—at the same time, free! But as what in those days was believed to be my "safe time" drew closer, he argued how important it was that we do well what we had already done once, but badly. We walked down the boulevards together, which had seen centuries of such arguments.

At the very best, he told me, less than reassuringly, we would have no more than one year.

"You sound like Stendhal."

"Oh, Abigail, you bore me, with your Stendhal."

"Then why do you give us only one year, after the 'crystallization,' or whatever *you* call it? What's wrong with a lifetime?"

"Because," he said patiently, "after a year, it would not be the same."

"What would we have then?"

"The sort of thing that *you* like."

It wasn't that they made love unimportant. Love was a thing apart. One could die of it, become heartbroken or demented from it. That was permitted in their medieval tapestry.

"Pheidias, if we *should* sleep together, please do not describe what I do clinically. I'm new at this, and I don't want to be typed in my first blunders."

"Oh," he said quickly, "I only do that to give myself a little sense of control, to regain some equilibrium, because—you are a god for me. I am like Odysseus with Nausikaa. I have to ask myself if you are mortal or a goddess. Parce que," he said on a long breath, "tu m'écrases."

I suppose that we crushed each other. Little shivers of delight started up my nervous system nevertheless, *although* we crushed each other, as we went down the dark streets together to the *station de metro.*

"Will you?" he said, as we parted knee to knee.

"Yes." My head bent slightly downward as if a wave crested over it. Embarrassed by the graphic nature of his kiss, I moved quickly down the stairs.

But there were other powers in the world besides the ones intersecting from time to time in this affair. Naturally, Pheidias had reckoned without my going to dine at the home of Anka Trivier.

Anka was French, but Polish originally. Her parents had been people of fortune, I believe, but since her youth she had led her own independent life and taken the great risks of that life. She'd had adventures, slept under the bridges in Italy, been a musician, disciplined herself in the life of the student and in a small business enterprise (fairly successful), and she knew the world. Her cooking was incomparable, her age indeterminate, but well past the midpoint. She was a thorough Parisienne, aesthetically keen, profoundly feminine, indefeasible, but with this one faint difference: She was Jewish. She was quite secular, assimilated, enlightened, and all that, but she had withal the Jewish sense for the steady push of universal justice in the slow, the true, the only way. With all the ambiguities of daily life intact. Without the impatience that needs miracles or violence. Without being fooled. With tendresse.

She'd been a friend from the time of my mother's youth, and a part of my mother's far-flung web of connections on the Continent, and Anka kept open house for me and for many, many others in Paris. "It's a madhouse," as a young Swiss had expressed it to me once, "but a house of the good Lord." When I would show up, unannounced, at the dinner hour, each of the other uninvited guests would have to give up something from his or her plate, while another chair would be dragged up to the table in her kitchen.

Once, when politely I stood at her door with some flowers, Anka informed me, "Did you not know, Abigail, that one comes to *my* house empty-handed? That is the rule, Abigail!"

For me, it was almost too heavenly.

That night, she had only her common-law husband as my fellow guest, and I thought it opportune to mention that I had become rather good friends with a young man and would like her and her husband to meet him.

"Oh, not alone, Abigail! That will make him self-conscious. Let us rather invite him with a group of other young people and see how he acts when he's with them and at ease."

I knew how he acted with other young people when he was with them and at ease. Badly. "He is a communist," I said hesitantly.

"Hhmmn," she sniffed over her shoulder, stirring the stew. "If he is a communist, he will convert you."

"He is Greek."

"Hmn! If he is Greek or Italian, he will not be satisfied with a romantic friendship, like a French lad. He will want *all*."

I did not know any French lads of her respectful description, but she was certainly right about Pheidias. He wanted all. "But, Anka, he loves me," I said in a puzzled voice.

" 'Mais il m'aime!' Girls seem to think that they have no defense at all to offer if the boy loves them."

Had I felt that way? I didn't think so, but I could not tell any more. There was a white line that ran like a scar through the series of my memories, dislocating their line somewhat.

As Anka's car drew up that night to leave me at my doorstep, which was only some few streets away from her part of Montmartre, she was warning me gravely against doing anything that I might "regret."

I had thought that she knew the great world, that she knew how to live — as the women of her generation had — an aestheticized life, in the grand style. She did. That was true. But she had not dyed her long upswept hair blond for aesthetic reasons. She'd done that to disguise (by offsetting) her Jewish features during the Occupation. And she felt that she owed my mother something: my safety.

I burst into tears. I was certainly under strain.

"Abigail," she peered at me solemnly. "When I told you just now to do nothing that you would regret, why did you cry? Etes vous déja sa maîtresse?"

I did not want to lie at that point. It seemed too demeaning. So I explained, somewhat brokenly, the gist of the circumstances, while her common-law husband listened up front at the wheel, commenting sagaciously from time to time, "But she is *very* weak." Now I did not like that, by any means, but I did not think that I had a clear place to stand, from which I could show offense. Besides, he was Anka's friend.

"Could you but know," Anka said solemnly when I had done, "the sufferings that you risk, even with the best precautions!"

What precautions? I thought desperately.

She told me a simply awful cautionary tale about the victim of such a liaison who had, despite all her precautions, gotten *enceinte*, suffered a miscarriage, and in the hospital had lamented to Anka pathetically, "Had I but known into what I was being dragged, I would *never* have begun it!"

It was a story in the tradition of my Russian novels. I was sure that Anka had read them. But I knew she was also a woman of the world, of the avant-garde, who would know how to advise another woman. "Anka, he thinks that we ought to do well what we have begun by doing badly. Do you *still* think that we should not?"

"Could you but feel how my arteries adjure you! Be chaste, Abigail!" she exclaimed vehemently and majestically.

"But, Anka, when one is young . . ."

"On the contrary, it is only the young who *can* be chaste. Later on, it is not possible," she added quickly and commonsensically. "Fulfill," she exclaimed, "the conditions of your fellowship. Honesty demands it!"

"But I will suffer, Anka."

She looked at me one last time. "Ce genre de souffrance vous enrichit." That kind of suffering enriches you.

It was the only part of Anka's advice that did come from the great world.

Pheidias would have been furious and scathing, had he but known of Anka's intervention. Indeed he may well have suspected something of the kind, though not her precise language, when he retrieved me at le Tournon, with more than his usual reproachful tenacity. He had brought my letter with him, the one begging off from our rendezvous. He intended to go over it with me, he soon let me know, in great detail. Point for point, in fact. He found my letter "arrogant" and riddled with informal fallacies.

"Whom did you talk to?" Pheidias asked, shrewdly and persistently. "What *person* changed your mind?"

"No one," I said, not wanting him to think me less than independent minded. Also, I didn't want him taking his aim at Anka, in
absentia. To me, Anka was not just any person.

While we quarreled, we wandered to the Foyer Israelite. "Jews
have done nothing for world progress since they wrote the Bible,"
Pheidias was saying, somewhat inopportunely as it happened.
"There are some very pretty lines of poetry in the Bible. But the
rest, the last two thousand years, has been a waste of time."

"I see. Einstein, Spinoza, Freud, your friend Marx, that was all
nothing."

"Oh, they were no longer Jews. They were freethinkers."

"So that's what you think," I replied frostily in English. The Jewish students listened to our quarrel. "I see." And so does the whole
group on the sands of Canaan, walking out of Ur. And so does the
alleged Davidic line of my ancestors, cast in the mold of the alleged
originals. So do the long rabbinic generations. We all see. And we
do not see that this is good. Or that it can go on much longer.

We drifted to a parting, full of ill feeling, and rehashed the
matters that divided us at some length in the days that followed.

Mostly, something had to give between us. Our worldviews were
colliding, and clashing inconclusively. He gave me arguments for
the strange modern things he said he believed in or could jus-
tify, having to do with the decisiveness of brute considerations. He
went back to antiquity for support of his moral modernity, reading
me Thucydides' Melian Dialogue, as if he were the living voice of
the envoys from Athens and I spoke for the "humanistic" islanders
of Melos who would soon be pathetically slaughtered. "You have
not used *one argument*," concluded the envoy from Athens, "that a
reasonable man would use!"

He gave me arguments, arguments, arguments that were meant
to drown out resistance. He'd take two paragraphs to make his
point, and, by the time he was finished, one had forgot one's rebut-
tal. He was arguing to win, not trying in a Socratic way to follow
the argument where it led, of course. And yet I always felt that, on
one side of him, he really hoped that he would lose. But not lose
against a better argument. Not if it was to come from me. He didn't
hope *that*. If I could have answered the dialectical challenge and
convinced him otherwise, I would have ceased to be precisely the
woman at whom those appeals were aimed.

But it was idle to imagine such a turning inside out or transfor-
mation. I could not have convinced him otherwise. Anka was right.
I was too young. I did not have the instruments. I had not paid the
heavy price of getting them. That would come, in a modest measure. But meantime, if I stayed, he would convert me with those

hard-edged, poreless arguments from his side, though I could see the tension of them briefly melting into spring when we would kiss, at the close of the second paragraph.

It was a moment I could not abandon, meantime. Despite Anka, despite everything, I could have sold the birthright for it, had the birthright been that kind of thing.

One night, I returned to Pheidias's room late, after an evening's entertainment at the theatre with Harper. We had seen Paul Claudel's *Le Soulier de satin*, and I remember being struck by its hyper-Augustinian hauteur and its premature renunciations. The play had its predictable effect. Pheidias saw at once, as I arrived, that I had set aside for one time *my* premature renunciations.

"Let's"—he fumbled with the idiom—"uh . . . make love." So we lay down together in the lost comfort of the nude. The grammar of *my* body he had not yet learned and at first slammed confusedly against its hidden commas. "Am I impenetrable?" I smiled up at him questioningly. He shook his head, gave me an explanation, and at length seemed to concede that I was not some other woman whom he had met before, and to let the punctuation that was mine slide home. Then he began to move inside me. Hovering above me, watching intensely in the lamp-lit room, his body argued at last with mine.

It hurt. Christ. It hurt very much, as I started to protest. Oh. I see. The penetration . . . it goes very deep. It doesn't lodge, as I had thought, just at the body's entrances. It travels upward, toward the very center of the circle that I occupy. And, from that center outward, there sweep these giant radii of feeling, through the belly and the lungs, transecting the breath. It's another world, inside the ordinary world, but somehow larger. I see. It's the whole corporeal entity that will move to admit, connect, thrash against, and extend this steep, steep Rise—even if sharply contested—of sensation. Ah . . . I see.

"You have a smile like I don't know what Mona Lisa," he hovered above me, afterward.

"So *that's* what she was smiling at."

"Of course."

We lay awake in the after hours and talked about everything under the pillowed sky. I kissed his folded hand, and moved gratefully along the length of his body. "Are you glad I stayed?"

"Oh, yes," he said, looking gravely into my eyes. "I am very hhhappy."

But when, after that long horizontal night of embraces that has no real end, we at last slept, we went on so late into the morning with our sleeping that our rising was perforce sudden, and in such a hurry. I was supposed to have lunch with my Czech friend Anna at twelve sharp. And Pheidias decided to come along this time, which he did not do ordinarily, walking not quite alongside as I joined Anna, reading a book of mine on art, but trailing the two young women friends peculiarly. Bantering, in a ponderous trade back and forth of insults with Anna (who had met him only once before, that being the time of our argument at le Tournon, and who disliked him intensely), he was so ungallant!

"For heaven's sakes, will you cut that out," I said, exasperated, as he actually swiped Anna's brown amulet from her neck and began to pry through its dried contents. "It's *hers*. Give it back to her!"

"Are you a fétichiste?" he asked her, mockingly. "*I* am."

"No," replied Anna scornfully. "I am *not*."

But I was just as annoyed with her, for not respecting a choice I had made, and sagged tiredly in thoughts of my private room and upholstered bed.

There was a lecture that I had to attend at the Sorbonne that day. So after lunch I went by myself to hear that. And afterward, I went to le Tournon, still alone.

"Let me see your eyes," said Richard Wright to me, at a back table.

I met his patiently.

"You are going through a *crisis*."

I smiled. "Richard Infallibly Right," I said, as sometimes I used to, jokingly.

"Abigail, I predict that you're going to marry Pheidias. I've seen this sort of thing happen before."

I pictured myself scarved in an old, green stocking, sweeping a dirty, brown room that had a kitchen adjoining. What I saw was shabby and devoid of lights, and I saw it quite clearly.

"I see The Pattern there," the writer said.

I was an hour late for the next morning's rendezvous in Pheidias's now intimately familiar chambre de bonne. By the time I got there he had begun, it seemed almost involuntarily, to lift down the red-broidered stuff from his slanted walls. He was embarked on a project of redecoration.

Why can't he keep his hands off the wallpaper? I thought. I did not think that we could take too much redecoration.

But perhaps he wanted to make some room for something new.

It was an odd feeling. I felt at once trapped and also very free. It was as if all spaces held him and me indissolubly. He could do what he liked. I could say what I liked. We could never, however, break up. Yet no particular space in the whole wide world gave us houseroom.

"Why don't you sit down," he kept repeating, waspishly.

If only he could hold me. But he had nothing, with which to hold me. We won't last. There is no way we can walk down the road of the years, together. I shook my head. His bed was the only seat.

"Oh, here is my sketchbook. I plan now to sketch you in the nude. If you don't mind, that is."

"I would mind, very much. No, thank you." God, they think everything is art.

"Why not?"

"Because I don't intend giving you any trophies."

Pheidias made a disdainful gesture. "What trophies? That is not for a trophy. Besides"—he grinned up at me complacently, from where he knelt, dismantling his walls—"the real trophies, I have them already." He paused, considering my possible "psychological" reasons for objecting. "Are you ashamed of your body?"

I looked at him icily and backed away, to balance on his door-knobs with both hands behind me.

He remarked, looking down at the things he held and not moving from his place on the floor, "There is no difference between you and a common prostitute. Except of course, as I see, you are more silly!"

I pulled the door shut with an unaccustomed slam and clattered down the six or seven flights of stairs, half hoping and expecting he would follow me.

But he would not.

I was free. I had always been free.

We were both, after all, persons of some will.

Chapter Seven

La Méthode éternelle

Dimly I can recall that I wrote him a letter, of explanation and farewell. It was emotional, as I recollect; I *think* it was loving; and it contained, I believe, these lines: "If I am wrong about our being the wrong ones for each other, then I am wrong about my very nature, and you should not be ambitious to correct a misapprehension so profound."

(From the present standpoint, I am much inclined to say that I *was* wrong about our being the wrong ones for each other, but that I was right about what our marriage would have done to me. It was not a situation that I'd ever read about, and I had no categories in which to enfold it. I dare say that it still tends to escape any categorizations with which I am familiar.)

He telephoned some weeks later, suggesting that we meet, if only for a conversation and a cup of coffee.

"No," I said.

"Do you detest me to *such* a degree?"

"It's not," I answered, conscious of my landlady's enjoyment of these sounds, "a question of my detesting you. It's a question of the whole course of my life."

"In that case, I cannot argue [je suis d'accord]," he said quickly, and—with *au revoirs*—he rang off.

I think that he *was* "d'accord." It was one thing he must always have known—each one of his faux pas (mis-steps in the literal sense) being proof of such ingrained *knowledge*. There was the mis-step of his ungallant ways with my friends. There was the misstep of his womanizing, the extent and incorrigibility of which I had (despite the nude sketchbook) only the dimmest of intimations, no doubt. There was his medieval "French" opinion that true love in the full sense had no more than a year to run. There was the misstep of the way that he argued: to win, not to see in Socratic fashion where the argument led. There were the missteps of his atheism, and his leftist extremism. All these showed prior knowledge of our being the wrong ones for each other, if by right ones is meant suitability as a married pair.

But from time to time I would see him, on the Boulevard St. Michel or the rue de Vaugirard, walking. I'd be with one of my American men friends, or women friends, and Pheidias would be alone, walking. We would not stop to shake hands, though our eyes would meet and my heart record the encounter in its fearful thudding code: stop-and-go, stop-and-go.

Of what was that impact made? After that first time in his room, I never quite entertained the concept that I loved him. In those days, in America, people regarded romantic love as an ethical decision, not as an autonomous force. So I could not conceive that I loved him. By the standards that then governed my culture, I *didn't*. Yet in after years, from time to time intermittently, I would suppose that, if there had not been—but what an if!—those insuperable differences of values and ideology, we two could have been . . . happy.

There was another aspect of the experience that made it especially hard for me to sort out. In the chapter "L'initiation sexuelle" of *Le Deuxième sexe*, Simone de Beauvoir says that girls who shrug off their virginity in easy stages, without anguish or shame, danger, or the sense of fleshly invasion, have not known what it is to know the masculine element.[1] Or perhaps her meaning is that they have not known what it is to be known *by* that element. So they remain, as it were, prefeminine. By that implicit standard, I had become "a woman," the very thing that Pheidias had, one late hour, commanded me to be. Therefore, for better and worse, I knew and recognized the masculine element in the world.

Pheidias's actions with me had left their mark. So much so that, years later in a museum in my neighborhood, a stone portrait of a man from the third century A.D., with the same curved high cheekbones, unsmiling mouth, and archaic eyebrows high above the same thin-penciled, distant eyes, could make my heart thud into its stop-and-go, stop-and-go, as if I saw him coming down the rue de Vaugirard again.

Of what was that impact made? What is it made of still, though all the flesh that men and women touch may petrify?

We met finally one long afternoon. It was a spring day, and the billows of green-scented air were wafting easily down from the Luxembourg Gardens to our crowded café terrace. A kind Black-American jazz musician had charitably ordered for me a great platter of ham and eggs, which, famished, I was just wolfing down when I felt the most imperceptible touch at my shoulder. The laughter and the chatter died away as I looked up.

He was standing there, slight in the spring breeze, looking at me in vague reproach. His eyes were unsmiling as he said hello in English. I could not eat another bite.

Pheidias took a café chair beside me uninvited and allowed himself some moments to leaf through an illustrated volume by Malraux that I'd been carrying and to address to me some desultory remarks about Malraux, pro and con, and Malraux's comprehension of art, which he thought rather good.

As I sat stiffly, people leaned over to address me with gentle teasing, or to urge me to eat. Paris is not unkind to what it identifies as tormented lovers.

At last, I pushed the plate forward—there being no help for it—and got up to take that one more stroll together. Anna got up from her chair too, to give me her affectionate triple kiss of parting, and the jazz musician tossed my deep red dress a sweet compliment.

Pheidias and I went on with small talk for some moments, walking down the rue de Tournon, then cutting through the side streets toward the Place St. Michel, as if we were both in a tearing hurry. I had just come back from a trip to Brittany with Anna, I told him, and we'd had a good deal of trouble getting rides. "Perhaps the drivers didn't care to look at Anna," said the envoy from Athens, crudely, and remarked that he was out of change, and, since he was, would I be so kind as to pay for the coffee that he suggested we stop and have together.

No, I said. I would not be so kind.

That was very stingy of me, he said indignantly.

I could not understand his emotional meanness, but I shuddered at it. Where did it come from? What did that make him? A lover? A seducer? Nothing? How did he figure in the epic of the world, or in my part of it? We had come to the metro station St. Michel when, hopelessly, I cut short our walk with a quick handshake, and an equally sudden *au revoir*.

He shook my hand in his turn, ironically.

One moment later, I was back at the open square, which he was just leaving. "Why did you pass by to see me?" I stopped him to ask.

"What is this? What do you think you're saying? I passed by to see you for no reason, just because it pleased me to do so, that's all!

If I choose, I can spend entire *weeks* without seeing you!" He was half gesturing, as if to push me down the metro stairs once again. We spoke French.

"Are you not aware," I said very distinctly, "that when I have seen you, it takes me . . . two . . . good . . . weeks to recover?"

"Wait a minute! What *is* this? Come with me!" He was steering me now across the bridge and toward that great, sprawling, medieval Notre Dame of our sometime joint pilgrimages. Once, Pheidias had used its multiple facades and flying buttresses to argue, by analogy, that I had never known *him* either, for the human soul turns up new facets at each stage of its self-disclosure in time, like that Notre Dame we two had circled while he made this argument.

"I was just starting to ask myself," he said, " 'but what has that girl got in her veins?' "

Ice? Yes, perhaps. We found seats in the rear garden now, for which the old cathedral served as a sheltering stone maze.

"That's a nice dress," he remarked, adding quickly, "in the American bad taste."

I grinned, a little embarrassed, as always.

He had come by to see me, he explained, not frivolously or idly, but because he absolutely required an antidote to a sordid encounter he had recently had with a very low character—another girl.

"Don't use me," I said, only too conscious that he had also used her, "even as an antidote."

We sat in the green spring shadows, with their cross-bars of light that patterned our knees and our hands.

"I am not using you, except in the sense that one might use a prayer."

"I am not usable—even as a prayer!" I cried, afraid to be ridden out of shape by misspent adoration and stranded when, sooner or later, his reserves of that had been exhausted. "What was so 'sordid'? 'Sordid' in what sense?"

"In every sense. There's too much to explain. But, for example, she said that she was virgin. She lied."

Oh that. Only that. God. These materialists. Have they nothing else to measure female time by but the quantity and flow of *those* molecules? "How do you know she lied?" I said sadly.

"Because"—his mouth went down at the corners in the French mask, worn to admit only evidence that was material—"we went to bed together."

"But with me there was also no—"

"Because you gave me a reasonable explanation. Besides, one can tell." He smiled in a superior sort of way, like an expert.

"What do you feel for all those girls that you sleep with? Is it contempt?"

"No. In general, I respect them. I want them to be happy. I hope that they marry some day. Yes." He shook his head at my look, which he took for surprise.

It was not that. I was seeing how unequal was the relation between the one man, who bestowed his soi-disant "respect," and all this *parade* of women in single file.

"That is my feeling for them, in the main. But you"—he peered ascetically at my seated form, backlit in the afternoon sun of the garden—"I want *you* to remain a nun. What egoism, eh?" He laughed at himself, shaking his head. "What a monster!"

We got up, finally, to wend our way out of the timelessly pleasant garden and exhale, into the parting roar of traffic, this brief suspension of the breath and this repose.

Finally, June came. One saw that the waiters got surlier, the streets more crowded with what the French called "dirty foreigners," my audiences with my Fulbright advisor thinner and still more contrived, if that were possible, and also that everyone who was not too poor for it was foreseeing a season of travel. It was time to pull out of Paris for the present.

In the course of time Harper *had* gone tranquilly home to Charleston and her long-anticipated wedding celebration. I missed her, but there was still a summer for me to get through here, however that could best be done. That was the project in aid of which Anna and I met two of our men friends for lunch, both Fulbright scholars. As one of our friends was an artist, he quickly sketched a map of free Europe on a white paper napkin for us. We studied it, the four of us, with all of our blandly wide-open American curiosity. There it was: *almost* the whole old world.

There was Delft. There was Amsterdam. There, traced by a vertical stroke down the white paper napkin, the Rhine valley, and across that horizontally the Black Forest. There was a highway that ran straight to Munich, and beyond that, to Salzburg, and one could continue right into Vienna, East-bound. At that point, at that time northeast of Vienna, the old world stopped—as Anna knew better than did the rest of us. So we looked south down the white paper napkin, and there was Trieste at the Adriatic, there the Dalmatian coast, and around there somewhere, Macedonia. The Yugoslavs had just opened up their country to foreign tourists, but it was still obscure, that Greco-Yugoslav interior. The pencil drew a series of quick grey striations. Then Thessalonica, in northern Greece. Then Delphi, as the sun came up over our white map. Then Athens.

"I can't make a choice," I said sincerely. "Let's see it all."

"We'd have to hitch," was Anna's view. "That is the cheapest way. Also, the easiest. It's door to door. You don't have to find your way out of train stations."

"There's no way you can see it all, girls," said our men friends in earnest. "That's just *impossible*."

As the party broke up, I looked at Anna. They would only have slowed us down, was the thought. It was easier for girls alone to get rides anyway. Our trouble in Brittany had been atypical. Then we made plans.

"Europe," Anna explained the situation to me, as one who had lived inside it most of her life, "is a garden. It's just small enough really to *see*. Just look around. You can see people, buildings, statues, places here. You can see bodies, and what the bodies are wearing. It's only in America that souls walk naked."

I saw her point with precision. She was, like me, *philosophe*. Yes, I thought. In America . . . it was all still unfinished and open-ended. It was stuff that had not yet worked its way into its defining *eidos*, or essence. But I liked Europe very much and thought I would *like* to step into those many-spired cities that make up the backdrop of Flemish triptychs, or to walk part of the way down their cobbled lanes, under their pale northern light. We could walk into the pictures. I thought we could do that if we tried, Anna and I, trained as we were to see essences.

John Armstrong had dreamed up his own summer plan. For him and for two other young men, one of whom was American and the other French, the plan was to test-drive a small French car, loaned by the manufacturer, down the whole spine of Africa from Egypt to the Cape of Good Hope.

When I told Richard Wright about my American friend, and that John wanted his advice in connection with the trip, the Black writer did not want to meet him.

"Where did he go *after* Amherst?"* Wright inquired.

"Harvard," I said.

"God, no!" Wright banged down a coffee cup. "Not with that background! He must be *teeming* with prejudices!"

John had asked me to arrange this interview. Would I really not

---

*Amherst is the name I remember.

be able to do it? "Oh, no," I protested. "John is an unusually fine boy. He's not like that at all."

"John is not *at all* typical," Anna chimed in at our Tournon terrace, giving one of her rare character references for an American male. It was ever John's intention to be gallant, and I think Anna sensed that. Besides, one rainy night in the fifth arrondissement, John had been crossing a narrow street when he caught sight of Anna, in trouble it seemed, being backed against a dark wall by a ring of tough young Algerians. He went to her side quickly and effectively, and later I would hear her defend him with a warmth she reserved for few Americans.

It was not a story I could ever have heard from John. And Anna, though she told me most things, would not have told me that story either. She never advertised her female frailties. Her physical strengths at least she liked to think of as sufficient to her needs. (I daresay we all liked to *think* that; but Anna was a refugee; her needs had been graver than ours, and she did not like to remind a person of them, not even a woman confidante.)

So I heard about it from Nancy. She was the only young woman among us whom John distinguished with his real confidences, as he distinguished her with intentions that were ardent but also honorable. On this, as on most other subjects, Nancy was very "sound." It was her view that marriage was a turn of the plot that they should both think over seriously—now, while they were together, and later, when they'd be apart and have time more thoroughly to sift, to sort, and to weigh it. That anything so private to both of them had figured in their friendship, offstage as it were, was not generally known in our circle. Nancy herself told it to me only later, after John was dead, and they two had no privacy any more to be lost.

In the end Wright acceded. "But you say he wants to tour all of Africa in a 2 chevaux? That's very ill-advised. They'll never make it past Egypt."

Nancy later told me that she never expected to see me again, either, after I left town with Anna. And to John she had argued emphatically that he ought to visit his relations in Scotland that summer, to find out where he came from, researching that interesting question of origins.

One day I accompanied John while he and his voyagers-in-prospect stopped at the different consular offices where they had to get visas and permits. Then John and I went on to have lunch by ourselves.

"I feel," John said deliberately, "that for me to go through with this trip is very important. You see"—he addressed what one could almost feel were the leaderless thousands of his young fellow seekers—"all our lives we are taught to believe that we have certain values. So we go on for years, always assuming that these values are really ours. You see, Abigail, I've got to find out whether I really believe all the things I say I do. Because if, in those critical moments, when you have to decide what to do, and there's no time left in which to pretend—I find that I've got to toss something overboard—then I'll stop talking about that value after that. Because it won't be *mine* any more."

It was the graduate English major's keen attention to the true but remote word. He went on to describe how he managed to exercise leadership. He did it by almost never openly seizing the lead. Rather, he would get the members of a group to rise to their own expectations. "With me, you see, it's always been the game that I play," he confessed to me now, smiling in naked candor. "You get it that this trip is my idea? *They* would have let it die. But always reminding, always putting in a plug, a suggestion here, a phone call there, lifting a slipping morale without letting it show . . ."

I pictured John at a steaming border station, arguing with the pistoled, helmeted guards, jettisoning *some* ideals that he carried, just so that the group could be waved on, but preserving at least one or two of his most high-flown values—at great personal cost. It was pretty. "John," I said, "I understand why you feel that you have to make this trip. I don't say to you, 'Go.' But I *can't* say to you, 'Stay.'"

Our eyes danced.

Anna and I bought backpacks, under her world-wise direction. We bought all-purpose knives to affix to our belts, workaday sandals from the five-and-dime (the Monoprix), and Basque shoes, for when we would need to change footwear. We would be laundering night by night at the youth hostels as we went along. "It's living," Anna explained to me, as grand master to bobbling apprentice, "like a turtle."

But when we got past our first and our second winds and settled into the mile-eating stride of our third, it was not turtles we thought of but trained field dogs, seeing the teeth of the wolf before he saw us. We stayed right on time down the highways, parrying and blocking our agile drivers who would be taking us meantime through Europe and paying with cups of coffee, or an occasional double meal, for that privilege.

With our paper-napkin map of Europe in mind, we could readily grasp its rock-garden contours. Tramping the rutted miles on a bad hitching day, the crabgrass rough, the highway hard, the drivers few and far between, we could still let the inner spaces and the outer ones jostle each other—by the way we two *talked* about these things.

Anna thought that most things reduced to some terminal absurdity. Sooner or later. And I thought one could retrieve a meaning from the whole skein of experience. I thought one could walk the path of one's argument, and it would lead one to God. So we walked along the inside/outside zigzagging miles of controversy over "mind" and "matter"—whether reducible or irreducible one to the other—and over "dialectic," as a path that either led somewhere or else did not, while we walked the burnished wheat fields or took shelter in roadside tavern-cafés from the driving rain. And, no doubt more at home there than elsewhere, we walked through the sober gorgeousness of formerly royal museums, blotting into our very cells those strokes of color by which all the world's fleeting things had been painted down by the masters into their permanent halo of signals: signaling mystery, signaling certitude.

We were getting hints, and giving them, of the cohesion of thought, adventure, plain living, and the enjoyment that the senses yield—and touch on such hints, if you can!

I can recall, after a crash course in the police-state mishaps of Titoist Yugoslavia, being barred from leaving the train at the first Greek border station that we came to, Idomeni, because all that land around the border had been mined. I can recall the Greek official who gave and—when we pleaded with him that we had to see the Greek countryside—*rescinded* the order of our banishment, showing us instead to a cafeteria inside the station. It was filled with music, and dancing men and women, though we were too tired to join the stamping, laughing circles that invited us, with arms outstretched. After we had eaten, the stationmaster showed us to a side room, small and dark, with a sink and cold water, where we could wash up privately. Then he locked up his waiting room for us to sleep in, as if we'd had reservations, and in English told us not to worry, not to worry, in the harshly sweet accents that Pheidias also used.

Anna and I—wherever she is now—must both have the memory of coming down to the docks of Thessalonica at twilight, with the sailboats tilting softly in that golden dusk that was just then settling opaquely over the cold, husky waters of the Aegean.

Both of us must surely remember the sweet Greek girls at the Y, virgins all, their peaceable eyes large and empty of struggle, for all their future copulations were marked out for them, and they were tender to us.

No doubt we can also recall the truck drivers, rock muscled, gritty voiced, nearly sleepless, who conversed with us almost incomprehensibly, since no one spoke a common language. But we were wandering students of philosophy. Did we know therefore . . . of *Socrates*? Did we know that three hundred boys had died here, at Thermopylae? Did we know what it was never to sleep a night through, just working to pile up enough for a sister's dowry? With true urbanity, they bedded us down in the backs of their trucks while they slept harmlessly inches from us—though their women, as they said freely, could not have done what we did.

We can remember Delphi. It was delicate. It was bathed in immense distances. Songs of birds led away from it, and its olive and silver birches were glistening in the fathomless dawn light.

We can surely recall, from however near or far, the shining Parthenon, riveting the heart on silver lute strings to its slender dividers. And how immeasurably blue the sky was over Athens in those days, with not a trace of green! Every other sky since has looked somewhat tarnished to me.

I came back to Paris at last, alone, with a last few brief days to call my own before the summons of the Atlantic crossing. Anna I had left in Genoa, from whence she'd gone back to Rome to rejoin an American whom she'd befriended at the start of our common travels. From Italy I had gone north by train to touch some of the family bases in Switzerland and then was able to take another train by night into my favorite, astral-twin city.

Cold, grim, grey, and semideserted in the ebbing summer, it traced all the routes of my settings forth, my dead stops, my reversals and involutions on its upturned avenues. For that reason, or for some other reason, it made me feel very free. I had no landlady, that week. Anna had given me the key to her chambre de bonne, from whose tiny box window the whole city spread out below like a miniature, incised in its own darkened ivory. A medieval jewel box for containing some precious thing.

On the empty rue de Tournon, a Portuguese *copain* of Anna's came round the corner on his scooter.

Hop on, he said.

We cruised the boulevards by day and by night went to see the best French films in a decade. While we watched these striking films (*Hiroshima mon amour*, *Les Quatre cent coups*, *Les Amants*), then new and not yet "classic," Chico would twist a left hand over my left shoulder teasingly, and I would edge away uncomfortably, gnawed by that awkwardly local lust that had seized my mind once or twice on similar occasions during our hitchhiking trip.

It really scared me, because I thought, if I can't be virgin, I must at least be chaste—and totally honest. I must have something in the way of purity, still to bestow as a dowry. I must regain as much of that as I can. This is very tricky, and precarious, my situation now. There is a lot at stake, and I no longer have any precise guidelines.

It sounds very existentialist, put that way, but I was not happy about it. I was a Jewish girl trying to do the will of the Absolute, not a character in one of *those* plays or novels. None of those people in Sartre's plays ever talked or acted like me.

The days ticked off. Three . . . two . . . one.

I had left a note for Pheidias with his concierge, suggesting that we two get together for our last goodbyes. Perhaps he was out of town.

On the morning of my final day in Paris, an answering note from him reached me at the American Express counter, where I had told him to write. It was very civil, in red ink and an impersonal, well-schooled hand. It expressed appreciation that I had thought to see him before taking my leave, and regret that he had retrieved my note only after a few days' delay, having sublet his chambre de bonne for the summer. Our meeting was confirmed by phone, for noon that day, in front of St. Germain-des-Prés. And for nearly an hour I paced there, waiting.

"That's a long time to wait," said a French boy who had been waiting with me, watching, for that hour.

Then I caught sight of Pheidias, running lightly down the milling Boulevard St. Germain, swerving his thin shoulders to avoid hitting the pedestrians, and coming up level with me. He kissed me like quicksilver, and my heavy head of hair bent under his dominion.

We took lunch, as the French say, in a small restaurant. "Why did you not get in touch with me before now? You are, you know, someone of importance in my life." He spoke with restraint. "Why could you not have treated me as you treat your copains, just seeing me from time to time."

"Because," I said distinctly, "I do not regard you as a copain. I regard you as a lover."

He swallowed. "And how many lovers have you had since we parted?"

"Not one."

"You have just given me the sole happy moment of my life."

Was that true? True or not, no American would have said it. It lacked all regard for the pragmatic factor.

"When I read in your note that you really intended to leave for the United States, I considered rounding up some friends with a car and kidnapping you."

"I would have been furious!" I said with enthusiasm. "And I would only have had to get a later ship. You know, I'm *expected* in New York! I have a *life* there!" We came out of the restaurant, walking now in quick time, dodging the traffic, and compressing the quarrels that might have entertained all those months that had passed.

Now he bestowed on me an alarming confession. It concerned a young woman whom he had not treated gallantly.

"What you have done to her, you have done to me!" I rejoined, with a sense of confusion that was practically scriptural.

The point he had wanted to get across to me was that he had been pursued by cascading *agonies* of remorse. And, as to my own case, he insisted, pleading, "You must forgive me."

"I am not a Christian," I said exotically and added, inaccurately, both in regard to Jewish teaching on the subject and to my own practice—but it had a certain éclat—"I never forgive," while he smiled about me to himself proudly.

The trouble was that I was due to meet some old family friends at two o'clock, in front of the old, dark Opéra, at the Place de l'Opéra. And so, in order to prolong our little tête-à-tête, my left-wing companion now steered us deliberately onto the wrong metro train, what with his ends still justifying any means.

"How could you!" I said, when once I had understood what he had done. "Older People? You are keeping *them* waiting, just to stretch out our time together? You see"—another moral lesson driven home while his eyes filled up with helpless tears—"you have gained nothing!" I don't know if he saw it or if he didn't see it. But he saw that I saw it. As we neared our moment of separation, we talked faster and faster. "You see, Pheidias," I continued, "you are not rich. D'accord. But have you any spiritual riches to offer?"

"I have," he said quickly. "There are women who have turned to me for a great deal of support and advice."

Goodness. What a city! Had they nothing better to turn to?

"And I have a side to my nature, of which you know nothing, because I never shared it with you, but which is profoundly mystical."

"But look at your *actions*," I objected. "You are a communist. Surely you at least would know that words count for nothing."

"But perhaps you are right," he conceded here. "I am not worth much."

Wherewith to retrieve his plummeting morale, what with the corner approaching? How could I even give him an angry kiss of parting, with the Older People now able to see us from where they stood? Still, we exchanged such a kiss, and he stood looking at me in stubborn defeat for long after I'd crossed the street and joined the others.

The people I was with that afternoon were extremely modest, kind, and unassuming. It was no strain whatsoever to be with them. All that they were and had was distilled, in my case, into mere banked, *emotional* wisdom. They took me in, and they left me alone.

We were now on a shopping expedition, situated among the swank shops around the Place de l'Opéra, and designed to load me up with lavish farewell presents and a sumptuous farewell tea. Gosh! The *things* that a young girl will take for granted! Into that tea party and shopping expedition, I had to wedge excuses for incessant brief exits to pay phones, where I placed unavailing calls to successive relations of Pheidias's who would answer the phone at the apartment where he was residing temporarily. It was not till evening that, the tea party broken up and *its* last farewells exchanged, finally I was able to reach him.

I heard his voice. But he could not hear mine.

I hung up and dialed again. "It seems," I said supercheerfully, "that the good Lord does not want us to meet."

He would have met me at my train in the morning with a note, he told me.

"Let's fix a rendezvous for tonight, nine o'clock, at the Turkish café on the rue de la Huchette, and I really implore you, *please* don't let me wait there alone, in the dark!"

I waited for an hour, in the dark, fending off the Turkish doorman meanwhile. Pheidias and I had been standing at different Turkish cafés on the same obscure, circuitous side street, not then gentrified. "Oh, please don't worry, don't worry," he cut short my recriminations. "We have already lost so much time!" As we talked, we went past the Turkish doorman again, who stepped back in his doorway this time, discreetly.

We went for dinner together, at a tiny restaurant that was crowded with a summer-night trade in students. I told him that nowadays I was always hungry until food was set before me. Then, right away, I'd lose my appetite.

"Then you are sick," he responded accusingly.

"Yes."

His mouth went down sharply. "You should stay with me. You would get well. I am a dietician. Stick to yogurt. What you have ordered, spaghetti, is nothing, and tea has no nutritive value."

It was all news to me in those days. I knew nothing about nutrition.

Pheidias darted a lightning kiss at the long, tanned neck that I was displaying for him. "It's a sin?" he grinned quizzically, as I drew back.

"You haven't the right," I said faintly, feeling my body stung alive. Changing the subject, I told him a story or two from our travels. "Oh, why are you a communist? It was so terrible in Yugoslavia!"

"If you knew how much worse it was before!" was the quick rejoinder.

They *always* say that. In that case, however, he may have had a point.

"Your country is very beautiful."

"Yes. Of course, had you told me that you were going there, I could have put you in touch with people for whom it would have been a pleasure to receive you and to show you many things of great interest to which they have access."

"Anna too?"

"Of course." He shrugged and put something on the table that he had been carrying. "I thought of what single thing among all my possessions would please you the most."

It was a large, exquisite book of color photographs, titled *La Grèce éternelle.* Now we leafed through it together. There was the charioteer at Delphi. "The very type of homosexual beauty," I said, and he laughed. A sexy remark, perhaps?

We got up, he paid the check, and we went wandering together into the summer night.

On pages in the air our conversation shaped itself, in a beginner's unfocused dialectic, but still and all it was the method of argument: *la méthode éternelle.*

"You," I accused, as we went toward the old cathedral slowly, for the last time, "when you talk of violence, you're talking about something you would *do*."

"That's right," he nodded sharply.

"Whereas I, when I talk about violence, all it means is that it's just *talk*." The street lamp shed its fan of light over our mouths— smiling. "You don't believe in Life," I went on. "What you believe in is death. So everything that you do is affected by that."

"Death *is* the end. For you too. I know that."

"You see," I gestured toward him, resignedly.

"How can you want to leave Europe? Look! Only in Paris can

one still see gaslights." He pointed. There was a stone-carved portal in a recessed angle of the street, lit vaguely at a distance by an iron lamp. It seemed now that we walked through the densest fog.

"I have often thought, and tried very hard to understand, my feeling for you," I said to him.

"Why do you have to understand it?"

"Finally I decided that it must have been some sort of vanity."

"But other men must have complimented you sometimes," he frowned, disagreeing.

"Yes, but you were the only one whom I believed."

"Why do you analyze so much?" Then, contradictorily, he revolved the entire matter in his mind analytically. "You did not disappoint me, you see. Oh, well, perhaps just a little bit. But on the whole, not. Whereas I, I disappointed you. When I thought of what I had done to you, I could not understand how I could have done such a thing. Finally I concluded that, at the time, I *didn't* love you. It was only a passion, obscure and confused."

"I always *believed* in your love for me," I replied, partly truthfully, partly scornful of myself because it was true, and partly proud of the heights he had touched by this—as it seemed to me—singular admission. We found a bench fronting the Seine and seated ourselves. "I don't trust your feelings for me," I hazarded, while the night currents poured buoyantly through the thin stuff I wore and skimmed over the shining water. My entrails hurt. "You make of me a god."

"But no," he countered gently, coaxing his fingers along my belly. "My feelings for you are quite carnal."

But one could be both. It was not an exclusive disjunction. One could be a carnal god. His countrymen had made a lot of them. Meanwhile, my shoulders were rounding to contain a literal pain of desire, so we stood up to walk onwards. I confided some of the theories I had worked out in his absence. "I think that I feel bound to you because you knew me as a virgin. You see, for the rest of the world, I have a very exposed position now. I'm a woman who has had experience." (Une femme qui a un passé n'a pas d'avenir, as my mother used sometimes to say. A woman who has a past has no future.) "But for you, Pheidias, I will always be *in*experienced, because you knew me at the beginning." I looked around me at the stone quais and the water, puzzled. "I don't see how I can go home at this point."

"But you are just the same. A year is not a long time."

"Yes, but I was a virgin before."

"But not now." He tilted toward me, reaching with one arm.

"No." I skimmed lightly out of reach for a few dozen feet. "Before, I was virgin. Now, I am *chaste*."

He found this hilarious.

I could have this discussion only with him. "Why are you laughing? Virginity is something very fragile, physically and morally."

Chastity, presumably, was not so fragile.

"At least it was with a man who loved you. I felt I could have lived with you those moments of complete and self-sufficient happiness that *women* dream of, more than men."

"Complete and self-sufficient happiness?" I echoed vaguely. "But that is bad faith."

"Yes. Women live a great deal in bad faith."

"Above all, in Europe!"

"Oh, yes. America is perfect. One has heard that. Still," he mused, "sometimes I think I could give up all work for the party, and go and live there, I who have always detested that country. You will even make me love America."

God. I could picture a congressional committee getting hold of this. "Perhaps"—quickly I sketched for him a mythical Greek patriarch, towering six flights high above Madison Avenue—"if you come to the States, my *father* will find out what you have done to me. And he will kill you!" Not a particularly likely story, but it served to indicate some of the difficulties I felt could proceed from that quarter too.

"What, is he that kind of an old type?"

"Oh, he's an authentic father," I explained airily. "None of your pseudomodern affectations. Have I aged?" I asked him, a non sequitur perhaps.

"You have become more beautiful. I was going to tell you in the restaurant. But it will come," he threatened, in the time-honored French style. "You should not leave me. For you see," he pronounced in my ear while we walked on and the gaslights still flickered indistinctly at the boundaries of our path, "there are profound affinities between us. You are for me what Goethe has called the eternal feminine. All other women have become a kind of neuter for me . . ."

The time that I had left to walk without those hands around me was fast dying out, but still I skipped a few steps more ahead of him, as if I'd been merely a flirt, and all this talk mere coquetry.

"You learned all those tricks in Italy," he remonstrated, catching up to me this time at his leisure. I put my things now, the picture book, the handbag with its money, its ticket home and its passport, on the wide stone quais very carefully and then turned to claim the one thing in life I had made my own.

"Oh, no, *don't*"—he raised one arm as if to defend himself, and he half turned away.

"What?" My arms half unclasped again in midcircle, uncertainly.

He laughed at himself then and turned back to receive his due. We met in one well-drilled legion of sensation, and a few words— like a sigh on the wind—but very strong, words that have stayed with me down the years. It had become unclear to me what might happen—what should happen, what was normative. "We must go to bed tonight," said Pheidias, as I slipped the latch that connected us and stepped backward, leaving desire poised in its pristine independence, waiting somewhere in the night between his form and mine.

"No!" I said and hit him hard across the face as he loomed against it. The desire.

His eyes shone wetly and he half smiled.

"I can't! I can't, any more." I could hardly go home pregnant, or even concerned about that possibility. This was real life, after all.

"But you spoil the very plenitude of life!"

"No!" I said, worried that he might be right, and feeling my entrails halfway decompress. "No more, never any more, I *can't*— without marriage!"

"All right, all right, don't be upset," he soothed me. "We will go now." And he promised to stop by Anna's chambre de bonne in the morning to take me to the Gare St. Lazare.

I lay awake most of the night, thinking on the topic of chastity, while steel tubes of sensation made their way noiselessly up and down the hollow insides of my body.

This can't be chastity was what I was thinking ruefully.

In the morning, I had just had time to wash, and to dress, using the enamel pitcher and basin, when his knock sounded. He was neither too late nor too early for a change but, at the crack of seven, at my door just on time.

Approving my light luggage, he pushed me gently back on Anna's bed, where the light of the morning streamed. "You are there, just as for so long I dreamed you were," he said in an undertone. And then his rapid hand moved inside my underthings to enclose, with an infinitely calming grip, that place where all the trouble and the thrill of living starts. Inside a moment more, and there was this entrance once again to defend. "All right," he said, after a struggle. "If you don't want to, then I don't either."

That was the kind of moral talk I liked to hear. Why couldn't he have said that sort of thing more often?

Impatient, he fastened his hands on my neck and slowly closed them, more and more constrictively, until I wondered *when* I would lose consciousness. Perhaps my widening eyes were noticed, for he released me about then.

"Did you think I would do in five minutes what I did not do for a whole night?" I was shaking my head as I got up.

"It can be well worthwhile in five minutes," he said, compressing the world.

Retrieving the scrap of underthing from the corner where he had flung it, I snapped it into place. "I certainly look neat and soignée," I said, brushing down my tousled new appearance in Anna's long looking glass.

He grinned at this self-assurance, meanwhile shaking his head at the waste of a room. Then we shouldered my things, locked up, and made our way down the winding back stair to the street below. Hailing a taxi without difficulty, he said to the driver, "Gare St. Lazare!"

"It seems so strange to me to be leaving Europe," I sighed in his ear confusedly as we stood there on the platform, next to my train. It was impossible for me to say that I loved *him* or would miss *him*. I did not think it would be *true*, ethically and unqualifiedly, to say so. But it is such a hard thing to know, how to say only what is true unqualifiedly.

"I have not even given you any worthwhile memories," he replied gently, understanding me.

"They are nothing, memories. Nothing!" I greatly hoped, against the chartless future, that I would not have to rely on them too much.

"No," he shook his head with the most intimate understanding. "They are very much indeed."

Truth, the classical Greeks had said long ago, is nonforgetfulness.

"All aboard," said the conductor, from farther down the track.

Quickly we ran up the platform together and clasped upper and lower lips in the hastiest of last kisses.

A cacophony of train noises rose, as now he took my hand through the window of my compartment, already far away. He pressed his lips against it, as though it were the stone foot of some idol, brightly painted, and he an especially enthusiastic local believer. "How long is your trip going to take?"

"Eight days."

"Eight days!" He looked disapproving, as he always did—but this time at the great length of my ocean journey. "When you enter your apartment in New York, you will find a letter from me."

I believed him. Vaguely, I thought perhaps we would marry after all. And then down the track the boat train inched, and it picked up speed, and that, poor god, would be the last I saw of him.

Part 2

Analytic

Chapter Eight

Of the Impossible Position of the Jews

It is all very well to be a sweet young woman with a "very Jeweesh" face that appears "very beautiful" to a young man who sees it that way, astigmatically to be sure, in the favorable lighting that Paris generously grants to its devotees for as long as that will be needed.

It is quite another thing actually to *be* Jewish. My father, who read an earlier version of this memoir, but one also written more than ten years after the events in Paris that it chronicled, said to me, "You have to face the reality here. After all, what did Richard Wright see? Pheidias was a seducer." He wanted *the benefits* of a Jewish girl like you, my father had continued almost in the same breath, almost as if it went without saying—implying by that a whole particular, well-differentiated climate of thought and culture—a vantage point from which to survey the terrain of experience. And, my father went on, he didn't want it to cost him anything.

At that time, I argued for a somewhat different view of the whole episode. Women, I replied to my father, are in the position of attracting to themselves erotic encounters with men whose particular level of conscious life is most fully revealed in what they *do* with the women who can bring out that level in them. The man's dialectical stage of development, or arrested development, is revealed through the woman, I argued, and for the woman it is in turn profoundly enlightening to come to see that—since together both form the known world. (That was the view of erotic experience as prolonged *éducation sentimentale* that I held then. There was at least one crucial particle that my quasi-Hegelian view of that time was lacking: the particle of tragedy. Otherwise, it was all right.)

My father had listened attentively to what I was saying. Then he'd remarked that, on my view of the matter, the role of women in the world was analogous to the role of the Jews. Jews, that is, show the world where it *is*, at any given stage of its conscious and unconscious life. And so they bring out whatever in the world is still underevolved, awareness of which it will seek to evade by projecting that defect of awareness, one way or another, onto its portrait of the Jews. So, with that sad analogy, on that note of "suffering/understanding,"[1] my conversation with my father resolved itself.

My mother, who had read the same 1974 version of this memoir at the same time, laughed when I told her of my father's original comment. Yes! Of *course*! He *would* say that, was her amused reaction. Isn't that just like a man! And a jealous, possessive father! For her part, she thought that Pheidias probably *had* been my true love, but that—since I could hardly have settled in Paris as the wife of a communist—the encounter had achieved whatever aesthetic closure was possible to it on its own terms and was therefore to be accepted as such. Such things were like that.

Both my father's view and my mother's were true. And each was one-sided. But how could they both be true? What really had drawn us together? And what was it that had "crystallized" (to use Stendhal's term) into all of those obstacles, and kept us apart? Questions with no easy answers. Like a gauze lining, those questions would lie around all the efforts of my life, from then on.

But first, there was the predicament of the Jews, to which my father had briefly alluded. Just what predicament would that be? It is one that is very simple to grasp, really, and it will be found to exist in all possible worlds that are fully developed, since, on the view I have argued for here, the predicament is part of what makes any fully developed world possible. First let us look at their (the Jews') role, then at their predicament.

The Jewish *take* on world history, we recall, included a dialectical argument between man and God on the topic of absolute justice, with the promised resolution to come at the end of the story, the argument being itself a sacred act. It also included a contract between God and man to work out this requirement of justice *in the narrative*, in "history," with the time and space of the contract serving as immovable point from which past and future could radiate out—not indefinitely—but in a way that memory would be able to compass.

That last point is where being Jewish comes into the story. They have a role to play. For, in any possible world, *somebody* must actually do this contract with God. Some particular, entire people with its real conditions of existence must do it. Otherwise, it's just one more program in retreat from the world—not a program that enters the world *as it is.*

I would have been happy, personally, for this people to have been the English, but it wasn't. I guess, as a certain kind of conglomerate, they didn't quite have the stuff. They are a beautiful, talented, and world-historically important race of people. But nobody gets it all. And it could be that—exceptional individuals aside—as an entire race, they were too entranced by their ancient mirrors, in which they could make out their fine bones and glossy hair, to get down in the desert with God and have it out. (I mention this because the preoccupation of Anglo-Saxons with their own beauty is seldom made part of the essays about them, or serious studies of them that I have read, and yet in my experience it is a significant, tacit factor in their social self-organization. Perhaps it is thought too trivial, or too frivolous, to be made mention of in serious studies.) Anyway, and however that might be, it was this olive-skinned, hook-nosed, dark-haired, Mediterranean, desert-wanderer people with a long view and an unaccountable sense of personal destiny who dreamed up the covenant: the Jews.

The Jews, or the ancient Israelites, had all their howlingly funny local customs, presumably, and they brought these with them— there being no place outside the camp to deposit them conveniently—right into the sacral covenant. Since all people have concreteness, even the English, and somebody had to do it, it was these people, with their concreteness, who did it. They made the covenant, between God and Israel. Without it, Christianity and all the religions that build on the Bible would lack historicity, would become just another branching arm of the global gnosticism. Likewise, all the failed political ideologies that the West has, for good and evil, ushered into the world, would have lacked their well-known messianic fervor—fervor of a pious patience that has snapped. It would be quite a different world. More pleasant perhaps, but more aimless. A place to tread water. A place to kill time. (The sort of place that Nietzsche extolled, when he wrote longingly about cows and children.)

Having made this covenant, the Jews had an immovable vantage point on something they had thought into being: human history, in the following sense. From that immovable point, they would be able to start counting—from time *t* backward, *t* minus one, and forward, *t* plus one. The whole of time would be short—for that reason exhaustively numerable—and they would be counting so that the questions could be asked (questions that never troubled Nietzsche): Who did it? Who killed your brother Abel? Who sold your brother Joseph?—these questions having, all, their necessary time frame.

When? Give me the sequence! That's what the judge would want to know. That's what he or she would have to know, if the facts of the case were to be determinable and the dispute fairly adjudicated. And, because it would be believed that the hand of God remained gripping the other corner of the contract document, "the case"—the facts of which would have thus to be established incontestably—would become the case of all humankind.[2]

With regard to this business of establishing the facts of the case of humanity, and adjudicating the rival claims about those facts fairly, one can admit that we all do that rather poorly. Especially when our direct interests are under fire. But we had still better try, and keep on trying, for without the far-reaching effort, there can be no story at all any more. So much for the role of the Jews, its irreducible part.

The *predicament* of the Jews had to do with the question of whether or not God really "chose" them.

Did God "choose" the Jews? Everybody seems to think so, else they couldn't possibly be so enraged. Or so malicious. Or so supercilious, as often the bystanders are. These quasi-pervasive reactions are, when you come to think of it, rather odd. For every people, every tribe, and every ethnic subgroup thinks that God chose it, *and nobody cares*. The natives of Borneo doubtless think so, and nobody gets mad. Why would Christian scholars have so persistently misrepresented Jewish doctrine on the subject of redemption, or Islamic scholars continue to deny that the ruins of Solomon's Temple lie under the Al Aqsa Mosque and the Dome of the Rock, if they didn't both fear and believe that, were the truth known, it would come out that God had actually chosen the Jews?

The struggle over the land between the Jordan River and the Mediterranean is not about patches of sand, of course. We all knew that, all along. It's a fight about whom God chose. If God had *ever* chosen the Jews, even at a time extremely remote from the present time, or in a place lying underneath the present surface of the land, then, being God, He is unlikely to have entirely changed His mind, even now.

Yes. That's what people tend to think—and tend to show that they think, in inverted ways. But what really *happened*? What is the true story here?

For Islam, the Hebrew scriptures on this subject require to be translated (or, as their biblical critics might want to say, "retranslated") into the underlying spiritual sediment of the Arabic, there to be decoded, once and for all, "reliably."[5] I gather that what has emerged from this decoding process over the years is that God *never* chose the Jews (in the sense here meant). He chose the Arabs. At first coevally. And then supersessionally. And maybe there never were biblical Jews. Better yet (as a Palestinian spokesperson has recently insisted, to international journalistic applause), Christ was an Arab. Presumably I am an Arab too—just not a very effective one.

Traditional, pre-ecumenical Christianity, whose case of Denial was not quite as heavy, did cough admissively and allow that God *had* chosen the Jews. Once. And then it went on to explain reassuringly to its parishioners: The Deity, since then, has pretty much changed His mind.[4]

As for the living faith of the Jews, of course—God and the Jews being still what each is respectively—for them the divine choice, the election such as it was, would still be *on*. On no other interpretation would Jewish experience be even thinkable to itself.

(About the religious import of this struggle over the land, it should be noted that the covenant was dreamed up at a particular time *and place*, there being no times on earth without their corresponding places. So there is, necessarily, both a holy sequence of acts and a holy land in which the acts happened, or in which something vaguely like what is reported did happen, if anything on that order ever happened. The struggle is therefore over what happened, and over *who gets control of the evidence*.[5] Not a trivial matter.)

But what did happen, where the essential fact of covenant is concerned?

The Jews thought up the covenant, and God cooperated, there being not much choice in the matter for any God. Once human beings wanted to live "historically," God had to help. What else *could* God have done? Could He have just said, "I am Shiva and Shakti; I am birthless, deathless, atemporal, and I don't even know who you are: What did you say your name was? Atman? Abram?" No, God couldn't have. God is primordial, utterly unsentimental, boundless Love. Once Love like that is importuned by a lover, however impetuous, talkative, and intellectually self-absorbed that lover may be, Love cannot but respond. It cannot but do what It did, which was to give the lover his own proper name, the name "he who wrestles with God." The name Israel.

In the case of the covenant between God and "Israel," it happens that its defining principle had long been among Love's well-hidden attributes. So it belonged to God's essence, as everything does, in one way or another. But for its existence, it had to depend, as so many things do, on a certain kind of human initiative. Had it been God's idea exclusively, it would not have been truly "historical."

So what actually happened was that God gave Her/His consent to a human agent who was pure enough to have heard God's answer almost before he had asked the question. Once again, *the question* was whether God would agree to form a lawful covenant with a certain people, who would move through its own time as if it were part of the world's single, connected, all-inclusive narrative. Since an affirmative answer to the question would serve to bring out one of God's own hidden attributes—that She/He is the God of history (the "God of Israel")—God was quick to give Her/His famous nod to the questioner.

So there is nothing, and everything, to envy. On the one hand, God didn't "choose" anybody. God was minding Her/His own business, and "anybody" (Abram) came along—and from then on the dance began. A two-step on the desert sand. On the other hand, an idea this good deserves more than a Nobel Prize. It deserves . . . just what it got.

What it got, for those who formed part of the group of original covenanters, was a position that was just impossible. On the one hand, everything that they did—worthy, unworthy, or plain mediocre—would be the target of envy, misrepresentation, and fathomless malice. On the other hand, whenever the covenanters did anything that was admittedly bad, it would look that much worse. Apart from the misspent, self-aborted, one-sided greed, delusion, or moral chaos that any private Jewish misdeed would reveal, it would also lack absolutely the glamour that wickedness can sometimes wear with such sincere pleasure. All the particular misdeeds of Jews would look merely disgusting and abysmal, because God, it would be felt all around, would have to regard them that way.

Finally, what with all that hostility coming at one from outside, and with the exaggeratedly high demands that one would place on oneself as the covenant bearer, and with the sheer drag on one of historical memory going all the way back to the projective "beginning" of the world that was created for the sake of the Law—one's Jewish identity would begin to be internalized as this great feeling of heaviness. Add to that one's resentment of (and mute pity for) the world's malice, one's quite realistic fear of the world's aggression from every quarter, and one's frustrated yearning to get to the end of the history of the world and to wrap this thing up—and you have the actual Jewish position. Impossible, from beginning to end!

Nor can Christianity step in at this juncture, as it would like to do, with the vaunted claim that the "heaviness" of "the Law" has just been transmuted into lightness, in Christ. This because the "heaviness" doesn't come from the "yoke of the Law." It comes from *the Jewish assignment*—in history—an assignment that can in no way be revoked. For Christianity, as it may even care to take notice of from time to time, has not just got Jewish origins. It has this Jewish-historical *substructure*. Which means that, even for there to be valid Christianity, somebody must live the Jewish assignment as such, on its own terms, and simultaneously with Christianity.

At this point in the discussion, the benign question suggests itself: Someday, in some way, can we not all, in good Hegelian fashion, get taken up and transcended in our respective parochialisms and flow like the river into some third religion, this time a universal one? Oh, quite possibly, we can all do that. Perhaps we are doing it now, on a silent ecumenical river.

But in that messianic "third religion," the essential features of Jewish experience will still have to be comprehended—not with transcendent pieties or other such moral evasions but just with the truth about the past, and the continuities to which it has given rise. Some people are naturally better at recollecting than others are. So, even come the millennium, those people (whoever they turn out to be) will be, for all practical purposes, back on the Jewish assignment. In sum: There really *isn't* any way out of the impossible position.

Perhaps it (the position) becomes just a bit more possible if one stays confined more or less inside the everyday Jewish reality, observing the practices (the so-called yoke of the Law) that somehow became part and parcel of the covenant, whether they did so from the beginning, or before the beginning, or only as time went on. Doing that, one can become stabilized in this activity of incessant renewal of covenant. But for most of my life, my family had not been doing that. All they had cared to preserve was the Jewish essence, the position itself, which I have tried to describe here in these formulas.

My parents, however, had come from some outposts of an actual Jewish community—carried over to Lausanne and Louisville—and they knew how to do the real practices. They also knew what the practices meant, in context, in detail, and in the original languages. So their final position, of private retreat and transcendence, still had concreteness, as mine did not. They could boast much more Jewish authenticity than I could. I look very Jewish to non-Jews. To real Jews, I look a bit borderline.

It is curious, yet unsurprising, that some of the classic styles of anti-Semitic imagination feature a sweet-faced young Jewess— charming distillate of millennia of Jewish covenantal existence— whose lissome form seems scarcely to have been touched by the sedimentary "heaviness" of that existence. And, in the novel or play, the proof of the Jewess's sweetness comes somehow to be manifest in her willingness to *transfer the treasures* of the parental household to her Gentile suitor, or counterpart. In that way we are given to know what a *nice* Jewish girl this girl is!

On the surface, presumably, this is meant to offset the image that the reader may have in his mind of all Jews as avaricious and dishonest. Beneath the surface, however, what this does is set up in imagination a state of things whereby the Jewish spirit can be enjoyed without paying *its* price. The price of conscious Jewish existence is suffering. (That is the real price of any conscious existence, of course—but here we are talking about something superadded to life's cup of suffering, whose definite character I have just tried here to sketch.)

Anyway, in these fictional representations, the cost-free enjoyment of that Jewish spirit will be made possible by the will to betrayal that the hero hopes he will find in the sweet young Jewess herself. Although her sweetness is what it is *because* of the arduous, long-term workings of the Jewish spirit within her (with all that such training, acculturation, and experience has cost everyone who has been concerned in her rearing), nothing of the kind is fairly acknowledged in these works of imagination.

To see what I mean, just imagine a play where a Christian girl eloped with her Jewish suitor, taking with her the Christian family's fortune! Could anyone suppose such a girl to be a *nice* girl? However much we excused it, on exceptional grounds, we would still have to see in the Christian girl's act a betrayal on some scale. Honor thy father and mother, as the book says. "Purity," as Léo Bronstein used sometimes to say, "is loyalty to origins." [6]

So there is the story: of the impossible position of the Jews. And that must have been what my father would have been briefly surveying when, years ago, he denounced Pheidias as "a seducer"— as someone who had taken advantage of a girl who was in that position.

Chapter Nine

Of Silence in General

When I reentered the apartment in New York, there was no letter from Pheidias. Fall term at Columbia was about to start. I had to go up there for registration. Within a short time, my graduate classes in philosophy would be in session. I would return each day and ask whether there had been any letter for me from Paris. But there had not been. And there would not be, as I began finally to understand.

He had asked for my hand in marriage, repeatedly and—as I believed, seriously—in a way that gave me to understand that it had been one of his fixed objectives. He had given me the beautiful embroidered comb of his mother—she who had died in the war years of his childhood—with its semicircular bronze mirror that you pulled out from the dark frame. He had spoken of me and to me with a gnostic fervor and natural poetry that I would never forget. He had promised to write. And now, there would not be even a letter!

He had then, it seemed, made a fool of me—a fool and a dupe. I had been converted precisely into what a woman had to avoid the fate of becoming: a figure in a tragi-comedy. Someone who, in the manner of fin de siècle Vienna, would be waiting all her life for a letter. Someone whose fate was "hopeless, but not serious." Of what was Pheidias *thinking*? What could he be *saying* to himself, now, in his heart? Could it be just: So goes the world, it's not my fault, and the more fool you?

He had spoken, to cite one example, of "the eternal feminine," Goethe's *ewig Weibliche*. That is an entity made of the stuff of the spirit, if it is anything. Materialists think they can go on construing the world as compounded of molecules, and perceiving the human experience as poised only to decompose when the molecules will, all the while taking their spiritual benefice when and as needed from such grand conquistadors of the realm of the spirit as Shakespeare and Goethe and Dostoyevski (or such exquisite potentates in that order as Jane Austen). Well, maybe they can, to some extent. A little bit of the things of the spirit is better than nothing at all. Without that least "little," you can't even survive biologically.

What they, however, ignore or treat lightly, is that the realm of the spirit has its own rigorous laws, as does material nature. Its sentences are not often revoked, save in special cases. They exact homage and submission. They are in force until time ends—and beyond time.

To pursue the same point for a moment: The realm of the spirit is quite an orderly place. It has its Swiss Guards, its ceremonial robes, its layered systems of precedents, its higher degrees, and its protocol. It is at the level, in the world's being, from which all those clumsy approximations that we call "law and order" originate. One cannot break its invisible laws with impunity. Not even *a man* can. The eternal feminine can do much, but just what she cannot do is what Goethe fondly supposed that she could: save the unregenerate from the effect of broken promises, with no special effort from him to repair what has been broken between the persons concerned.

There are, it is true, numbers of women who would not have been devastated by the way this affair of mine ended. They would have said, with a shrug, a single raised eyebrow, and a lopsided smile that mocked—both at themselves and at men in general— "Well, that's how these things go" (Ainsi va le monde).[1] But Pheidias, insofar as he *had* loved me at all (and there was in me the intuitive certainty that he had), must surely have known that I was not like that. I was made of the kind of material that retains for a long, long time even the faintest of impressions, that expects a good outcome (continuity and trustworthiness), and that has a frightfully hard time dealing with disappointments of the heart.

There is great power in this kind of male silence that can come down like a curtain abruptly over its own most fulsome expressions of love and desire. Shut up, it says to the puzzled object of its former devotions. You are merely ridiculous. You are a familiar figure in a novella. By Schnitzler. Comedic and pathetic. You are not inside the high walls of our sanctuary. You stay outside. Ring the bell, if you like. See the porter, perhaps. As of now, there is nothing you can say. You have nothing that can recommend you. You dare not raise your voice, here in our courtyards of silence. Stay there, please. Wait for me, there where I left you. Toi, je veux que tu restes nonne. [I want *you* to remain a nun.] Never forget me. Lead me above, on that day when I, even I, will have need to supplicate heaven. But I will go on now, and, incidentally, make quite a good life for myself.

And that, more or less, is what happened. I did not understand it, of course, at the time. This understanding has come to me later, and (like all understandings) through suffering. (The allegedly "less sensitive" women will come to it still later, and with still more suffering. There is nothing else to discover, here. It's not enough to say that "so goes the world." What would be truer to say is that it is wrong to default on professed love suddenly and without explanation.) So while he, as I would learn later, went on to build a life that had its own internal logic and, yes, happiness, I, who'd on instinct rejected the "French" view of love as a moment forever frozen in time, was unable to do as much for myself.

Although I never quite faced the fact, *because* he had hurt me and disappointed me, the truth was that I had really loved him. It did not depend on my convenience. My very structure was apparently bonded to his. It was not based, as I feared at the time, on the freshness of the experience in its Parisian setting, or on the Greco-Jewish contrast between us, or on all that romantic lighting. It was not based on contingent facts (that he was the first or that he had hurt me). It *was* a profounder attraction, as indeed he had said.[2] It was also unlivable. He would have darkened the very lights in my soul, without any question. So I did right to leave him.

Even had he not sown the ground between us with bristling stakes as he did, I would not have done well to stay. The disparity in aggression between us would have prevented me from testing my purposes and my strength, and therefore from earning the right to say what I do say in my life and on paper. I would have been far less achieved, as a human being. So, in this sense too, of companioning a long pilgrimage, he was not ready for me.

Men are not ready for women—even for the women they love. Yet. The exceptions exist, and more power to them, but they are exceedingly rare. The movies mislead us. Men are not often like what we see on the screen: tender and constant, noble and brave. It's all very sad. But very widespread. I am not alone in this understanding. Men have not had to grow up *internally*. They've been catered to, overmuch, for every male thing that they did. As a result, they've become at some points very brilliant and dashing, but inside—fairly raw.

The result is that we are *all* mostly alone at this time. Men need women, of course, as lovers and companions. But, once these are won, they convert them into mothers. *Their* mothers, I mean. And women need men and long for them. But on the whole they must settle for these peremptory overgrown children—or memories. It's tragic. But not unalterable. Ainsi va le monde, it is true. But history has not ended yet.[3]

What did he owe me? (A question for the moral philosophers, perhaps.) What ought Pheidias to have done, since, after all, it was I who had left him? Only a letter, that's all. A letter explaining just what had caused his decision to withdraw from me now. A letter without a false note. I would have respected that. And it would have left me, too, just as free as he was.

Just that. But why *that*? What would have been so important about some faded pen scratches on a sheet of paper that would have long since turned brittle? Only that those pen scratches had been *promised*. That's all. A promise was broken. He left me alone to deal with the fact that I had been lied to, and he had not been. And the "liar" had been someone of great importance to me on a number of fronts. He was angry. Yes. Understandably so. But he also had power to burn.

So, between me and my lover, there now moved these thick walls of silence, built on the fact of male power. Which meant that I could do nothing about it, without letting myself in for something just a touch awkward, just a trifle obscene, that tinted me with just a shade of embarrassment. It was unthinkable then, unless I was going to accept his proposal, just to make renewed *inquiries*. I never faced the fact that behind that "unthinkability" lay power, raw and clear.[4] I read Kierkegaard, and vaguely I understood that I had been lied to. So, in the deepest instincts of my heart, I had been proven a fool. After that, what else could have mattered? Could even a Nobel Peace Prize have made it good? Hardly.

Is a lie so important? They got tired of hearing them blared forth in eastern Europe, and of having to speak them. Communism collapsed, because it had rested on Pheidias's twin props—of force and deception. Force and deception are not props enough. The smallest lie, whether noticed or so far unnoticed, is of tremendous importance.

My own situation was going to demonstrate that, since, for the first time in my life, I was having to lie systematically.

"I have something to tell you" was what I decided to say to them at the pier.

"Yes?" It was my father's Kentucky drawl.

"We never took any buses. We hitchhiked to Athens."

"Yes." And here were the muffled giggles from home.

"I have something else to tell you."

"Yes." The semicircle of home was revolving in my direction.

"The two boys—the Fulbrights?—they didn't hitch with us. At the last minute, they backed out. So Anna and I went on by ourselves, without them."

Ironic, deprecatory laughter, and they were now peering at me attentively. "Go on. What else?"

I explained the intestinal facts.

Emphatically, this was more like it. More medical. "And? What else?"

I put a talent that I cannot even reconstruct into an utterly guileless look. "That's all."

They chuckled grimly, cross-questioned me a bit further pro forma, and they accepted it. Anyone would have. Clearly, I was lying for keeps.

The posture of emancipation that my parents had found by the time they read the account of this that I wrote in the 1970s should not be confused with their posture in 1959. Then, had they known this much, they would have been absolutely appalled. A great block of their parental love would have plummeted from the building, leaving a gash they could not have concealed, try as they might.

For one thing, in those days, they were possessive. Unabashedly. Also, they had certain favorite ideas about me and my womanly future—ideas that were *wholly* conventional, that were cut from the common pile and were not even given any special polish with a buffing cloth. And it would not be an exaggeration to affirm that my family, which so far I have praised to the outer galaxies, was not only unable to save me from the abyss toward which I would now be traveling. It did a fair bit to push me there, and to close off other exits. We did it in unwitting partnership, one might say, though we did not have too many options.

To explain this, the situation of 1959 has to be reconstructed. If one cannot see what the situation was in those days, one will have to fall back on those tired Freudian formulas about the unconscious predation within close families, which do nothing to sharpen the understanding and do so much to blunt it. (This caveat will not slake the thirst of the armchair Freudians, who have already been seen to lean forward in their armchairs, and to smile for the first time in a long time.)

Here was the situation—first of all as regards intercourse. From the present vantage point, some people who are beautifully self-accepting on the plane of the flesh may want to say to me, "You were very *inhibited*. You had all these complexes about sex. You must have been raised wrong." But these people have not understood something very simple: One of the main things one worried about in those years (once virginity could no longer be saved) was getting pregnant.

Although my friend Harper had soothed me with the fantasy that she would "go with me to Sweden" in such a case, that left some questions unanswered. Were we supposed just to board a train headed north? And what were we supposed to *do* upon our arrival? Buttonhole strangers and ask for directions to their abortion clinic? Or were we supposed to have stopped first at the Swedish consulate in Paris, to explain to the personnel there what one of us—the Jewish-looking one as it happens—"needed"? And where would Pheidias be in the meantime, really?

Readers who can easily picture such things have perhaps never moved through the world *without* social sanctions supporting them. Or, if they have done so, they have at least been *self*-approving. But I could not have approved of myself in such circumstances. No principle that I could think of would have commended to me self-approval, in the midst of that trouble. (What I mean is, I thought that abortion was a sin.)

No. It compounded an impossibility. To get pregnant was, quite simply, the end of everything in those days. It was *the* trap, from within which there was no coming back. You were caught. The fine, walking-the-high-wire act of being female was ended, and in a broken heap, and irretrievably. That was all there was to it. No postmodern person could then argue that life showed no plot line, or no definitive interpretation. Pregnant out of wedlock was *quite* unambiguous. One showed a plot line all right. A bad plot line. Once, twice, *maybe*, I could play Russian roulette. Not oftener. I knew it. And I was right.

What about contraception? But unless one had a superrealistic boyfriend, which I hadn't had, or a mother who was very "advanced" (nearly unpleasantly so), contraception was just not accessible. One was without a clue as to how to ask for it, or whom to ask. There were doctors, of course. But how would they treat one, if one crossed that line in the sand? And the idea of unloosing an inquiry among one's *friends* put one on such a level! This would not be something to share with most of one's friends, in any event. If one did, one had to put on a hard shell of emancipation— *extra*hard because this was long before the then undreamed-of era of sexual liberation—a shell that would have sat most uncomfortably on my superthin skin. No. A search for the right contraceptive device would be out of the question. And that left a girl with a fear of ruin that was 100 percent realistic.

All these constraints belonged to the era, and I shared them with many—though not all—American girls. Now put that together with being Jewish, in the sense that my family understood the calling. You are the shining hope of a jeopardized and tenuous, yet absolutely portentous, future. Pregnancy becomes then more than bad news. With regard to bad news, it's the bad infinite.[5]

Even to *risk* such a thing would have been to play Russian roulette with hopes and affections that *I* believed were legitimate. The recklessness, by itself, would have been felt as betrayal. One could not afford the vacant-eyed, long-lashed, photogenic sort of naïveté. The Jewish predicament does not permit that. When Jews characterize someone's conduct as "dumb," they are declaring that it is bad. Reckless stupidity is incompatible with the heavy demands of the covenant. One simply *must* stay alert, in the currents of time.

Besides all this, my parents did perceive my virginity with the eyes of a future bridegroom. I was the light of their life. They wanted me *virgo intacta*. They could not let go of me. They were too scared. Being Jewish was scary for them too, as it is for almost anyone who is Jewish and thinks about it at all. And they were both mavericks, even from an ordinary Jewish perspective. So they held on to each other, to my sister and me, far, far too tightly.

I don't make a federal case out of that. I don't think it's a matter for endless psychologizing. It has to be seen in the larger historical setting, which also had made it possible for them to be people of an extremely rich texture, of many, many layers.

Physically, what my mother had located early on in my childhood was a low-rent apartment of six thickly constructed rooms with French doors and high ceilings, at the top floor of a building that rose only to six flights above Madison Avenue. The neighborhood where we lived was at that time solid and (as it seemed) changeless. At midcentury, the neighborhood had hovered somewhere between the top and the middle, on a genteel scale of privilege. But the prominent decorative motifs of our building (the roof turrets and the lion's head over the portal) had been carved in the nineteenth century, and, under its thick stone eaves, the building seemed to conserve personalities—quite in the style of that previous century.

Usually displaced persons, the friends of the family would find in my parents' apartment a near substitute for the places they had lost—a small, guarded universe. Some had lost countries, others less evident fragments of private or professional lives. What they mostly had not lost was their high personal culture, their wit, and the *charm*—so mystifying to me at that time—of personal insight: hard bought and finely distilled. For that very reason, the friends of the family might have felt lost to themselves in this epoch, which is hardly devoted to the talent of strong personality. It appears to have been a nineteenth-century talent. But such were made much of in my parents' home and preserved there to crowd my childhood, leaving me already spellbound and at odds with the world's thick, obscuring flood tide.

For it held tales, that pretty apartment with its blue walls: short stories, novellas, unfinished chapters of much longer works—held these things securely, as a canyon may hold its reflecting bay of rainwater. The building has been leveled many years since, but whenever I dream about us as a family we are all still there, and the problematic of our common lives is still taking shape . . . from room to room to room.

It is nearly always in the apartment that I hear my father's voice, when I still hear it: pointed, savagely witty, undying, truthful, deep ranging with its southern timbre, up and down the toilsome indices of the historical vocation as he self-correctively understood it.

I see my mother there too, in the setting she had made that was so charming and so original. I see her as the lovely, chic young woman she had been at the beginning, and in storm and shadow almost to the end (when her face lost all of its feminine quality and the last traces of youth, but *dissolved* into stern and timeless love), who had lived everywhere: in Palestine when Tel Aviv had three streets, in Berlin when the kaiser was still in place, in the Hague, in Lausanne, and in Rome; who had known Elsa Triolet and Lilly Brik; who knew Jabotinsky and Bialik; and who was rooted, or so I felt, in the deep-dyed nature of things historical. She was intuitive (almost to the mystical point, but that side did not interest her overmuch), literary in at least four or five languages, coquettish by natural instinct and also by conviction, but consecrated by some blend of personal vocation and the forces of happy circumstance to the nineteenth-century, feminine virtues of wifely and maternal devotion.

It seemed very clear to me that God must have tied the knot between my mother and father, albeit from His usual troublesome distance.

The day would come when it would all resolve itself into boxes, cartons of books, papers to be sorted, furniture tagged for the dealers or for their still-standing house in Maine—all to be lifted out and carted away. And I would be kneeling in blue jeans on the bare floors, weeping sometimes, packing, and pondering too an en-quoted remark I had found on a small sheet of paper, penned in my father's clear and elegant hand: "The future is the past entered through another door," his note had read. But all that was to come to pass far, far in the future. In 1959, their whole system of life was in vibrant full force, and I could have done nothing to tarnish it, or to dislodge myself from it, then.

Why did I not lose them later on, then, in my thirties, when they at last understood—both what had become of their *virgo intacta*, and what was by then a rather free life? Well, for one thing, I was older. Also, the culture had changed, and they were smart enough to perceive that, and to see that certain gates had swung open that had been closed to young women before. Besides, their private, secular principles had never been quite so old-fashioned as they'd made them seem. They both had another side to their vision and had always had. Naturally. Had they not been themselves double, my own nature would likely not have been quite so divided.

It was only that, in the fifties—that conformist, precarious de-cade for women when all this had first come about—they had wanted to see me safely through the tunnel of a closed youth to a closed female contentment, if they possibly could. And, with all that they were and represented, against so many currents and grains of that time, they had been stretched too thin for them to have entertained the other side of their vision, where I was concerned.

They could not have borne it. And I could not have risked it.

Later, when I was in Portugal with my brainwasher, they had my old black trunk shipped home from London. Although my tor-menter had seen to it that I jettisoned everything large and small that belonged to my past, there were, as it happens, two pages of journal entry left in the trunk. But two pages that made it all clear. And these were what they found. So they could read them and see the key part of what had been driving me. They knew that I would have found it utterly fraying to have felt obliged to lie to *them* about something so consequential for me.

The proof that they really did love me, far more than they loved their constructed image of me, or the "role" I had played, was that at last they drew the right inferences. After that, when I was home and well again, they let me be. They got the point and allowed me to draw my own boundaries around the life that I chose. And therein lay the profound and free adult friendship between us—a friend-ship amply displayed in the remarkable conversation that I have described in the previous chapter. This friendship lasted until their deaths, for ten years in the case of my father and thirteen years in the case of my mother.

Overall, what was the moral in my eyes, in those days, as all those obstacles were gathering, like the objects that had whirled at my feet in the Seine at flood tide?

> Qui pourrait ne pas frémir en songeant aux malheurs que peut causer une seule liaison dangereuse![6]

Was *that* the moral, as I then saw it? That any reflective soul would tremble, who kept in view the griefs that could follow from just one dangerous liaison?

No. Not exactly. Somewhere, beneath all the icy, dark currents on which these obstacles floated, there was another view of the matter to be taken. We had staked some kind of a claim on each other, Pheidias and I. On the banks of time, it was rather deep, perhaps even eternal—anyway, of that order of fact. We could not now be joined. And my realistic sense of that would force me to view my life as a journey through the dark labyrinth of our separated lives— guided by the dialectical thread of Ariadne—to an as-yet-unseen entranceway where the things that had kept us apart could be seen through, and to that extent perhaps overcome. So my whole life had received its half-conscious erotic contours and its stirring theme.

Though I might not quite survive it, it was impossible for a person like me to regret that.

Chapter Ten

¡Venceremos!

What does the confrontation with raw power make of the "historical" project? Many men in particular may find this question puzzling, since for them "history" *is*, largely, the amassing and moving about of blocks of raw power, for which the words are provided as mere stage directions. When Achilles says to Hector that he will first kill him and next hold back his body from Priam, the words have force because he can and (as we know) *will do it*. The words are the counters of power, in such a context.

But the question is not out of place if "history" is regarded as the religious quest that it was in its text of origin and still is, transcendentally. Given that optic, the use of raw power to silence the fight for fair dealing is a *frustration* of history, not a manifestation of it.

One way that men will try to conserve their inherent masculine force, *without* having to shoulder this backpack of too much unfairness, is by taking the unmarked path of high risk. If one goes mountain climbing or deep-sea spear hunting or journeys to a given edge of the world, one will be trying to honor one's youth and its hopes, rather than sullying these. At the same time, one will not be trying to push anyone *else* around. One will be authentically masculine, yet harmless.

Now there were many things that my friend Nancy Sendler may not have known about the fine lines that people walk in hopes of connecting their present life forces and their future deaths in the way that will make most sense to themselves. But she had known enough about the young man she loved vehemently to *oppose* the trip that John Armstrong proposed to take through Africa. Her alternative suggestion, no doubt much more Jewish because "historical," had been that he visit Scotland first and trace his family's line through that space and time.

"Tell me anything you want," John had written to his mother. "But don't tell me not to go." The masculine force will need an appropriate vent, always.

So Nancy had dared to do what even his mother had not dared. Yet later they would not be assigning her to her rightful place beside themselves—those large-boned Scottish women who would be wearing black for John.

What had he meant, when he'd spoken to me of testing his ideals? *His* ideals were not then in jeopardy, since he at least had some, and was prepared to put them to some test or other. The problem, for John and his friends, would lie in the ideals that *never visited* the men on whom they would all have to rely, in the places through which they would soon be traveling!

Had Richard Wright known that? Probably. Wright had said to me that he himself could never live in Africa. "It's too *primitive*."

Did I know that? Yes, in a way I did. Anna and I had known that we could hitchhike from the North Sea to the Aegean, but that we couldn't cross over geographical boundaries, beyond which lay most of the planet.

In most of the lands on this earth, a foreign woman cannot walk. She cannot walk alone, or with a solitary friend, not even if the solitary friend is male, tough, and well armed. She'd need an army. I knew that, sight unseen. (Here I don't speak of women whose particular force of soul or character would give them safe passage through hell. I speak of the rest of us. And I don't speak of certainties, but of risks.) Perhaps I knew it as a Jew. Perhaps just as a woman who, despite all the philosophy, was not in every respect a fool.

But John Armstrong did not know the corresponding fact—that he too was, for many of his fellow human beings, a walking target. He could scarcely have conceived it. It would have offended his idealism, even to suggest it. And he was largely concerned with the ongoing progress of his own idealism, not with the defects of other people's.

John was the only friend I ever had who was the subject of a front-page story. In the *New York Times*. And the problems of moral identity that he had gone out with his friends to meet had resolved themselves by fall into mere problems of "identification." They had been three friends and a local guide who had set out together, crossing the Nubian desert of the Upper Nile, in the borrowed small French car. Only three bodies were found, however.

The Egyptian authorities claimed that among these three was the body of the guide. From Paris, Anna wrote, "*Le Monde* says that the guide was shot and traces of violence were found on two bodies. The whole thing is terrible in its unclearness." But Nancy told me that an American relative who had flown to the scene had identified the third set of remains as *also* those of an American. So the likelihood is that they were all murdered, either by the guide or some others, for a few Egyptian coin.

Officially, the proximate cause of death was "thirst and exposure." The Egyptian authorities were an unconscionably long time about releasing the bodies (which were found "in a state of disintegration"), and they kept back most of John's diary—making public only a few of the terser lines of defeat that he had allegedly written in it at the end.

The reports in the weeklies sensationalized the story, painting the dead as a trio of harebrained youthful losers who had tried to cross the desert without adequate supplies and had lacked common sense. Their mistake, however, had been of another kind. They had shown, if you will, too much "common sense," so much that, although they had carefully planned the trip with respect to supplies and the route and (from what I was told) the weather too, they had neglected to sound out the worst elements in Paris—among those who knew the Maghreb and points south—to get from them the detailed and graphic straight story about what they'd be getting into.[1] John Armstrong and his friends would have thought that to do that was condescending, or slumming.

In that belief, they would have been wrong. Had they gotten the right information, they could have made up their minds from there. Had they believed what they were told, probably they would have had the sense to turn round and go home. Home to Scotland. Home to anywhere but where they did go.

John's privileged background did not incline him to form adverse prejudgments, as Wright had feared. Rather, it inclined him *never* to do that, even where it would have been a very good idea.

"I *didn't* love him," Nancy said to me, refusing to be more or less than honest. "He wasn't, as my French professor put it, 'mon jeune amour.' It was only a *possibility*. That's all it was."

But isn't that all any of us are, old ghost?

"I only know that something young in me is dead for good," Nancy went on matter-of-factly. "*That's* all I know."

It was a point I could not dispute. Since, in her youthfully "sensible" way, she had refused John a virginity she could never surrender so aptly again, her grief at least would be unalienable now. I wished that she would not make that excruciating a use of it. But it was hers, the grief, to do with as she would. And perhaps she had less choice than I imagined.

On the rue Monsieur le Prince, Anna wrote me, she'd met Richard Wright walking and had taken out the clipping from *Le Monde* to show to him. "I *told* John not to go," Wright said, shaking his head, sorry. Wright was much thinner, weakened, he told Anna, from an intestinal disorder, also as it happened consequent upon a trip to Africa.

Stop crying, Nancy, I thought, and looked away, for the face of her grief was almost washing off against the sleeve of one of John's Fulbright friends, the only one of them I knew who used to say outright that women were genetically inferior. She sat huddled in the back pew, at the memorial service for John, and John's friend was standing behind the last row and extending the wool of his dark sleeve for her to use as a handkerchief. Oh, please, don't cry, for there is no one here big and masculine enough to laugh away your tears . . . and they merely follow John down the leaderless path into the past.

John's father having died some years before, we were met after the service by a household of tall, gentle, grief-stricken women, dressed in a black they had worn on other occasions and prepared to be anything but maudlin.

"This is Nancy Sendler." So John's sister introduced to his mother the girl to whom John had offered their family name.

Mrs. Armstrong looked puzzled at the tear-worn face.

"You remember," said the sister. "From the Bronx."

"Nancy from the Bronx." John's mother nodded, smiling to his sister, who smiled back nodding brightly too.

Oh, that's not who Nancy is, I thought wearily. *Only* by what de Maupassant has called an "error of fortune."

"Well, at least you *knew* John, Nancy," Mrs. Armstrong later cried out in her heavy Scots accent, across her crowded, subdued front parlor.

"I knew John *very well*," rejoined the strangled girl.

And then there is the pitiful fight for the remains.

He is not here.

He is not risen.

He is not palpably and justifiably fallen.

He is not here.

My part of the spoils was a postcard that John had written, to thank me for arranging the interview with Richard Wright, and which he sent after Anna and me to Amsterdam. He wrote that we'd been missed at the farewell party, which hadn't seemed the same without us, and he said this as well: "You are a fine woman, even if I don't agree with all your theories and views. See you in December—unless!"

Nancy herself died at around the age of thirty. She was in the Midwest, the rut-carved American heartland, where she'd gone out to teach after she'd gotten all her degrees. As I heard the story at thirdhand, from a midwestern woman friend of Nancy's some years later, she'd been in a car that had stalled on the highway at night. Another car had piled into it, and she was killed. She had not been at the wheel. Others in the group were also injured, I was told. But Nancy was the only one who was killed.

Well, John had waited long enough for her.

What is a man to do? What is a woman to do?

Had John not gone on that trip, but instead taken Nancy's advice and "gone home to Scotland" for that summer, to reconnoiter, et cetera, his ability to leave those markers made of deeds that tell what you were in the world would have been sadly diminished. In his own eyes at least.

It is not only women who have their scripts for this life handed to them. A man who wants to live historically (that is, consequentially, with importance) also has a script handed to him. That script says that he must move to the forefront, to the cutting edges of the syndromes of his experience.

Scotland was not on that cutting edge *for John*. He would have found it boring, I suspect, to retrace a family line and almost equally boring to retrace in that context the lines of his own motivation. Whether there were wild border-lords or Celtic kings to be found in those misty hills, they would not have returned him to a confrontation with a past that was sacred.

They could not have done that for John, that is, unless he'd retained the Christian belief in a supernatural transfer of the covenant between God and Israel—transfer of it to the Gentiles in and through their acceptance of Pauline theology. If John could have fixed such a doctrine in his (nontheological) mind, then perhaps, looking back through the mists, he could have seen holy grails, King Arthur's questing knights, or whatever there is to be seen that is sacred in Scotland. It certainly seemed to me a romantic heritage.

But John was no longer a Christian. So he couldn't fool himself about things like that. He was too historically niched in his own tradition to go in for the Vedas or Zen. And he was too decent a man to take pride in a British *race*, likewise too sensible a fellow to get much out of ancient Druidic rites evoked in imagination. (Homer's people, from whose example he got more, were not *his*.)

So he needed to wipe the slate clean, to believe in nothing more than the natural order. Yet, as someone who came from a Christian land and culture, he was left with history as the place from which grace has been withdrawn and in which sin still prevails. A place from which one has little to take and nothing to leave but one's marker made of deeds. John was an idealistic scholar by training, not a man of action. But since history was not for him safely sacred, he couldn't allow himself to be a mere scholar of it. In sum, an impossible position! Men too are (many of them) in an impossible position. Gentiles as well as Jews are in an impossible position. John would naturally have written to his mother, Tell me anything, but don't tell me not to go.

And Pheidias, with his communism, and his male taking-of-advantage? What was he to do, in reality? He too had lost a child's faith at some drastic point in his early development. Being Greek, he could not neglect history. The past was already delivered as sacred. And it would have been unworthy of his critical intellect merely to revere Greek antiquity, like the truck driver at Thermopylae for whom "three hundred boys died here" as if they had died yesterday. Besides, philosophy—that anciently Greek enterprise—had carried him where it carried so many Parisian intellectuals in the fifties: to Marxism. So he kept the hope of sacralizing history alive, pegging it now to the only available script, Karl Marx's, that promised to bring in the real golden age, the real millennium, by the exercise of high risk. Revolutionary risk. With as large an umbrella of intelligent rationalizations as could be found for all that, as if being intelligent were enough.

As for the uses of force and deception, lust, and perhaps infidelity, by which I suppose he continued to dominate women—and was in a certain sense to dominate me in absentia over much of a lifetime—the alternative would have been a more true intimacy, and for *that* one needs to be able to face oneself. To face oneself, one has to have something to stand on, a vantage point. Men are less purposeful and convincing than they once were, partly because we no longer live in an age of unfalsifiable (because mythical) masculine vantage points (though we still have some merely false ones). And I still do not see what could have provided a true masculine vantage point to Pheidias, at that point, situated as he then was. In the case of Pheidias, as of the far more moral John Armstrong, we are talking about people who are gifted with tremendous original passion, and who absolutely require an outlet.

The reason most people don't feel that they are in an impossible position is that they don't look.

As for me, an analogously narrowing circle of predicaments was closing around me in those years. First, as has been noted, there was the still "impossible position of the Jews." To which now I found added the nearly impossible predicament of women, in the special form that it took in my case. I couldn't forswear life as a woman and still live as I had to, "historically." Yet, quite simply, at that point, I could not live as a woman.

I could try to. I could make strenuous efforts. But Pheidias continued to hold my life strings in his hands, albeit invisible strings, seeming so tenuous if I asked them to give utterance to their rationale, yet so tenacious and strong, stretching from the shores of New York to the quais of the Seine. Meanwhile, my desire not to be ousted from or pushed to the margins of the "only real" covenant and its "only real" lineage kept me silent about this main fact of my youth. But that silence, with its attendant untruths, *nullified* my effective presence in the world. And each ineffective moment ricocheted and reechoed along the lines that otherwise would have connected my past to its future. I had to live historically, if I was to be myself. And I couldn't, if I was to remain myself.

It was a crisis of major proportions, going unspoken and unremarked.

For each moment of ineffective presence that I lived in those days, or witnessed in others, I felt inclined to take most of the blame. So I felt the most awful guilt for John's ill-fated trip, since I had said to him, "John . . . I don't say 'Go.' But I can't say 'Stay.' " Now I felt sure that I should have sided with Nancy, about his going to Scotland instead. And I could not remember *why* I'd neglected to do so, at the time. And, as I knew better than anyone, he had led those other boys outbound to their deaths, who without him might never have left their homebound shores. So these invisible threads fanning out from the words I had spoken that gave John permission seemed to have ended up soaked in all that visible gore and "disintegration."

To be sure, I could not have stopped him. Not even his mother could have. Nor Nancy, whom John loved with all his serious lightheartedness. But those empirical, commonsensical exculpations did not go very far toward the business of giving *me* absolution. Had I tried to prevent this tragedy, I would not have succeeded. But what stood out in my mind was that I had not tried. I had misread the signs of the times. And that to me was very serious.

(Now I think that I did not misread all the signs of the times. His position *was* just impossible, read from the inside. And I had read it right, from that angle. On the outside, I had thought—mistakenly—that he could probably get through this journey safely, where I couldn't have. On the inside, I think I saw that he was in a corner and could not back out. But, oh God.)

By February of that second year in New York, when I was well into my solitary preparations for the written comprehensive examinations for the doctorate in philosophy at Columbia, Anna had been home from Paris six months. And she too had entered a crisis phase.

Her fiancé in Paris had become unacceptable, and she'd broken off the engagement. Why unacceptable? He was young, good-looking, very French and, one may suppose, quite intelligent. What was the problem, then? One *marries, n'est-ce pas*? Almost everyone marries. Why not Anna?

What she'd told me, when we were both in Paris, was that he had become something inauthentic, or, as she said then, "unreal." What I gathered she meant was that he had acquired airs and graces, sophistical pirouettes, cultured sinuosities, most of which were incompatible with the youthful promises and sentiments that they had once exchanged. And what was a Parisian to do, after all? Whatever he did, it had to be accompanied by spinning centripetal spirals, by scrollwork and ornamentation—affectations of bohemian nihilism and superb discernment, for just one example— whose aim was to make sure one did all one's spinning in place, the place being Paris. Aesthetic and aphrodisiac city. So he had done what a man had to do, in Paris. And Anna had not liked it. She called him "unreal." And some other, worse names.

And she, in her turn? What had she done next? After I'd left, she had turned to certain experiences. Perhaps they were turned to in sympathy with *him*. What they were doesn't matter. This is not about gossip. Almost all women, if they've hung around life with no love of their own for enough time, have had certain experiences. The point is that these experiences tarnish somewhat the feminine side of one's sense of honor. Something is compromised, and it becomes harder and harder to get it back. It's not impossible. But it's quite a puzzle, even to see what the problem is. One can be nearly suicidal and still not see why. The culture has got rid of the concept of honor, or thinks that it has. But the instinct for honor is innate. And especially for erotic honor. It may be the deepest thing about any of us. And it certainly cannot be wished away with a downbeat phrase.

When Anna returned to New York, she told me her particular story.

"Well, we have to think what you ought to do now," I said.

"I don't know," she said. "That's why I had to tell you. I knew Abbie would know what to do."

There is a spring near the sea, where the goddess goes once a year to bathe and become virgin once again. That much I had learned from Pheidias. What he forgot to tell me was how to get to that coastal spring. So I avoided Anna, uncomfortably but helplessly in New York City, till she found her own shore, on her own.

"When I first landed in New York," said Anna half a year later, "I didn't look around me. I paid no attention."

So these inchoate American spaces had found no answering stare.

"But then, six months later, I opened my eyes. I really looked at where I was." She moved her lips back in that questioning nonsmile of hers. "In hell."

In hell, finally, you had no *body* that you could call your own.

At that time, we were both following the new developments in Cuba with some interest, although, true to my early reaction to her after that first New York conversation, I didn't in fact see too much of Anna. Then one day she rang me up to tell me about her new days, which were mostly being spent at the Fair Play for Cuba Committee.

"I wish," I said, troubled, to Anna, over lunch at the Metropolitan Museum, "that they wouldn't take little boys of twelve and train them to carry guns."

I remember that she had leaned forward, her mouth pulled back in that smile of a person who doesn't really speak English. "Those who say that don't know what it means to be a small country. You have to use *everything*."

Anna had taken a lover now, whom she'd met at the Fair Play for Cuba Committee. He was a Cuban. His name was Juan. He was as black as the moonless night, and—as Anna told me—"absolutely beautiful." The only bad thing was that he would be leaving for Cuba soon.

So. She had taken some measures daring enough either by those means to recoup her sense of feminine integrity (assuming she really cared for the man) or else to mix up her underlying and real sense of jeopardized feminine honor with the "false consciousness" to be found in merely conventional prohibitions against interracial affairs, and then to defy both (real and conventional honor) together—thus layering over with dry leaves and dust the trail that might have led her back to herself. I breathed in the recklessness of that kind of action, in that era, in my stuffy America! It suited her. No settling for merely *bourgeois* ambivalence here. This here was a *radical* mixup! "So he's beautiful, Anna?"

"Absolutely. We've been meeting, the last few days, on the picket line. At Herald Square. It's so funny, Abbie. You ought to see us. There are a lot of cops, and a strange bunch of seedy fascists waiting to yell hate slogans at us. And, when we meet, we always exchange a Russian kiss in front of the cops. The cops just don't know what to *do*."

She had lots of good things to report about the Cubans she had met down at the Fair Play.

"Oh Abbie, it's the first time since we left Greece that I really love a whole people."

There is a coastal spring where the goddess goes once a year to bathe and become virgin again.

"Abbie, you can dance with them! You know how I always hated to go to a dance, because you felt like something for sale in a market? Well, now I *love* to go to Casa Cuba, and dance all night! In fact, that's how I met Juan. He was new at the Fair Play, and we were all working there one night, and I just kept *staring* at him over my shoulder. Finally, when it was time to go, he said, 'Hey! Are you coming to Casa Cuba?' I said, 'All right.' So we went. I'd never been there before. And we danced there. And danced. All night, till they closed. I never could dance with an American boy. How can you dance with a cold fish?"

It is a very curious question, how the despair of one's erotic honor shifts, at a certain moment, into the eros of revolution. Both Anna and I should have had built-in immunity to Fidel and his siren songs. In Paris, she'd been consistently *anti*communist. She had been born in Czechoslovakia and interned in a Nazi-managed D.P. camp in Germany after 1948 (the U.S. army having apparently misunderstood the provenance of the camp director's job qualifications). It was what taught her some things that students of philosophy don't ordinarily know. "To some people," she had once explained to me patiently, "*words* are absolutely meaningless."

Her father, whom she had loved—like mine, a professor of philosophy—had died in the refugee period or shortly thereafter, and her mother's resiliency had been broken at the same time. Some people are not meant to have to travel.

The ruin of her country, her family, and her childhood, she had understood to have been brought about by the communist takeover of 1948. For her, there would have been no derouted idealism to be traced in a communist lover, only the bitterest, traduced reality. And she had despised Pheidias for his communism above all.

For my part, Pheidias had not left me an objective presence to oppose, any more. So my silent, suppressed longing for him was sliding into identification. "S'il est communiste," Anka Trivier had once said, "il va vous convertir." Well, she was right. But the process was indirect. Because he was no longer there to be resisted, he was converting me.

What happens in these cases is that the proper objects of lust, its original desiderata, become inaccessible. I use the word "lust" in the broadest sense, meaning the erotic élan of one's life, one's possibility of realizing what one wants. The way to these objects is blocked. But lust, left to its own devices, does not then evaporate. It displaces itself, naturally and automatically, to another object or objects. The shift is sudden, direct, and almost devoid of supporting mechanisms—although of course one reads plenty of books and articles while the whole shift is taking place, to explain (to oneself) this shift. The new object of all this failed lust is the "revolutionary" hero, the one who will make the world safe for one's original desires, desires just at the moment rendered inaccessible. It seems quite natural at the time. But it's very sad, because so vicarious. People die, and people kill, and it's not for anything that they really *want*.

> Si Fidel es communista
> Póngame en la lista.

I didn't join the Fair Play for Cuba Committee. Not joining it was a happy accident. Also it was Anna's reflexive protectiveness toward me, one that she did not extend to herself. But I did go with her a time or two to the little café-restaurant on 139th Street and Broadway where they used to serve lovely Cuban drinks, soft or hard, anything you dreamed up, and the jukebox was always going, cha-cha-cha, and so also were the slim boys and round girls who were the native, unassuming habitués. Merry, good dancers, solid to a man and a woman for the revolution, they brought photographs and films of that green-and-blue island that was being washed down and made new. Why, in Cuba you could hose down the sky. You could do anything. You could get all the soot off the sky.

Sartre and de Beauvoir visited Fidel, who told them that the only true humanism was a humanism of need. What if the people told you that they needed the moon? queried the sage of St. Germain-des-Prés. If the people told me that, Fidel answered them gravely in the same poetic register, then they would be entitled to have it.

By spring of 1961, I had finished my course work at Columbia and was pouring through the enormous list of readings to be covered for their June examinations. While I was doing this, in mid-April, there was the Bahía de Cochinos, the Bay of Pigs invasion. In front of the UN, Anna and her friends carried placards and yelled their imprecations in Spanish. Anna was just learning that language.

"When the next invasion comes, *I* don't want to be carrying a sign in front of the UN. *I'd* rather die on the beaches of Cuba." So Anna had said to the man from the "26th of July Movement," then barricaded behind iron mesh at 139th Street, who was handling the immigration permits. "After I said that he didn't argue any more," she went on in her sing-song voice. "He *knew* how I felt."

It (the revolution) was the great romance of her life. And it was to make up for the failed romances of her youth. I could not stop her. Just because I *could* have, I could not. Not with my own arguments. I was at that point too Fidelista to have any. But I could have taken her—poor Czech orphan—to my father. He had been her favorite American teacher and man. *He* would have stopped her. Decisively. Since the purge trials of the 1930s, my parents had been unambivalently anticommunist. Since the Hitler-Stalin pact, they had even broken with friends who were still sympathizers. They would not have been bemused by any pretended new-style communism. They had already seen the new become the old. But the fact that the secrets of *my* life were being concealed from my father put me, I felt, in no position to do otherwise with Anna's.

Also, on some level I suppose that I sensed that *these* secrets were not the first-order secrets. They were second order. They concealed others that were the real secrets. One can take one's real eros to one's father and ask him to accept it. But a passion that was in its essence vicarious? To take such a thing to one's father and ask him—not even to accept it but rather to suppress it—would be a humiliation. It would invite shrinkage of the spirit. I had the same problem that she had, of deflected eros. I couldn't have that second-order eros whipped out of me, too, and couldn't stand to see it whipped out of Anna.

"I finally made up my mind not to speak to my parents before you go," I said to her, during her last few hurried days in the States. We were on the Fifth Avenue bus, speaking a discreet French, going downtown from the Fidelista café. "Because I believe that my parents would not understand."

"Uh huh," she said, disciplined by secrecy.

But I thought I observed a shade of disappointment cross her tanned, irregular features.

The last thing that she gave me was a copy of Che Guevara's *Guerrilla Warfare*, with her inscription, "Guerrilla should be like hitch-hiking. ¡Venceremos!" (We shall conquer.)

Fidel has proved to be one of the most influential of the hubristic bad men of this century: a liar, a brazen face-to-face killer, a betrayer of virtually all of his intimates, a man who—on his own say-so—was pushing the world to apocalypse, a man for whom nothing was real, finally, but his ego.[2] In sum, a master of the fake romance of the revolution, who outfitted the youth of the world with wax wings for their Icarus flights.

I didn't know this. It would be years before I would get a deep whiff of this brimstone. Nevertheless, some things could be known, in the next weeks and months, as I watched the situation unfold there with growing alarm and shock.

It was only *after* she'd gone that it occurred to me that I'd waved one more friend, besides Armstrong now, down the road of a fearful mistake. Cuba turned doctrinaire. One could see that from here. Anna had become a Marxist in order to give her soul that yardage without which it would have had to walk naked—as she said that souls had to do in America. She had gone into exile in Cuba. I let her go, when (through my father's intercession) *I* could have stopped her. And from week to week it seemed Cuba hardened, despite all the forecasts of its friends, and became the small island where I could not wish Anna's soul to walk *at all* now, lest it attract the wrong sort of attention.

Anna had not been my feminine confidante, like Harper. But she had been a philosophic companion. We'd shared dialectical conversations at le Tournon, and on the road, though we had differed about whether such dialectic led on to enlightenment or had to curve down toward some terminal point of absurdity. She had been sceptical, I optimistically rational. Looking back over the whole graph of our friendship, from where I stood at the edge of it after she'd left, it seemed to me that I had not won the main point in dispute.

She had. Oh, Anna!

But despite that silent cry of my heart—so horrified to see Anna's philosophical scepticism "justified" in that irreversibly actual way

—this was not really an instance of "the absurd." Neither of these episodes were that. They were only instances of the truism that in history, at any given stage of the process, a happy ending is not guaranteed for the parties.

Anna had done the very best she could, by her then lights. And so had John Armstrong. And so had I. And it was tragic, not absurd.

Chapter Eleven

Of Women and Philosophy

Philosophy was for me the long way to get home. But it was still the way home. There was no other way—that I could see.

What I did at Columbia, philosophically, was look around. The place had a technical, philosophy of science side that wasn't suited to my interests or capacities. Meanwhile, its relation to the epic of philosophy, its history, seemed amply encyclopedic, but unfocused. Therefore, from my standpoint, *intolerably* boring, like a long story where they mention everything but the plot.

There were brave exceptions: a course in aesthetics that I remember as actually exemplifying a sense of taste. And there were courses in analytic philosophy, taught by some British visitors who later went on to eminence, and those courses did have real plot. They were self-plotted, as it were, by the arguments that came in, one atop the other, bringing with them ever nicer, more discrete distinctions. But this plot seemed so dissevered from philosophy's long history as an eternal discipline that carried consolation, correction, and connection to the human story, that for me even to *follow* it in those days was to feel oarless and becalmed on an open sea, empty from horizon to horizon.

The place seemed to be about careers. Among those who'd achieved one, it was about that fact. And among the graduate students with a fair sense of smell, it was about making one. That was fine. I had no objection. But I did not think it was romantic.

I took the written comprehensive examinations that conferred doctoral eligibility, landed among the rather small group that had survived them that year, and decided to exit from the place with a master's degree, before I became too distracted by its irritations to remember what it was that I'd been seeking.

There were women of my generation who recollect the snide remarks about women that Columbia professors used to make in those days—remarks that a later vocabulary would describe as "sexist." For me that was the problem only tangentially. What I felt as putting in jeopardy my very sense of *being* at that place was its erotic deadness. The words that I've used here—"boring," "unfocused," "careerist," and so forth—are designed, however awkwardly and (I dare say) tactlessly, to get at that fact about its life. I don't know how else, or how better, to put this.

I had come back from Paris with a certain erotic authority. There was definition, in spite of everything. There was form. So I would feel *escorted* by the muses of desire, by a whole band of muses in fact, as in my first days at Columbia I let "them" usher me across the concrete sameness of the mall. Atypically for me, I felt no shyness at all. There was a burly young graduate student whom I remember asking for directions, in the course of my first day on campus. When he'd wheeled, inside his thick jacket, as if he were dodging a bat's wing that was scarily dipping and circling in the vicinity of his short-cropped hair, I was quite disconcerted. Goodness. Could he not answer a simple question from a young woman? Where *was* this man? "Behind Low Library," he replied to me shortly, pointing a fat finger toward Philosophy Hall, over the heads of the stone bestiary.

Passing by half a score of men as I walked that way now, I looked from face to face more searchingly. As if scoured by something corrosive, their glances would meet mine, start back instantly, and then ricochet, only to sink somewhere behind the ragged edges of the ill-matched buildings that belonged to that fine old campus. But where were their glances sinking? Where did they want to go? How did they visualize the process of history, the process of men and women? That, I couldn't fathom. But perhaps there might be among them a suitable partner for me, after all? And perhaps someone Jewish?

I have described the Jewish vocation in the most world-historical terms imaginable, because it seems to me that only in those terms *can* one truly imagine it. But what about the case of someone who lacks the hardihood to keep imaging forth that transcendence-in-immanence that is the Jewish vocation, but who is nevertheless "born, by an error of fortune," Jewish and male? So, worried about sex performance and—what is nearly the same thing—worried about maintaining an edge, like most men. But we specify that this hypothetical person lacks it (the courage to find transcendence in immanence) and is nonetheless placed in what we have described here as the impossible position. What sort of a *style* is available to such a man? Specifically, what sort of erotic strategems?

The heart sinks, even as the question is raised.

"Everything," a young male coreligionist said to me one day where we were having lunch in the Viennese café below street level, "responds to pleasure. If something didn't give you pleasure, you wouldn't do it."

A boring generality, as well as a brief for moral decomposition, I thought.

"I think that your view is oversimplified," I said aloud. "What about the people who have sacrificed their lives for some ideal which to them was more important than what you are calling 'pleasure.'"

Shrugging. "Oh, *that's* easy to explain! They got more pleasure out of that than out of any other thing."

"I think that you're misusing language," I said, as I struggled on up the hill of language alone. "An experience can't give pleasure and pain at the same time and in the same respect. Clearly, such an experience must have other dimensions."

"I don't care what kinds of dimensions they are." His lips, bereft of definition, were stretching way back in a tired grin. "They are all types and aspects of pleasure."

And apparently his type and aspect lay in causing me pain. But I felt anger rising. "Listen, by such standards it will not be possible to condemn *anyone's* actions, even a Hitler's."

"How could I condemn him?" he agreed, with that admirable pseudo-Socratic consistency that would have put him naked into the gas chambers. As a volunteer. "You're perfectly right. I might not *like* him. But I would have to grant that by his own lights what he did might have been right because it gave him pleasure . . ."

As he was speaking I was getting up and getting into my grey gabardine hitchhiking jacket. But, before I left, I leaned down to look into his gunsights, which were his eyes, in this case, directly. "You"—I smiled—"are a worm." I looked him up and down, from the ground to the crown of his head. "An earthworm." And at the door, still unsated, I turned back to wave. "Goodbye, worm."

His expectant, appetitive leer had changed by then into the

rather glazed smile of an earthworm about to be served up as part of the icing on a very rich Viennese cake and not quite sure whether that was his type of pleasure.

In any event, the conversation with the young man in the Viennese café was atypical (and perhaps for that reason I have remembered it) in that in it I had the last word. The fact was that such men often told one explicitly to "shut up," or to "make it simple," and not say what one had to say in "such a complex way." (Maybe he failed to shut me up because, *that* time, I really did make it awfully simple.) In other words, however and whenever they felt that they needed to, they cut one down to size. Their size.

So what I did at Columbia finally was decide to get out with an M.A., writing a master's thesis titled "Action and Purpose in Merleau-Ponty." Merleau-Ponty looked to be my intellectual Ariadne, who might thread the way for me through the maze-world where Pheidias had roved, with its strange vagaries—from humanism to terror and, in Merleau-Ponty's own case at least, back again to pragmatic humanity.

Along the damp, half-dark way, on that Frenchman's mazelike journey, one would at least find reference to all those radial concerns that in those days fanned out from Paris as their center: the alleged contingency of values; the alleged indissoluble irrationality of certain phases of experience; the shaping of identity through risk and self-commitment to a public dialogue that might or might not communicatively work; the sense that outcome alone determines who has read the moving forces in the situation (read "history") aright.

When I reread my master's essay now, it reads like nothing so much as my search for a way out of the labyrinth—to some no longer to be concretely expected reunion. If in those years I was asking myself where Pheidias was behind his silence, what I find now in the master's essay are the likely answers to such a question. Better answers than I knew then. It was a long love letter. That is all. Eighty-three pages in typescript. Nicely done, too, as I see somewhat to my surprise. I should have padded it out a bit and made a book of it. It would have "helped my career," as they say. It's a useful introduction to Merleau-Ponty, anyway.

Part of the trouble was, I had not yet managed to become an American again. I was in New York in what a Bostonian Fulbright acquaintance, on the eve of his trip home to Cambridge, described bitterly as our "internal exile." I was trying very hard to come home from exile. But it was complicated.

I had left Pheidias for the values that my father represented, to put the whole thing in a slightly oversimplified formula. Yet I could not seem to find those values here—find them abroad in the land, I mean. I was not trying merely to hang around the apartment on Madison Avenue where my parents were. I had my own life to live. To do so was imperative. But, so far, I was not succeeding at what I'd set myself to do: find the Absolute without Pheidias (find it and bring it *back home to Pheidias* in one world or another), since I hadn't thought that I could precisely find it with him. I was going forward in philosophy. Those were by no means wasted years.

But it seemed that my heart did not agree with what I'd done. And it refused to come along.

My father's image in my life was not my image of the Absolute. (I dare say that he didn't confuse himself with It, either.) His life had its own imperfect convolutions. But that influence was a reminder, and it acted as a sharp inward imperative: to compare the true directions on the compass with the accessible calculi of personal advantage, to steer home through uncharted seas, and not to be ready to give up. One was never counseled to be cynical, neither directly nor by indirection. And his influence did not come down, except in the most superficial sense, to a style that could be copied, to an address book that could be used, or to a chart (whether portentously wide or abstemiously narrow) of the philosophic waters. It was a style and a method almost inherently inimitable, as object lessons in how to be an individual must be.

It seemed to me that, if the main lines of my life were to be dragged forward across choppy seas, I would have at least to put in at some other graduate department of philosophy, even if the men there turned out to charge me the landing fee of crediting as little as they decently could of the course work I had just done.

The risk involved in staying at Columbia was that over the long haul I would lose my way. I would get bored and blunted out of compass. I would learn a great deal—indeed I had already covered a simply savage amount of reading—but in the process I would forget why I had started. I might become a salvaged professional, but that was not precisely what I had set out to become, and, in these chartless voyages of the spirit, the whole point was to remember what one had set out for.

Since I was now "home" in America, and not Paris, and *still* searching in my Jewish way for the Absolute in the context of real history, what I would have to be after now was the deep-buried essence of America: the romance of America, in other words.

> I do believe the average American to be an Indian,
> but an Indian robbed of his world.[1]

So I naturally longed, like every child and former child, to be a Native American, by way of getting to be a real American. Inevitably, I would want to make contact with that great American corrective to its Puritan repressiveness: our "frontier" unfinishedness. In *that* the New England transcendentalists saw their recovered Eden, and a new-style redemption that would fit the rest of humankind also. (Whereas in that frontier what Hegel saw was mainly open space, confusion, and the postponement of an eventual reckoning.)[2]

The Swiss philosopher Jeanne Hersch was spending two terms in New York as a visiting professor in my father's department, that year that I was writing my master's thesis on Merleau-Ponty so as to get my exit visa from Columbia. The first time she came to dinner, I said something to her that caused her to respond to me, gravely and attentively: "That is the mentality of Paris. I think that you are wrong. But I see Paris in you."

Jeanne Hersch described to me a quintessentially *American* department of philosophy. It was at the Pennsylvania State University, where she had also been a visitor, and it seemed exactly to fit my rather inchoate requirements. There were its European ties—the influence of Kojève and of Leo Strauss. And there was the nearly pervasive "poor man's Heidegger" (so the local jest went) attention to the out-of-doors, to the American grain in philosophy, to the transcendental.[3] "And also, Abigail," Jeanne Hersch said to me, in her wistful, absent, tender tone, the place had "the American sadness."

So, in the fall of 1962, I began graduate studies in philosophy almost anew at Penn State and also took on my first teaching duties.

One late morning, on November 22 of the fall following, I was having lunch at the usual sort of off-campus eatery in State College, Pennsylvania, called (as one might expect) the Corner Unusual. When the waitress brought the check, she said, in the flat accents of rural Pennsylvania, "Isn't it terrible. The president's been shot."

"Where?" I said, half rising. "Where is he?"

"He's in Dallas."

"Is he hurt?"

But she had gone back to her under-the-breath adding up of the numbers on my check. There was a radio, however, in the Corner Unusual and someone must have turned it up. The first few bulletins were inconclusive and confused. But a head wound! It sounded serious, quite possibly.

It was in the context of what were probably advance notices of the Warren Commission's September 1964 report that my parents had the visit of André Philip, some months later. Philip was a French economist, staunch advocate of European unity, finance minister for several successive governments in France, and hero of the French Resistance. He was a lovely man. We had met him through Jeanne Hersch, and the friendship had continued on its own thereafter. I must have been back in New York from Penn State for the midyear break.[4] "All Europe," said Philip to us, "is sure that the death of your president was the result of a conspiracy involving official levels."

"Oh, no!" went all the polyphony of our patriot's chorus. "From all accounts, the Warren Commission will issue its report after what promises to be the most thorough and responsible investigation. It looks as if they are going to find the assassination to have been carried out from start to finish by one man. That's always been the American pattern. With Lincoln. With Garfield. America is not like Europe. We have our unique historical configurations. Whatever would lead you to think otherwise?"

"Because," replied Philip, "I know that *carabine*," meaning the old-fashioned, bolt-action Italian Manlicher-Carcano rifle with which Lee Harvey Oswald would be found by the report to have killed the president and wounded Texas governor Connally in several places, getting off three shots in extremely rapid succession from the sixth floor of the Texas School Book Depository building behind the motorcade—doing all the wounding with a purported single bullet that emerged undamaged and the killing (from the same rifle) with a second, apparently "frangible," bullet. The laws of physics put on a real show that time.

"They are going through all the evidence. No one at that level of government would conspire to cover up evidence. That's not the way things happen here." So we continued to assure our French guest in good faith, with all the civic piety of 1963.

"No. But your CIA . . . ," Philip responded, with an amplifying gesture of both hands, pronouncing the letters in the French way, with equal stress on each syllable.

It would be years before I could begin to credit what Philip had said that evening. However, I suppose that on a deeper level I believed it just as soon as I heard him say it in the way he did. Why else would I have stored away his words, accents, and gestures so minutely? What I did not know then was what on earth I was to do about it.

If Philip was right, then the project of recovering the deep-buried essence of America—the transferred project that was supposed to keep me on the track of world history even here—would be far more dangerous and difficult than I'd imagined.

But I had come to State College, Pennsylvania, in 1962 partly in search of that untarnished wilderness with which the whole world still has its unspent romance. Like "the average American," I was still an Indian manqué.

(An Israeli cousin, back from her first tour of the real West, has commented: "I *see* what you have done with your Indians. You have put them on the *worst* land and left them to starve!")

But despite all that, shortly after my arrival at State College, I telephoned a young professor whose romantically "deep silences" and wirey mountaineering had been kindly (and even pointedly) recommended to me by Jeanne Hersch, in the context of what she had wistfully termed "the American sadness."

My question to this mountaineer-philosopher had to do with how one actually got to "the country," meaning those wooded hills that one could barely discern from the town. I had tried to walk there, I explained, but had not yet managed to drag past the regress of gas stations that seemed to stretch just about to the horizon.

He gave me a few long moments of those wirey "deep silences" of which I had already heard so much and then laughed laconically. "I guess you'd better just give it up. I don't think . . . yer gonna git there."

I didn't persist. My weary heart no longer took much to discourage. It was tending to take bad things as omens. And a lot more than a trip to the mountains got settled in that conversation.

Aside from that longed-for trip to the mountains, Penn State gave me whatever else I had gone there for. It put me in touch with the American philosophic grain, its hopeful astringencies, its dry paradoxes—everything in them but the private heart—and its slightly self-mocking transcendentalism. Most significant, it helped me to reconnect my private history (which by now had to contain those opacities that so many white lies and silences had dug into my psyche) with at least some of philosophy's more resonant articulations.

Stanley Rosen, who was one of the more influential presences during my time at Penn State, had counseled me in this way at the small welcoming party that the Rosens had given for me when I first got to the small town of State College: Find the philosopher, living or dead, from whom you think you can learn the most, and then learn everything that you can from him and about him.

That was superior advice, as far as it went. It beat anything I had heard at Columbia. It assumed that the philosophic tradition could be mined—for its *secrets*, for its depths, for its stories.

Pushing past Merleau-Ponty, I had already noticed that he had been made possible by someone earlier and possibly larger, who had first (or at least most effectively) crossed philosophy's eternal strain with the historical. I was not an enthusiast of Hegel when I first drew up alongside him at Penn State. What I could sense, however, was the size of his influence, and that it was something to try to understand. But he seemed to want to take away life's mystery, to collapse the transcendent into mere dialectic, and what I wanted was to get inside that process of his, to find out why it was both right, and wrong.

Once I had sat beside the River Seine at flood tide and felt, with the sadness of anticipation, that it would be my destiny to learn philosophy, to sit in the cafés, to watch the river-flow of feminine existence from the dry margins of life.

That my real assignment, then and later, was strictly the feminine assignment, I did not then consciously realize. But there are some assignments that are hard intrinsically and would be almost as tough—even were one to "know," with complete consciousness, that one had been posted to them.

My charge was to find the means of reconciliation between Pheidias's worldview and mine, so that I could see how he could have got to think what he did—how he'd got to formulate his values as he had—and could then make my way over to his thinking processes and back to mine. If I could do this—find the mental road between our outposts in this world—then he could do it too, in principle, whether or not he ever would. In any case, this much my love demanded of me, as I felt it.

It was the same assignment that all women have, more or less. The fact that it went forward without visible evidence that it *was* my real assignment only brought out more starkly the element of blind faith that belongs to the feminine as such, in the real world.

But at Penn State what they told me, both directly and by implication, was that the mind as such was masculine. What this said to me was that, if I ever reached Pheidias, with the mind's bridge-of-understanding, he might well refuse to recognize that I had done so. He would refuse, if he too needed to believe that the mind was masculine. And if that were so, my feminine assignment was so structured that I could not succeed in it.

Perhaps I sensed this with a kind of dread whenever I would board the train for Lewistown on that five-hour lap of the journey to State College and would feel the night wind howling through the hollow at my back. At Lewistown, one waited for an hour in the rural bitters of what used to be coal country until the local driver wheeled his little bus into the station. It was then another hour's winding drive into the town of State College, which had grown up to service that land-grant university. The trip from New York was neither pleasant nor interesting to me in those days, but it allowed plenty of time to be alone and think, and watch the land change from formless eastern industrial into the sloping rises and concavities of the central Pennsylvania hill country.

I could scarcely even *see* the hills from where I lived and plodded along on foot. But if sometimes I got a lift, then, driving over the white-striped rise of highway, from certain angles I could glimpse a long, low, indented ridge that, like a distant black fortress, seemed to police the town. To the right of this ridge, in the November afternoons, I saw how the sun glinted off the clouds like a burnished steel skillet. It gave a solid clear light, so clear that in the full-length mirror that I got from Woolworth's and had hammered up in my white-painted efficiency apartment, I could see the fine lines that were starting to form around my twenty-five-year-old eyes just a day or two before they got there.

The way to feel the power of the town in full force was, however, to get out of it for a brief spell and then be driven back quite ineluctably (I had committed myself to this place, after all, and to the whole exhausting schedule of its higher degrees), riding in from Lewistown on the night bus through the hills.

My country, my America, sounds the full range of its lonesome cries now, with its white moon clanging and rustling like tin eaves. And overhead, reflected darkly in my eyes, there are the needle-breasted stars that I can see, against their aureole of frozen milk. As for the populace, those whom my country holds in trust, why they sleep on, in houses whose windows go winking insanely, like dreadfully mottled, sightless tissue in the chill November darkness. And the pines—oh, have a care!—how they pronounce themselves so blackly over against the ashen backdrop of the lower sky!

No fear. My land cannot be wholly unguarded, for strewn here and there about the darkness I can discern its wooden houses, unpainted, standing like weather-beaten sextons at the borders of what looks like a vast but untenanted cemetery. The cemetery is perhaps not wholly empty, for by the roadside I can still see piles of stone, by their shape looking to be neither ruin nor relic but, rather, derelict. Yes, there are derelicts creasing these sloping cement shoulders! But will this land fail utterly to stand for anything, so that the snubbed hills will just sink flatly into their surrounding curvatures? Or will the whole country take its stand from time to time and allow its remote sky to curve into the V of its hillsides—to say what? What could it say? Never. It could never say it. At least, not to me.

I used to pace the cracked uneven sidewalks of State College, with their weeds atop small mounds of dirt pushing the cracks apart. I would be counting the cracks, measuring the distance —God, how long?—between the utility-white walls of my apartment and the gigantic campus, framed all about by a soul-freezing wind, tenanted by widely divergent buildings, in some of the oldest, newest, nearest, and farthest of which, over a period of two years, I taught philosophy.

In some ways it was freedom for me. Like a little black-winged insect I flew down the airways above the cracked walks, made it into my classrooms, flew in circles and figure eights all round the inner spaces of my classes, my rooms! and I still see, beneath my weary eyelids, the soaring flight of that cheerful bug until, whop! It's dead. The poor thing is dead. A huge, invisible hand has crushed it, and it sprawls back on the chopping block—more stick figure than bug now—and, in a slow, dying gesture drapes an elbow backward over its fatalistic eyes.

Now the bug is getting up, angry and menacing, its dangerous bug tusks curved garishly upward from its angry twisted eyebrows—but it is too late to charge forward. For its eyes have protruded conically out and out, until the vertexes have opened and are dripping blood.

Poor bug, nothing seems to work for you, and perhaps it would be better for you not to see at all, and let your lids, like tired, dopey caps, fall down over your black eyes.

But no. That won't work either. A big hook, or is it a fingernail, is reaching under your lid and actually rubbing your pupil, scraping and squeezing from top and from bottom, so that your eyes get no rest! And they pendulate to and fro, and turn till they become sightless disks, and then revolve fleeing but trapped in the eye sockets of your head.

Oh, what is it, poor bug, can't you tell me down the telescopic sights of time? What is it that pursues you like a fire in the very expanding inner tissue of your head?

The bug is perched on a rooftop now, bowing and waving, with one weary, affably formal gesture of the hand, its diaphanous wings folded against its black joints. Now it has somehow acquired a metal visor that is fitted to its head and permits only its staring eyes— transfixed as if by an intruding double—to greet its social context. And what is that social context but a huge eye, incandescent like its own but without a pupil, and sometimes terrified like itself but without a motive; sometimes visored over like itself but without a body, and therefore sinking in shadows that rise climbing out of nowhere; sometimes weary like itself but clamped in place and without the means of fleeing into the jaws of the gnawing burning interior—the black pit of fire that consumes from behind the eye sockets.

For a dim shaft of purple transfixes my bug's eyes now, and sets them alight from within, and wafts and billows and becomes seas— seas of purple striated with purple lights and shadows; and my bug walks or shall walk in the seas of purple, teetering for balance like a maimed man. And deep under the seas my bug reaches or shall reach for the carapace of another creature like himself; he shall be in love, the poor fellow, and he tugs at its carapace and goes after it, but teeth and eyes close over the scene in avenging judgment, and massive stones around which the dried weeds twine now reach to high heaven.

It is the largest, highest building ever made, and the very night is no proof against it. But be silent, my future, for I am busy. Penn State calls—the thin steel blades are sucked into my eyes and re- turn them to their normal shape—and, dear god, I must prepare a class.

But all this must sound almost like madness! What in the name of the good Lord had happened to me? I'd been a normal young woman, when this story began. How had I got to that edge? I had got there, as it happens, most reasonably.

Let me recapitulate. What I had wanted, at the start of my year in Paris, was to enter into the Jewish relation to God by penetrating the historical setting where I then was. Only from full congruence with one's time and place can one make the "historical" effort au- thentically, the effort to bring about justice and mercy (by small or large increments) in the world narrative. This is assumed. This goes without saying, ordinarily. I say it here only because of my present assignment, which is to make these assumptions stand forth explicitly.

Of course, one should try to find one's *proper* place at a given time. Not stick it out in the wrong place and time. But I was in Paris. On my U.S. government grant to find definitions of man in aesthetic experience. At the very beginning of my time as an adult. And it felt to me like the right place at the right time. Which tended to mean, since I was a young woman, and (in the Jewish narrative) women's lives are to unfold in concrete complementarity with men's, that I would inevitably be drawn to some man who would fully express, to me, in "aesthetic experience," that historical setting.

Pheidias did, and I was so drawn. He was a modern man, Greek and French, with his mix of yearning, homesickness for antiquity, nihilism, and utopian violence. He was very sophisticated and intelligent. He was, by birth and training, the heir to all that high culture. In some far-buried corner of himself he probably carried the hyper-Augustinian conviction that he was condemned. In some inexplicable way, we were powerfully drawn to each other. Neither time nor space could have affected it. Only the power of ideas could.

In forcing on me a sexual initiation before I could agree to it, he both saw correctly that I *never* would have agreed and therefore—in the logic of our intimacy—was "asking him" to do that, and also that *he was incapable* of finding that sane and befriending discourse that could have won me over without sacrifice. Our two incapacities met.

That event compelled me to become "historical," but in the mode of what Hegel calls diremption, self-alienation. Not in the sense I had envisaged. First, in that era and the setting of my family, the fact of my new unsought sexual status had to be kept a secret. This was not because my family was especially distorted. One should avoid the temptations to oversimplify, fix blame, and evade understanding. The virginity of a loved daughter was a weak mesh in the network of their own defenses within the larger nets of the Jewish assignment in history—about which they had all their intelligent sense of its having placed the whole lot of us in jeopardy. I don't blame them now, and I didn't then. One ought to think of these things with one's heart, not just with one's clinician's eye.

In its own turn, this secret subtly dislocated all my relationships with others. For someone who had sought the Absolute via self-transparency and truthfulness, *it put a lie at the very center of her seeking.* I could no longer reach others, and, by the same token, less and less could I reach myself. When I tried to write in my journal, I couldn't get *me* on the line any more. The words had become hollow, drained of power.

Also, Pheidias's "modern" lack of erotic follow-through, the fact that he did not write, his easy surrender to reductionist realism ("l'amour, c'est eternel, mais dans les circonstances favorables"), meant to me that all this forfeiture of purity on my side had not gone for any good that I would live to see triumph. My feminine honor had been staked on a cheat.

I looked, therefore, for other ways to carry that feminine sense of honor forward, in real time and in real relations. "Historically," as I said. There were my friendships. I have not chronicled them all here, only the ones with John Armstrong and Anna. But they will stand in for the others. With those two it seemed to me that I had sent friends on some trips that I was not taking, and—they had not returned. Whether or not I did in fact bear some guilt for what had happened to John Armstrong and Anna, the point that I sensed about myself was that *I* must have been dislocated, or else I would have put up some resistance to their projects. I must have been suffering some failure of insight, or else I would have seen the right way and sounded the right note, when it was called for. Because of this secret I kept, and the lies that concealed it, I was out of step. I gave bad advice.

I had sought asylum in the *politique* of the radicals (it had seemed another way of rejoining Pheidias in absentia), and there I slammed up against the bankruptcy of that whole nihilistic investment of life's youthful energies. Once again, I was seeing in the mirror of events my own deflected eros and inability to find my right path through time.

Finally, there was the realm of the intellect. In the academy, the house that Plato built, I had always felt at home. Philosophy *was* my real home, and it had always been that. Yet it too would be, for me, not a self-standing enterprise, but my preferred means to this engagement with the God of history. So, in and through it, what I sought was to go on with what I had started: to discover the mind's bridge-of-understanding between me and whatever *au fond* (in the realm of ideas and values) had separated Pheidias and me. For I could not and did not forget him.

(Did you want to remark here that I was "far too sensitive" for a modern girl, and that I should just have healthily "got over it"? But who or what has assured you that you are right? Why should love be that kind of thing? Why should anyone get over it, if it is real? I did not choose to be transfixed in that way, in history. Yet for all I know, it may have belonged to my task in this all-too-modern world not to get over it. *Not* to be that modern.)

It was here, in my effort to live the feminine vocation on the plane of the intellect, that the message of those times drove me straight to the edge of my mental resources. For my more hard-driving professors and peers either told me outright or else strongly hinted that the mind itself was masculine. What that meant was that the exercise of mental powers would be defeminizing, in-trinsically. (In those days, that was widely believed in America, on Freudian and other grounds.) I was in nearly thoroughgoing feminine self-contradiction, therefore. In order to continue to be feminine in my sense, I would have to become defeminized in their sense.

I had already read de Beauvoir's *Deuxième sexe*, in Paris. All my women friends had discussed it with each other there. Betty Friedan's *Feminine Mystique* was circulating while I was at Penn State. So, I did not necessarily *agree* with the culture when it so de-fined the gender of the mind. And I had, from my father, masculine support that other women did not have for pursuing these projects of the intellect. But it did not matter that the culture might be wrong. For the whole point about seeking the Absolute historically was that one could not just transcend, by a mere mental somer-sault, the culture one was in. One had rather to work at justice and mercy in and through that concrete context. And, in so doing, one had to take care not to become unreal oneself. If one became un-real, a mere abstraction, one would have lost the game in any case, whatever the scorekeepers later decided.

What I feared here was that my feminine energies might get so worn down, in the struggle to survive as my sort of *philosophe* and somehow prove to those most concerned that the culture was wrong, that my energies would be as good as vanquished, and the culture proved "right" by that very consequence. I would prove it right in the very effort of proving it wrong. Even if the exercise of the mind was not (as was thought) intrinsically defeminizing, it would prove so, empirically, in the time it would take me to live it, in real time. History was not a thought experiment. I could see what all this was costing me in every mirror.

So, by the time I left Penn State, I was indeed at the edge of my psychic resources. I was at the brink. And it would be at that point, in London (where I'd be residing while doing my doctoral re-search and taking a breather), that I would meet Suzanne. She was a young African-American student, doing her graduate research abroad, like me.

I met her just at the point where I was about ready to abandon the "historical" project, the Jewish vocation, altogether. And she was Black. "Negro," as we said in those days. And she had never had that project. And she appeared to offer me another way. By the time I met her, I was all out of ideas. But, as it turned out, she was a great destroyer. So this is the brainwashing part.

One last question: If my reserves of sanity were so nearly exhausted by then, how did I ever get back from that brink to where I am now, well established in my sanity and in the profession of philosophy? I got back because I had got there—to the end of my rope, to the brink—most reasonably.

The way up and the way down are one and the same. So said Heraclitus long ago, and not untruthfully.

Part 3

Another Paradigm

Chapter Twelve

By the Narrow Way

Some readers might want to say soothingly at this point that *writing* well is the "best revenge." But have such readers ever considered what an insignificant and weightless thing revenge is?

It is true that the self-appointed mentor to whom I was now about to turn would develop by stages into an utterly implacable and fathomlessly clever adversary. The worst enemy I ever had, in other words, and I have had several since then. You can do a person no greater injury than to abscond with her soul—her moral "identity." (By the largeness of the injury to it, we can measure the reality of the target, on our philosophical side.) Bodily harm is pretty bad: It's an attack on one's place in history. But the other thing is worse yet: It's an attack on one's place in eternity. So we're talking about a bad enemy here.

But at this point in the memory game I have a much better idea than revenge: It's the idea of nonviolence. It's *ahimsa*. It was good enough for Gandhi. It was good enough for King. And it'll be good enough for me, who still is a well-intentioned American, with a lot to remember. I'm harmless and could not hurt a fly, no matter what might be unlocked from the chambers of memory. And I certainly wouldn't *want* to hurt her. Hurting her wouldn't make my life any better. It wouldn't turn any gears in the life that I've still got to live.

However, since I can't necessarily say the same for her about me, I'll pick one of our favorite American hedge-the-bet styles of

action: driving by someone (that we want closure with) *in a car.*
She'll be standing on a street corner. I'll drive by her in this car with
one window down and tell her exactly what I forgive her *for,* item
by item, and, if I can just get out of there in one piece, I know I will
find some ventilation for my feelings: some relief.

But my target? The beneficiary of all this spectral largesse? Ah.
You noticed. Still inviolable. Still untouched. Even primed.

Never fear. These are the kinds of frustrations within the com-
municative circuitry that philosophy was borne out of Athens a long
time ago to handle. So we who love her (philosophy) are permitted
to make the wholly transcendental supposition here: She admits
my case (my bad enemy does that), whatever my case might turn
out to be! She breaks down and confesses that she is quite culpable
in my case.

In the event, what would confront us would be a wholly new
case. Breathe in the new, breathe out the old, and *now* where did
she go? My old tormenter would have been, so to speak, exhaled.
In this transcendental supposition we surprise her, like Actaeon
surprising Artemis at the hunt, peeling down layer on layer of her
onion-skin hatreds till she gets to the core of common humanity, at
which point condemnations will necessarily stop. They must stop,
else we cannot get on with our lives. If for some reason they did
not stop, I would have to step in myself and put a stop to her self-
condemnations.

Why would I have to do that? Is it by reason of some sort of
squeamishness in my spirit—some fear of the truth—or what? Is it
by reason of a desire to win in a contest whose prize would be niceness? No. We are all a long way from nice, on this road. And a long
way from home. Well then, perhaps just to avert some future's re-
tributive judgments against myself, as these tremblingly sensitive
scales of justice shall be balanced, upset, and rebalanced, as long
as our common humanity shall be weighed in them. Besides, even
a bad enemy is not all that bad. From the worst of them, one learns
most of what one can later be said to know.

Revenge, by its very nature, is built to be frustrated, because
it *is* nothing but frustration, acted out. Forever *un*avenged, therefore, I stand, with the eye of my enemy equally unexpunged. I can
pledge the last part of this memoir only to a different kind of revenge: Only memory can be my "revenge." Memory is divine, for
the conversation of the soul with itself is divine at the very least.

So wake up. It's wakeup time, you serried ranks of the dead, for
here comes the last long recollection. Put your flesh on again, for I

have come back for you. And, as I see, you are all there, right back where I left you.

My search for the Absolute had been an experimental one. I'd never *felt* that there was a road mapped out for me in advance, though for all I knew there really was one, and I had been walking it the whole time.

At any rate, at the point in this story when my course work at Penn State had been completed, and I had come across the Atlantic once again, to London this time, to do the reading for my dissertation on Hegel and be sometimes "advised" by a British Hegelian who was at King's College in London, it seemed to me that there was one last global hypothesis about the Absolute that I had not yet tried.

This was the hypothesis that there *was* none and also, by the same token, that there was no meaning in history—my own or anyone else's.

Perhaps I was driven there, to that point in my pilgrimage, by erotic despair. Or by (what is nearly the same thing) despair of my historical purposes. Or perhaps I was hoping in this way to surprise God out of His apathy where I was concerned and force Him to a confrontation. In any event, the hypothesis that He and His providence didn't exist was not a mere thought experiment, in my case. It was enormously consequential. And it cut to the very quick of my existence.

One reason it did this was that the hypothesis was for me virtually self-contradictory. It was as good as my saying to myself that the God who had all along been taken by me as the Cosigner to the agreement that this story of mine be entered as a small but perfectly real part of the historical struggle for absolute justice and mercy here on earth—that this God of history never had been anything at all to anyone at all! From this it would follow that the self, who had (as I had long believed) undergone all this narrative in the sight of an absolute Witness, never could have done so, in the sense intended. Finally it had to follow that the yearning for a certain particular love that had grounded that self in its heartbreaking but purposive personal history never could have done *even that much* for me, if only I had seen the matter clearly in the white light of day from the first. I would have had to see the whole thing as a childish crush, a hormonal agitation. An accident.

For someone like me, to deny (even by hypothesis) the existence of God was not to step into any merely intellectual vacuum. It was to issue an invitation to lesser gods to step in and take over. I could not live as myself without a fairly direct relation to the Absolute. It did not matter that I was not sure if the transcendent Object of this relation was or was not imaginary. Whatever God was or wasn't, whether or not He was something that I had made up, the point was that I had imagined Him fairly *consistently* up to that moment. Without Him, what would be left of *me*, to hold on to, to come home to, and to send out to fight the real wars?

It is understandable, in that denatured mental context, that I could not record undergoing the amorous "stroke of lightning" for London that I had for the city of Paris, although the powder was very dry. It was certainly not because the English were mean to me that I failed to fall in love with their country or its capital at that time. As a matter of fact, they were rather nice in their way, the professors and the students that I met. It was only that, viewing all of life as a strictly contingent encounter with givens of sense experience and linguistic practice, which I was now attempting (atypically) to do, and human relations as mere ramifications of these coincidental complexities, was viewing reality much as *they* did. And it is hard to fall in love from that episodic vantage point since, about love, there must always be the gathering of storm clouds, winds of striving and yearning that will blow up and down the years and, through it all, the flavor of "destiny."

One's first sight of a place that is going to be important to one, like the shock of birth, can be awfully vivid. Crisscrossing the Waterloo Station, as I made my own way toward the taxi stand with my baggage in hand, were some of the men of this great English city, each man contingently situated in his niche on a descending scale of societal inferiorities. A scale given in sense experience and linguistic practice.

Most prominently, there were the men of the City, the financial district, the bowler-hat men, who were bobbing sightlessly (or so it seemed) through the station's giant lobby and were wound (like crepe paper around pipe cleaners) into their dark, fitted clothing and umbrellas. What had moved any of them to look like that I could not know. But this uniform kept them well above the people whose attire seemed to be two cuts beneath theirs: the men of the lower middle classes, whose clothing did not quite fit, whose connections were not quite so habitual, and who looked to be teetering on the permanent brink of discomfiture and vulgarity.

Meanwhile, far beneath them strode the POOR, their ankle-length grey coats flapping like the pouches of old-fashioned vacuum cleaners that carried and disbursed on their ankles the street soot, their hats sagging at the brim and sinking as if to ward off the very opprobrium that they attracted, their gaits shaken and uneven as if astride the great wind of ill feeling that had piled in draftily from the street.

And surely there must have been women there too! So they must have been hugging the interstices of this cavernous station like ciphers. The women were being presented in code, no doubt. Yet the atmosphere here was not devoid of a feeling for sex that could yet attach itself to those women who were happening by, already partly concealed in their fall coats. It was as if the small patches and particles of societal inferiority that were floating about could alight on the female erogenous zones, if the women were not very careful. Which would be the *embarrassing* genre of turn-on. A bit S and M. Something that was likely to bore one before very long. It would be tainting, but not very important. It would belong to the givens of sense experience. Entirely.

Commonwealth House,* to which the taxi was taking me now, was the female residence of an international students' housing complex, funded by subscription in Commonwealth countries. It had what were very possibly the best accommodations (for the purpose) of its class in London and was patronized, as they said, by the queen.

Ensconced in a labyrinth of gated and padlocked parks, childcare centers and playing fields, alleys leading away from the area, and a lengthily low-roofed, eighteenth-century street that led up to it, the ground plan of the neighborhood's walkways simply could not be memorized. At best, I saw, it could only become habitual.

The supervisor who greeted me in the lobby, Miss Blood, as I shall call her, was a wraith-slender Englishwoman whose collarbones protruded over her bosom and who seemed to belong like a shadow to this place that she called, with a smile wherein diffidence and slight self-deprecation were mingled with steel-rod authority, "your *home*." Concluding her brief tour at my doorknob, she had added for my particular benefit, "There are really no *rules* here."

Maybe not. But there are habits as deep as the English Channel. And as silent.

Bathing and laundry facilities were down the corridor on each floor, as Miss Blood had shown me. Also a grill for one's minimal cooking. My room—a long, white rectangle—had almost all its furnishings upholstered in a hideous yellow-and-brown-flowered stuff. There was a small desk, a small bookcase, a big heavy arm-

---

*Not its real name.

chair, a long narrow bed, a sink behind a partition with hot running water at all times and — inducement never to leave — the whole place was centrally heated! So is the room that I'm sitting in now, but it can never display the effect of enclosure that Commonwealth House gave off, encircled as it was in those days by an almost official *English* cold.

"How do you like it here?" the English would smilingly ask me.

"I'm finding it . . . a bit cold," I would answer, fighting back tears.

"Did that *surprise* you?"

"Well, yes. English literature does not seem to advertise that."

"Have you read Pinter?"

"No. I've read Dickens." And Jane Austen and the Brontës. People whose patch of earth and time was different from my own, but who were *also* locatable in narratives. Goodness, I was out of date! "What do you hope for?" I asked the English girl who had read Pinter.

"For England? Nothing. For myself, just to lie in the sun on a rock in the south somewhere. In Spain, perhaps."

Everyone seemed to have health problems here, of one kind or another. That did look, despite what Miss Blood had told me, to be the one general rule. Mine was the problem of "glandular fever," as the English poetically named it. Mononucleosis would be its more scary, prosaic American name.

In those first days in London, when I was registering at King's College, meeting the British Hegelian, and getting my card for the use of the library at the British Museum, the glandular fever would occasionally overwhelm me. One time, at the Russell Square branch of Barclay's Bank, I had almost fainted, a near event that summoned forth from the teller's side some unsentimental, soft-spoken, and thoroughly accurate nursing. With no dillydallying! It was so good, it was almost as if one were *supposed* to be ill here. If only one were ill, then everything else would be all right.

"Your trouble is Total Physical Debility," said the private society doctor whom I saw next (thanks to emphatic recommendation from one of the names on the list I had carried to London), and who looked just like Humpty Dumpty. "Your organism is sound. It just cannot stand *up* to anything."

Well, good Lord. It *has* to.

"All the same," Humpty Dumpty drawled on, "I really would not worry. Despite your present picture, time *is* on your side."

The only way to get time on my side, Doctor Dumpty, is to knock over the hourglass.

"You *will* get better." He looked at me curiously. "Don't you believe that?"

I shook my head, smiling through glistening eyes. Better than what, Asclepius? What did I owe you, old god of healing? And how should I have paid it?

I had been sitting alone in the lounge of the Commonwealth House on one chilly fall afternoon when someone who was moving in back of the couch put on a record. It was a George Brassens record, and his voice sang out a pretty tune:

> Y a des petit's fleurs,
> Y a des copains . . .*

Not that I had seen much of either lately. Not much of the small flowers of life and not much of comrades.

"Is the music bothering you?" asked a slim, dark-skinned American girl as she came into view and slid into the seat beside mine on the couch. She wore dark glasses and did not look at me.

"Oh, no. How in the world could it bother me? I've liked that song ever since I first heard it, years ago."

"Oh, do you really like it? I bought it in Paris. I came back from Paris just yesterday."

"Just yesterday?" I turned my gaze toward hers, which was still averted. "How did you like Paris?"

She seemed to consider her possible answers. "It was so beautiful," was what she said finally. "It made me ask myself how I could have come back to . . . this awful place."

"Oh. Don't go 'way!" I reached out to touch her skirt in the sketch of an imploring gesture. "That was exactly my first impression, at Waterloo Station. 'This is just terrible.' That's what I thought to myself. But all the people that I've talked to here in the House assure me one gets to 'love it' after a while. Anyway, meanwhile, as of now, I just can't see *why* I should ever 'love it,' even after a very long while. But they say I'll get over that."

She gave a closeted chuckle, as if at something all too familiar and clearly macabre. "Hang on to your first impression," was what she advised me.

Before long, we had adjourned that first part of our meeting

*From *Au Bois de Mon Coeur*, paroles et musique de Georges Brassens, © 1957 by Editions Musicales 57. Used with the kind permission of PolyGram Music.

in order to go get some four o'clock tea. She was sitting at one of the small tables while I carried tea for us both from the cafeteria counter. I moved slowly across the great, tattered emptiness of that dining room toward her nuclear tailored figure, watching for me behind black sunglasses, unsmiling, like some hard, knotty destination that—in the opaque seas of unjust experience—would not be moved.

Chapter Thirteen

A Competitive Conversation

When one cannot find a way to go forward in the direction of continued self-liberation from inside the perimeters of one's own culture, one quite logically will move up to those perimeters to peer over the edges of them.

At the margins of the experiences that I had lived stood all the ranks of those who had been pressed to the margins, and African Americans most glaringly. In the circumstances I was in (with nothing working for me very well and the inner trajectory virtually halted), it was inevitable that I would find Suzanne,* with her victim's status and her open scorn for everything that might have victimized her, very interesting. Had she been graceless or ugly, I might have found another way to describe her presentation to me of an antinomian option. But she was not ugly. She didn't look like a failure to me, particularly not a feminine failure. She didn't look like an angry rebel. She was well-groomed and graceful. And I thought she moved and spoke with an utterly magnetic presence, even when one disagreed with what she said. She had some kind of fathomless authority, quite apart from all her expressed views.

All that was left *to me* in the way of authority was my intellectual training and the philosophic project that had brought me to London. So I should not have been quite as surprised as I was that

*Not her real name.

those things should turn out to be the topics of our first extended conversation.

"What is important," Suzanne said to me, "is simplicity." We were in her room for the first time.

"Ideally that might be so," I agreed. I agreed absolutely. I had loved Thoreau in my teens. "But, Suzanne," I went on with a backward glance at my unresolved past, "I'm not simple. I just can't help it. I am complex." And so, I thought tiredly, is the culture that Western philosophy has partly the task of interpreting. A task it has given to me, among others. Worse luck.

"You know, Abigail, people use words as if they were things. 'Complexity' is a word."

"Words are things."

"Oh, Abigail, when liberals talk about civil rights and don't do anything about them, Negroes *know* words aren't things."

("Black" was considered an insult term then. And "African American" would have been thought an intolerable insult—by her at least. "Negro" was what you necessarily said in those days. So it would seem that some words were perceived as thinglike. Like sticks and stones.)

"Uh, no." I felt confused to have been misunderstood by her. "That isn't what I mean."

"I don't believe in complexity," she continued penetratingly. "Complexity is confusion. You know, people misuse words a lot."

"Yes. But the 'confusion' is something I have felt that I had to clear up. For a long time, I've been committed to a certain"—my right hand described a wavering line that continued indefinitely in the direction of the future—"quest. And that quest is bound up with philosophic problems." (This was the literal truth about my life, as I knew it, to date.) "And philosophy just isn't simple. It takes years of training before you can get any sort of grasp on it. And I don't think that it's all been for nothing," I finished sincerely, if uncertainly just at that juncture, putting all my cards faceup on the table in front of her. It might all have been for nothing. By now I wasn't quite sure, after all.

She sat, small and dark in the center of her room, considering me. "By 'quest' you meant that you have a destiny."

"Uh, yes, that's it," I nodded uncertainly, wondering what that word committed me to, and feeling that in my case it (my quest) was hollowing out by this time, whatever it might once have represented.

She shook her head. "You know, Abigail, Negroes don't need philosophy. *I* don't need philosophy."

I wasn't the type of academic philosopher who interrupts people to ask them how they can make good on whatever it is that they utter. Clearly, one person had no license to speak in the name of her entire race, or people. But we all do it. And I knew that what she had meant to do here was at least speak for herself, as one such member of her race. So I tried to address the substance of what I guessed that she'd meant, as best I could.

"Well, that doesn't mean that *I* don't need it," I said diplomatically, which is to say humbly. "Philosophy is about human freedom. It's about getting untangled from the confusions that beset the culture. But, if you're fighting for freedom directly on the political level, I agree that you don't need to find your way to it through the conceptual maze." That there were many roads leading to wisdom was something I had always been willing to grant, even if I was no longer sure that wisdom itself could be found at the end of those many roads.

Suzanne stared at me gravely. "I have *never* seen such fear," was what she told me.

"That's extremely insulting," I said heatedly, looking down. It was true that I was very scared. Never before had I been so unable to *say* where I thought I was headed, in my life. So, never before had I stood at such a brink. Nevertheless, a discussion like ours—meta-cultural—had certain boundary conditions, and she was breaking through them uncivilly.

"But, Abigail," she returned, sounding both reasonable and unmoved, "I didn't say it in the least to insult. Don't you think it's possible that in my whole life I simply *have not* seen such fear?"

That it was possible, sheer honesty would force me to acknowledge. Something might well have been working to toughen her and all the people who would have been likely to stay in her circle for any long stretch of time. That "something" could have dowered her with experiences more scorchingly exigent even than mine. Whatever it had been—her experience—I didn't think that it could have placed us on wholly disparate moral terrains, however, with no contiguous borders. The pieces of the moral map, or the geopolitical puzzle, would sooner or later have to be fitted together, was what I believed. I still had that much residual Jewish vocation for "history"—the global narrative under the one God—despite my newfound atheism.

Bearing that vision in mind, I said to her that I thought there were quite a few people whom I stood "head and shoulders above" on the score of refusal to sell out. My intent was to tell her where I thought I could be found on the aforesaid unified moral map. And there *was* just a touch of the truth in what I said. But the fact that I stood in some *moral fear* of her was not, as our analytic philosopher friends might put it, a "truth-maker" for my assertion.

"Mo-ral judgment!" she pronounced unhesitatingly. "That's moral judgment!"

"What's wrong with that?" I said, with authentic Jewish puzzlement. God, one never knew from what rafter she was going to fly down next, this small, grey owl of Minerva.

"I can't tell how much progress you've shown in your life, Abigail," she answered very softly, "because I can't tell how far you've come."

Neither could I, I thought, trying reflectively to rouse myself from a new depth of blankness. Where were we? Where was common ground? Perhaps the New Testament? "You know, Suzanne, I get the feeling that you have been speaking 'not as the scribes, but as one having authority.' But you know, you really can't do that in the context of friendship. There have to be common terms between friends. There has to be fundamental equality."

"There is never any equality," she replied quietly, in one of her truer hard sayings. "I have a friend who is ten years older than I am, and every time I see her she has gotten more beautiful. She has grown tremendously in our religion. And I have another friend who's a cellist. My friend Chauncey. When we go to concerts together he's way ahead of me in what he understands about music. But I don't find that discouraging, Abigail. To me, it's wonderful! It's so inspiring!"

"But the superiority of your cellist friend just functions inside one discipline. It doesn't pose any challenge to you *as* you." Whereas superiority on the spiritual plane could lay claim to authority absolutely. How could one "admit" to inequality absolutely? Where would such an admission leave one? "I don't know, Suzanne." I shrugged, temporarily stymied. "Maybe you are much more 'evolved' than I am . . ." Evolved as a soul, theosophically. I didn't think so, really, but it was one hypothesis. And a flattering one, for her.

"I don't know." She shook her head gravely, not looking at me. "Maybe you are ahead of me." Then she continued on the same topic, still looking elsewhere with muffled emotion. She loved her God very much, she said almost childishly (the same One that I didn't, I thought discouragedly, believe in any more). "You know, people set limited goals for themselves. And then they limit *themselves*. I don't *believe* in limiting myself."

Well, I thought briefly, your race is a present limitation, if we were to talk about common history and not just about qualitative changes in private experience.

"I want to be perfect," she said solemnly and naïvely, looking up at the electric light overhead. "Perfect. I want to ascend. I think that's legitimate."

Ascend?

That there was a mechanism that made unconscious use of religion to compensate for historic deprivations, I was of course well aware. But, even granting its usefulness in maintaining a person's equilibrium under outside assault, this I thought was stretching that little unconscious gadget a bit too far. Still, I didn't want to waste her time or mine by asking her where she'd got the idea that she could "ascend." Escape *death*? Who, professedly, had done that in the Bible? Was it Enoch? Elijah? I couldn't remember. As with her claim that "Negroes don't need philosophy," my aim in the conversation was to move ahead to whatever she'd had in mind in saying that, and then try to address my remarks directly to that. One has to decide what to consider crucial, in an argument, since one never gets time to address everything that is said.

So I thought, anyway.

"You know, Suzanne," I went on reasonably therefore, "your religion is more otherworldly than mine is." (I meant my religious culture, since at that moment I could no longer honestly claim to believe in God.) "What Jews try to do is to steer a middle course between an otherworldly transcendence and sheer reductionism. We believe that no one who is human gets to be absolutely perfect, or needs to be perfect. You're not faulted for not being perfect. And we think that every religious question must be resolved within a human conversation." ("A human conversation" was my shorthand for the moral-historical dimension, and as I spoke I was sketching a rectangular frame in the air—like a proscenium stage—to indicate that it had a spatial component, this "conversation.") "We don't think that you can descend from the 'other world'"—here I sketched a deus ex machina coming down on the putative stage—"to break up the conversation by claiming to speak 'with authority.' That's why being Jewish is just like being human." I opened both hands from the frame in the air now, in a kind of smiling, shrugging, general disclaimer.

She smiled cuttingly. "That's soo-periority."

"That isn't what I meant," I said now for the second time, beginning to feel that the machinery was wearing down, however.

"You know, when Sammy Davis Jr. converted to Judy-ism, all the Jewish women in our neighborhood came up to my mother to tell her that they didn't consider that he had become *really* Jewish."

Ugh. This one was complicated. On the one hand, it's likely that they thought they were saying something *reassuring* to Mrs. Pines in telling her that origins couldn't be wished away so easily. Tribal origins. Ethnic origins. One's character in the whole human narrative. But this one would be hard to convey, to Suzanne. And on the other hand—"There are," I began heavily, "complex historical reasons for the Jewish suspicion of the proselyte . . ."

"These were RACIAL reasons."

I shuddered, probably visibly. Probably audibly. "I think a distinction should be drawn between a folk attitude, which may be ignorant, and a religion's established teachings" was the reply I now mustered.

"Well," she conceded after a pause, "I see the justice of that."

From which I inferred that her coreligionists, whatever the doctrine to which they officially adhered, had their fair share of "folk attitudes." And I also inferred that—except where she couldn't quite do it—she would be making me sweat, in this little conversation. No Marquis of Queensberry.

"You know, Abigail, nowadays Jews are getting quite nervous, because they've been assuming that the whole world is white and that they had to make friends with the white man. And now they're beginning to sense that most of the world is nonwhite. And, since by this time the nonwhite world is starting to come together and unite, they suspect that they're going to end up on the outside."

Well, I thought. Yes. And it won't be the first time. Or the last time. You can join the longest queue for the longest hatred if you want to. I shrugged. Was she naïve? Or did she not care that this conversation was getting very dangerous? That it was moving toward war?

"No, it's quite serious, Abigail. Negroes are going to have to accept this. My best friend is Jewish, Abigail, and one night she came home from an evening at CORE, where she'd been working for months on the problem of slums in New York, and she was just sobbing. She cried in my *lap*! And I kept on saying, 'Judy, what *is* it?' until at last she told me. 'Oh, Suzanne, it's so awful! The landlords are Jewish. They are ALL Jewish, Suzanne!'"

She turned her gaze away from *her* proscenium stage in midair, on which her recollection was being dramatized, and she looked at me quietly. "I'll never forget that experience," she concluded, in a stage whisper.

The landlords were Trinity Church and Columbia University. Or so Bayard Rustin had told me and a group of other young people in our high school days. And the *agents* were Jewish. Or so Rustin had said to us at the time. The ones in the front window were Jewish. Because Jews may have many things in this world, at one time or another, but the power to purchase invisibility (to look good while they did something bad) has never been one of them.

But what the hell did I know? My information was not fresh. This wasn't my specialty. Maybe the landlords *were* Jewish, every last one of them. What did it prove? And this "Judy" was Jewish too. And so was I. And so were most of the whites who were working in CORE. And so what. And some were bad, and some were good. But they weren't perfect. Not one of them was. That wasn't their job. They weren't supposed to be, though one could wish. They were just human beings.

I slammed down a fist, as tears came to my eyes. "Dammit!"

"Oh!" she said, all solicitude. "*Don't* cry!" She sprang up to extend one long skinny arm in my direction. "Here! Have a pear!" It was green and hard. It was not comfort food, though I guessed that she'd meant it to be.

"I don't care if the landlords are Jewish," I sputtered, biting into the underripe pear. "What can *I* do about it?" I exclaimed in exasperation.

"But, Abigail," she responded in her most quiet voice, the one that came up from her marrow. "The reason one talks about these things is because one can change them. They can be changed. Don't you believe that?"

"No."

What a thing *for me* to have said! What a terrible thing. That sort of belief (that we human beings can improve) had been nearly the deepest one of my life, up till now. How had she taken possession of it, leaving me to hold out for empiricist stasis? The future will resemble the past, was what I had just said to her. And she, with her victimized race, was precisely the one to whom one *couldn't* say that. To say it would be almost a provocation!

With my old relations to the Absolute in process of fraying, I was coasting downhill on leftover intelligence, and getting very tired. I felt Jewish fatigue, but no Jewish consolations. But I could still remember the moves. I could still remember that there was a fine strong thread of recollection between past and future, out of which all sorts of improvements in the future-tense narrative could be spun. I remembered that it was the thread of human intelligence.

Thus, if one could not figure out why particular Jews, caught in their well-known predicament and often hard-pressed as outsiders, were taking deplorable shortcuts for themselves or their families, and if one "did not know" that other particular Jews, who were taking no shortcuts whatsoever, were abiding in the essential Jewish vocation, then one was taking in that whole picture without the requisite human intelligence. It was *unintelligent*, what she had said to me.

But it would be very difficult for me just to speak these lines to her. For one thing, although I took in—as she did not seem to— all these resistance factors of our common history, I still shared some utopian tendencies with her. I also wanted, in the Kabbalistic phrase, "to repair the world." So I was far from complacent about those moments when the highest ideals of the Jewish vocation were being honored in the breach only, by such well-publicized individuals.

For another thing, if one went in for this kind of detailed decipherment of the cultural contexts in which the human repair jobs were being called for, and then went on from that point to compare Suzanne's cultural background with mine, then one might just find that her culture had not contributed *quite* as much toward global historical progress as mine had.

The concept of "history" that I still carried around with me was linear and universal. So it implied a common moral, intellectual, and social standard, meeting which would be the goal of history. The common standard might be transcendent, invisible, and, so far, ineffable, but toward it the various civilizations of the planet would be advancing at their different speeds, in their different kinds and degrees, and to some extent (people being what they are) competitively. As in the Book of Genesis, where competition isn't mandated or desired, but is found to be very nearly primal.

An instance of this nearly primal fact had been my very conversation with Suzanne. It had been a deeply competitive conversation! I was aware of that, and it troubled me to the point of agitation. It was disgraceful morally, I felt (or anyway hopelessly unsporting) to point out where one's chariot *really* might be on this world-historical racecourse. The only ones I'd heard of who could be found doing that were the rednecks, and they automatically lost points in the same chariot race for the way that they did it and were in 1964 often found doing some other things as well, for which they got (or deserved to get) long prison sentences.

So to get into the precise questions of why some Jews were to be found doing what they shouldn't while other Jews were to be found doing what they should would be to get into questions of culture. And from there to comparisons between cultures would be but a short step. And an even briefer step from there to competitive comparisons. Which could have results just the opposite of the ones that were intended (by me at least in my residual Jewish vocation), universally. For my understanding of the Jewish historical assignment was that one was to strive to include all humanity in a narrative that concerned and helped to bring about universal justice and mercy.

It was a tricky situation. For Suzanne was very ambitious, in her naïve and youthful way. That was evident from our conversation, and I felt inclined to honor it in my heart. What she wanted, quite naturally, was to "win" what she seemed to discern as a great international competition. Unless she could "win," on her own view, she wouldn't get into it. And it was my self-given Jewish assignment to get everyone into the narrative of world history. So if someone was going to tell her that she ran with a handicap, it would not be I. I wasn't in it, myself, to kick dust in anyone else's eyes.

There was one other little touch on this canvas. The touch of color. She was a young woman, like me. Somewhat younger, it seemed (in that she looked ageless), and a bit prettier, some might find. But her *skin* had been converted by a significant number of the world's cultures into this wax tablet upon which anyone could write his or her message of rejection. Write it verbally or through consequential actions. But *at least* write it mentally.

This was so outrageous. It was so very insufferable from the standpoint of erotic self-esteem that, even if the rules of chivalric conversation had permitted me to speak the thoughts that were passing through my mind at this moment on the subject of cultural contexts and competition in history, there was no possibility of my doing so in the face of her skin, its color, and what these things *meant*. And that was the heart of it.

(Her color was in itself no worse and no better than other colors, of course. What I was picking up on, however, and seeing as coming to her from the world, was her own strong, well-nigh-implacable current of self-rejection. But, since this was her internalization of the world's sensed rejection, it came to nearly the same thing in the long run.)

So, for all these reasons, this turn in the conversation had reduced me to silence. "No," I shook my head. No, I don't believe that things can get better. I left it unfinished, what I had to say. I left it at that.

She smiled tiredly and got up to pace her rectangular room with slow steps, straight backed and diminutive. "I expected that this would happen," she mused, in measured excoriation. "I *usually* give more than people can take."

"But, Suzanne," I put in, on behalf of my now only partially voiced contribution, "I'm exhausted too."

"Oh," she burbled, "I'm not in the *least* tired!"

"You're *not?*"

"No," she said lightly, superlightly. "Not at all."

Gawd. Wot was she made of? Not tired? Feeling fine? And convinced that *she* was my spiritual benefactress? Imperviousness like this could be the stuff of legend.

After a pause I shook my head and replied in tones of wry celebration, "Suzanne, what you remind me of is Galahad. You know, in T. H. White's *Once and Future King*? Galahad's purity has made him the best knight, do you remember? He can do miracles and raise the dead? So he races around on his charger saving people, never stops to be thanked, and defeats all the other contenders at the Round Table because he's much purer than they are. And nobody can stand him. He's just *des*picable. After he's completed all his local exploits he rides off in quest of the Grail. Which leaves nobody to sit with Arthur around his Round Table because all the other knights struggle after Galahad, trying to catch up. And Sir Galahad never looks back. He doesn't care. He's just not human!"

Instead of explaining that she had to catch up to me and couldn't (which was what I really thought, in part), I was pretending wittily, sociably, and tastefully, I thought, that I had to catch up to her and couldn't.

Suzanne was, however, furious. Her teeth showed oddly and distinctly as she stood there, eyes on the door—not on me—and replied. "You're not talking about Galahad! What you've been saying to me is that 'Suzanne is inhuman and cruel! Suzanne is despicable!' You know, *you* are the one who's been insulting."

She shook her head now, in broken-voiced, childlike puzzlement. "I've never *talked* to anyone like you before. You actually doubt a person's *goals*, when the person has *stated* them!"

But, lady, I don't doubt your goals. That is, I don't doubt that you have them. I just doubt that you have any means (above all, supernatural means) of reaching them. And I did not say you were Galahad. What I was suggesting, in what was meant to be a good-humored reductio ad absurdum, was that this would be the logic of you, if your eerie "tirelessness" (or apparent immunity to the resistance factors in a historical situation) were to be carried to its limit. Anyway, it wasn't an insult to be compared to Galahad, even if I hadn't been joking. Goodness, but she was volatile! And easily hurt. Explosive, it looked like. How could a human conversation push past such misunderstandings?

(From my present standpoint, I can see that there had been no important *misunderstandings* on either side. Ours had never been a "failure of communication." Rather, Suzanne had seen as far into me, deflationarily, as I had into her. She had surely not missed the condescension behind my vaunted "tact"—condescension in that I neither took her to task for her crassness toward my then situation in life and her incipient anti-Semitism nor told her what I then thought of her gifts as my would-be spiritual benefactress. Behind all that tactically crucial reticence on my part was moral condescension: the belief that, with all she'd been up against in her life, she could not take it. But perhaps she really could not. I was trying hard to be fair. Her unusual arrogance was a symptom of felt weakness, I surmised. I didn't want to break down the defenses I saw that she needed. And she in turn must have noted how conscientiously I was making my way through this excruciating conversation. For, had she not seen that, she might have written me off as poor material.)

In the meantime, Suzanne was winding the whole evening down. "Now I've been talking to you all night when I had something very important that I had to get done. This conversation has given me nuh-thing. It's of absolutely no importance to me whether we ever talk again, or whether or not we become friends."

Now she was pacing along the back wall of her room by the radiator with its glinting metal teeth and describing her path in this world. "In my whole life, I have never betrayed a friend. While I am with a person, I give all the help that I can. But"—and there was that scary effect again of her mouth suddenly seeming striated with teeth—"it's a flaw in my character that, once a person disappoints me, or BETRAYS THE FRIENDSHIP, they drop out of my thoughts completely, just as if they had never existed."

She said this in a preternaturally mild tone, staring at me with her round, black eyes, while her pale ghosts stalked by us.

I stared back. "That's how I feel about friendships too," I replied. But what I said was not true.

For behind me fluttered, like streamers on the complaining wind, all my unrepaired human relations. There was John Armstrong—and Nancy, who had lost him. And I could be made to answer for it, on some day of reckoning. There was Anna, in Cuba now, and I could be asked about that too, when it came time to balance my accounts. And there had been others. There was Pheidias, and the uncanny spell he had woven around me. Unfeasible

to live under it. Impossible to outlive it. And there was philosophy, whatever that was. It should have helped me, by providing its
countercharm. But it had not done so. It had an unfinished claim
on me. But there seemed no reciprocity between me and it. I should
have been talking *to* somebody, dialectically. But I seemed to be
talking only to myself, when I talked philosophy. And there was history. In which one had to remain a player, not a figure of comedic
pathos. But I didn't feel to myself like a player, any more. And there
had been my relation to God. Wherever He now was. I'm lost, now
You get lost too—that was what I had told God.

That in full armor on horseback like Galahad she had flung
down a gauntlet to me where I stood was quite clear. But our ground
rules for this joust were quite different, it seemed. Why was this
person, who thought so little of me, of philosophy, of Jews, whom
I scarcely knew, and who made me so very uneasy, issuing ultima-
tums to me about "friendship"? Who said I had chosen *her* for my
friend?

But perhaps I already had, and she was righter than I knew. For
she knew something that gave her this impervious skin and internal flame in the cold midst of England. And, at least in the near
term and present circumstance, I had chosen to try to get to know
what she knew. For I did not know where else to turn.

In the days that followed this conversation, I kept to a newfound
resolve to avoid her as much as I could, while she on her side would
single me out with a marked and one-sided friendliness. There was
a didacticism, also one-sided, that went with her friendliness, but
that seemed to be just her character. Or her style. Or a tic, compen-
satory, that belonged to her racial predicament. Which made one
hesitate to say "Who asked you?" when she'd let fly with one of her
unscheduled lessons.

For example, she volunteered the information, which I'd not
requested, that in her discipline, anthropology, people tended to
marry across racial lines. They intermarried, she explained, partly
because in that line "people have no prejudices," also because "in
the field, it's a help," and lastly because (and here she smiled crookedly) "it gives pretty children."

She must be insecure, I thought. But that by itself did not account for the sense I also had that there was something in her that
was radically repellent to me. Sometimes she caught me staring at
her with a look on my face that caused her to start and me quickly
to rearrange my features. I could not tell if I was accurately sens-

ing something noxious in her, or if I, unlike her teachers and her colleagues "in the field," *did* have some prejudices. (That last possibility would make me wary of trusting my own moral intuitions about her, from the first.)

"You know," said Suzanne to me on another occasion, "there is a belief in this house to which one must keep very, very alert: It's the belief of Old Maidism."

I've heard of them.

"You know," she had continued without smiling, "women think that having a 'style' will save them."

What d'ya mean "save them"? I thought, looking wildly for the exits. Isn't "save them" a bit strong?

"And so," she'd gone on, "there is this extraordinary concern with finding a style. And yet, style is of no importance."

"What *is* important?" I had gotten to the point where I would have been glad to settle for a style.

"Being na-tural," she had said, striking metallically hard on the first syllable. "And, you know, everyone talks about femininity as if it were 'sensuality.' " Here she gave me a keen look. "But that's not so either. Femininity is honesty."

Well, whatever femininity was, and whatever her motives (altruistic or catty or both) for needling me like that, I needed another handle on the entire subject. Especially here, where, if the present situation continued much longer, I could lose the whole thing. I had taken my tray to a long table where a group of young men were sitting, having their lunch in the women's cafeteria of the Commonwealth House. They had stared with the roundest embarrassment, risen as if on a signal, and all left the table at once. Yes.

As Miss Blood had said: There are no rules here. What she'd meant was, they didn't post them. It was not a good feeling.

The American girls, with their faux-marble accents and rolling stares, looked to me like so much bright-polished glacial detritus, rolling right down the rocky mountain of life. And the Indian girls walked hunched over. Their saris were soot stained, and they'd mention—in arch, lonely accents—a sudden problem of tooth decay that sounded to me almost English. I did not think that it was the food, since they mostly cooked their own.

There was a deficiency of something here. Could it be nothing but calcium?

The Canadian girls were looking more swollen and white in the legs from week to week, and they seemed to have stopped taking daily baths. Could I be imagining that? And if so, why was my imagination taking that surreal turn? And if not, if I wasn't imagining it, how long had they looked that way? Was this no country for young women?

There was an older American lady, an art historian, who could not find her slides in her luggage—her *slides*—and who had been found meanwhile instead by anemia. On the BBC, the prime minister said again and again, "We have got to stop the bleeding." He was talking about their economy. Yes. There was a deficiency of something here. Could it be merely the clotting factor?

Not far away was Charing Cross, where the poet had seen Jacob's ladder. What had he seen in it? Not far off was the Thames, where the poet had seen Christ walk. What had he seen in it?*

"The English, you see, do not play fair," Suzanne lectured me. "An American, if he wants to put someone down, he'll let the person *know* that he's doing it, and why. Whereas *here*, a person will smile in your *face* while he is insulting you to his friends, just to keep you from realizing what he is doing!"

There are times when an oversimplification, even a crude one, can be useful, and hers turned out fairly useful that night. I'd been invited to dinner by a couple on my English list. My hosts were making their introductions to the fellow guests, who included a smiling Englishman, immensely tall, slouched on his dark couch like a long-necked blue heron and plying me with drawling questions about my aspirations to education and breeding.

For heaven's sake! Had it not been for Suzanne's "they do not play fair," I might have tried to pretend that he was not doing this and become finally rather uncomfortable. A small moment, one might say. But I was feeling quite fragile, and at such times small moments get large. Forewarned, I was able instead to block every one of his feathery thrusts with quick, light counterstrokes against his long neck and his beak, while nudging him up to his feathery neck with seemingly tireless affability.

He was, seemingly, charmed.

I was not charmed. In America, I thought with disgust, we don't just slouch back on a couch and count on caste to pull us through social situations. Not even a Boston Brahmin will do that, ordinarily. We have to be faster and funnier than you were, Lord Haw Haw, just to lose social ground *slowly*. The way I had been doing in fact, in America, over these past five years.

So I came home from the party that night feeling grateful to Suzanne. She had shown me where some of the fight was.

*Francis Thompson (1859-1907) in "The Kingdom of God 'In No Strange Land.' "

After about three or four weeks of observing the scene around me and getting acclimatized, I felt that my new goal in London was no longer to find the lost threads of my life. It was to find out where the local fight was. The English seemed fairly determined not to show you. Perhaps they could not show you. They did not know themselves, possibly. Or they knew it too well, and they thought it was hopeless. The fix was in, the social game rigged—since 1066 at least. But it was a matter of urgency, my new goal. For you could lose ground very fast here and not get it back.

"Those people!" Suzanne said when I told her the story. It was the next morning. We were walking to breakfast, at a café she had tagged the Green Nothing.

"How did you know about them?"

"Well, I have many friends, Abigail. I hear many stories, and I see a great deal. People turn to me naturally. And you know, one friend introduces another. You see," she added disarmingly, as if not to take unfair personal credit for her successes, "I am a Gnostic Christian."

Chapter Fourteen

A Conversion

We took a table by the plate glass–covered street view. I ordered a danish and coffee. She did too. They were cold and tasteless, but they were better than the bacon, cold eggs, and brittle toast at the Commonwealth House cafeteria. Better, because not so routinized. Not quite so dead.

Tell me what you are.

"Tell me," I said to her, "all about Gnostic Christianity.* Do the members of your religion believe in the Trinity?" I asked, full of focused curiosity.

"No."

Good. There's one barrier down, to my task of understanding her. "How about St. Paul's doctrine of Original Sin?"

"No. The belief that man fell is the basic illusion. You heal just by claiming the unfallen state that in fact you have never lost. That's *all* Jesus did. That claim is 'gnosis,' hidden knowledge. But it's very simple. It isn't 'complex' a-t-all. If you follow Jesus, and you cannot heal," she said to me rhythmically, "then you don't follow Jesus!"

"Suzanne, how can you be sure that what have seemed to you to

---

*Not the real name of the faith she professed. I have left its key doctrines intact, but changed some of the names that it gives to these doctrines. ("Gnosticism" is a generic name for the tendency, ancient and modern, to consider social or physical norms as illusory—and to try, by secret knowledge, to penetrate to a spiritual reality hidden behind the norms.)

be healings weren't just coincidences, or reactions of the kind one calls 'psychosomatic'?"

She leaned forward, caught up in her characteristic excitement. "Oh, Abigail, I have had so *many* experiences. Not just physical healings! I've been able, in seminars, to discuss *books* that I haven't read. I've gotten the answers to exams! I've seen job situations work out. When I had a different problem of scarcity—not having a scholarship—that's come. I saw my mother, when we were young in this religion, healed of a broken arm that just slid into place in front of a nurse who had been urging her to go see a doctor. *I* was healed, instantaneously, of a burn in a chem lab, which had covered this whole side of my face!" She touched her cheek. "Oh, Abigail, I have *never* known Gnostic Christianity to fail!"

I looked attentively at her seamless brown cheek. There was no sign of a burn, certainly.

What had happened, then? A spontaneous remission? Or what?

The body has extraordinary powers of self-renewal, which could sometimes be tapped into by nonstandard approaches. This much I remembered having read here and there. The yogis of India had anciently systematized such approaches. But who knew any yogis who were bona fide? She could be just lying. But I didn't think so.

Watching her with a half smile, I was shaking my head. "I don't know . . . about getting the answers to your exams. It makes you think that you don't have to study. And it makes the ones who do study . . . look like they've missed the boat somewhere."

She smiled melodiously. "It's a humbling thought, isn't it? That God is Mind."

I gathered from what she went on to say that what she was involved in had its own "system," like yoga. It had its particular grid of explanations or "principles," with their practical applications, and you worked your way through these impersonally, just trying to understand and to use them. The system had its "discoverer" and was of fairly recent gestation, not tested over time. But time-tested yogis with their alleged, immemorial, mantric, Sanskrit teachings were not so available, unless one had access to caves in the high Himalayas. I guessed that her system was more like a patchquilt of notions with different sources than a coherent whole, therefore. It came with no guarantees. But then, what did? If one merely "tried it"—for want of a better idea—it would still be trial and error, all the way down.

Since it had been articulated in its own texts and practices, whatever she had there could be learned. My early supposition was that what she did have was one of those crude, presumptive technologies of the realm of the spirit that work just at those borders of human experience where science will no longer serve. When the doctor could not cure you (but could assure you that your physical system was now pretty much indefensible), when the therapists such as they were couldn't get to the bottom of it, when the politics of experience had just collapsed under you, you could punch one of the keys in this "gnostic" system and it might just produce a beneficent outcome.

Some of it would be quite worthless, I supposed. Other parts of it might be worth something but still be fairly crude. And some of it might have hit on a truth or two that the men of science had yet to discover or incorporate within their own ecosystem of received hypotheses. But her point, I gathered, was that all of it was accessible to anyone who could read. So no one could justly complain, not having read it, that another was gaining advantage from it at his or her expense. If enough students learned it, and it made that much difference to their exam results, the schools would just have to devise different kinds of exams, that was all. Such was the gist of her argument on the score of exams.

She had one other response to these notes of wariness she could hear in my voice. The whole system was founded on "Love," she said. Love was its ultimate "principle." If one neglected its most basic axiom, then soon enough the subordinate propositions would be unusable. So the system had its purported internal checks. On its own terms at least, it wasn't bad witchery. Of course, since its algorithms were in the domain of motivation and will, any sort of unclarified *motives* would yield uncertain results.

I imagined, however, that, if Suzanne suffered from personal problems of any kind, the usual modern medley of motives would not be the sources of them. The whole point about Suzanne was that she was winged like an arrow for one swift homing flight. What she wanted to do was "ascend," after all. And if in the end it turned out that she'd failed to do that, it would be because she'd bumped into something. There had been an obstacle in midair. It would not be because she'd felt ambivalent. She wasn't that trendy.

"Why do you have to call the thing 'Christian'?" I asked her, in some embarrassment. "If there really is such a mental 'principle,' which can be used to solve practical problems, then it's got to be universal. Jesus did so many peculiar things. Like driving those Gadarene swine off the cliff."

She gave me a grim look. "He knew what he was doing. They were swine, after all."

I shuddered, remembering how on a recent evening we had

gone to a concert together with her friend Chauncey the cellist and returned here to the Green Nothing for coffee afterward, where two burly young Englishmen of distinctly Hogarthian, porcine appearance had joined us at our table. Uninvited.

"Let me handle this," she had said to me under her breath.

What? I'd thought, puzzled. Handle what?

"They are fighting boys," she'd continued, "and I doubt very much if Chauncey could fight his way out of a paper bag."

They are? He can't? I'd never heard that expression.

Chauncey was one of those lanky, bloodless types who were, in those days, the prime candidates for the "transfusion" of interracial relationships. But he was a gentleman down to his shoe soles, and from good, old New England stock. As to a fight, I'd thought it at worst a remote possibility. But it was conceivable that, if one broke out, Chauncey would need more protection than he would be able to give.

Be that as it may, Suzanne had driven those two local swine off her metaphorical cliff with no more than the brush of her feminine fingers on the sleeve of the larger one. Her exorcism had owed something to the way she'd been joking with them. I'd found the joking neither witty nor funny, though both sides had been smiling quite broadly, with a large show of teeth. Apparently she had foreseen the worst and had therewith touched something in them. Was it their pride? Or their latent aims with regard to their café initiative? Whatever it had been, they were gone, quite suddenly, having first been made harmless by her.

Dimly I saw what she'd done. She'd jumped out of the present tense in the sequence. She'd got ahead of the worst before it could take up positions. Perhaps it had never intended to do that. But if it had, and events proved her right, it would have been too late to call up reinforcements.

It was not the first time that I'd witnessed her doing that. She would wear her best suit, and no one dared spill coffee on it "accidentally." "Unconscious" hostility, "thoughtless" remarks—"insensitive" social missteps from white people—all these didn't get off the ground that she walked on. She moved through the milling, muttering multitudes, who did not necessarily trust her (any more than I basically did) or care if they wounded her (unlike me, for I did care, awfully, not to wound her), and they didn't find openings.

Had I been much freer, myself, of insecurity, I would have been somewhat less impressed. No doubt. Nevertheless, at that point in my pilgrimage, I was very impressed—almost thrilled for her. I had never met a woman who was able to move through a hostile social context so imperviously.

I returned to our present-tense interfaith dialogue. "And what about all those apocalyptic threats in the gospels?" I asked her. "'There will be weeping and gnashing of teeth'? 'If you don't receive me or receive my apostles, you will wish you had never been born'? What about all *that* kind of talk?"

"Well," she responded reflectively, "with Jesus you have to separate the principles that he taught, which can still be proved, from the prejudices that belonged to the time when he lived."

The principles that he taught, which can still be *proved*? It is hard in retrospect to lift out the components of the wind that went rushing through my head at that moment. But it is clearer to me today than it was then, what that wind was doing in there. For a moment, one brief moment, I had identified with her strategem. I had jumped the tenses of the historical sequence. Had I had just a bit more vision, just a little more patience, and just the tiniest touch more faith, I would have been able to steel myself and to wait. To wait: the gesture of faith.

Wait (my better angels must have been crying). Someday your lifelong desire to make sense of your youth will be vindicated. Someday your position, relative to others' in history, will be so much clearer to you. Someday God will show you what He has had in mind in these labyrinthian years, what you've been learning, who can be helped, and what it's been for. You know perfectly well that you don't really trust her. You know perfectly well that she's insecure—that she goes in for miracles, real or imagined, because she can't stand to acknowledge the kind of rickety chariot that she's been handed in the big chariot race we're all in. And you also know that you haven't the heart or the courage to tell her what you really believe about her generalizations for the most part: that they are startlingly clever, but imprecise, and not deeply intelligent. Lastly, you know that you've made your mind a blank tablet with regard to religion only because you are angry at God. In your heart you still search for Him and you love Him, even as you make your way through this blinding *ḥamsin*⁎ of your twenties. Wait. Don't jump the tenses. Have patience. Just wait, a little longer.

But I didn't wait. There was a small, scarcely perceptible mental jump—and I was self-propelled out of my place in my time. I

⁎Hebrew name for the dry, hot wind that blows through the land of Israel at certain seasons.

still thought *historically*. I couldn't help doing that. But my mind wheeled out of its orbit and turned back to another time, to a place on a hill in suburban Jerusalem where, fatefully, a man hung on a cross between two thieves.

Maybe, I said to myself as I wheeled in the air above him looking down, maybe *we* should not have crucified him! Oh, maybe.

For the first time in my life, I was attributing guilt for the death of Jesus collectively. To the Jewish people and to its nation, as a whole. It was sudden, and it had to do with jumping the tenses. I had not waited my turn. I was out of order, in time. So, with the same small, imperceptible motion, I had got out of sequence in the process of distributing condemnations and vindications—*justly*. I could no longer determine who had done what, and to whom, and when. It was not a matter of information. It was a matter of will. *I had turned my will another way.*

Yes, St. Augustine. That's what I said.

That was the conversion.

Chapter Fifteen

Thought Reform

What did her Gnostic Christianity mean, doctrinally? To what had I been converted? The doctrine here was that one could liberate oneself from all the negative limitations on one's life—whatever the nature of those limitations—simply by keeping in mental view the "affirmation" that the Spirit alone was real, one's own being an integral part of that Spirit, and all the empirical obstacles delusive.

Liberations of every kind Suzanne called "healings." Did one feel exhausted erotically, worn down as a woman, to take one example? If one kept affirming the "unreality" of this exhaustion, it would all come back, one's erotic authority. One would know what to do and say, how to dress and move. And it would not depend on the culture. Neither would it depend on one's personal history.

Was one deprecated or rejected on account of one's color or cultural background? If one just affirmed in one's mind the "unreality" of material skin and its color, and the delusiveness of cultural origins, and the extreme delusiveness of any competition between cultures, one would find one's equality on the plane of the Spirit as something already accomplished. Apparent barriers would melt. Courage would crystallize. One would move through the worlds of culture as if one owned the places.

And so on. It's clear enough. "Now we see through a glass darkly, but then face to face," as Paul said. What her Gnostic Christianity did was insist that the "but then" could *also* be transmuted into a "now" when the human spirit reconnected with its divine Substance through the medium of these affirmations, these mental acts, this gnosis, this divine intuition.

There are many denominations and sects that have some gnostic tendencies.[1] Any approach to the social order that inverts its system of ranks, making the last first and the first last, is implicitly "gnostic," if one wants to call it that. Elaine Pagels has argued that many of the original gnostic Christians were feminists. Feminism itself may be deemed a species of gnosticism, since it seeks to replace—sometimes to invert—the traditional ranking of the sexes. Many systems of Eastern meditation that make the phenomenal world unreal ("mayiyic")* are gnostic insofar as they do that. And European romanticism, with its preference for the nonrational as the way to transcend phenomena and contact the noumena, has a gnostic tinge, coming to it directly from the Vedic tradition and indirectly from German philosophical idealism. The American transcendentalists had it.

The term is so broad in its possible applications as to empty itself of concreteness. If we drained the culture of all of its gnostic influences, it would be the poorer by a good deal. A particular claim is not necessarily deluded because it is somewhat gnostic in feeling or tendency. In the trials of life it makes good sense to speak of a hidden reality, ideal and imperceptible, which must be affirmed in one's mind and heart before it can be worked out in the daylight.

I have used the generic term, rather than identify the particular sect to which Suzanne in fact belonged, because that sect has some respectability and should not be taxed with what would become her private excesses. She did not induct me into a cult. She was her own cult.

How was my gnostic turn un-Jewish, particularly? Why do I term it a "conversion"? It was un-Jewish because it treated the cultural and historical context as delusive, as something to be willed, prayed, or "affirmed" away. So the past lost all its authority, and human memory its restraining power. The temporal sequences in which real actions had taken place got blurred, under the mental poundings of these "affirmations." And it became that much harder to tell what was fair or unfair, since one was no longer quite sure *what was happening*. One was too busy affirming that something much more divine, pure, and holy was the hidden meaning, soon to be made manifest. The result was a scrambling of moral intelligence.

---

*Adjective from the Sanskrit noun *maya*, meaning the illusory phenomenal world according to Indian idealism.

By the way, was I quite devoid of practical shrewdness at this point in my life? Had I become simply daffy? Not quite. I think that the practical side of my wager, in trying on this hypothesis experimentally, was that Suzanne's savvy about living—her street smarts—would rub off on me if I continued to watch what she did and the way that she did it. The simplest thing to say about what I hoped *practically* was this: I hoped I would learn how to be cool. For surely the reader has noticed by now that I wasn't, very. I had noticed it too.

(In this ambition, Suzanne really did help me. It's no small thing. But the price was rather steep.)

My loss of heart about history was sincere, however, not calculated. And the act of conversion was the very act whereby, instantly, my historical judgment was self-blurred. But—such are life's paradoxes—I suspect that I took on her gnostic refusal of moral-historical judgment in order to learn how to cope with my personal history more effectively, and to get fresh light on it from her. If I had to worship God in some other way, in order to get light on my God of history, if I had to betray Him to understand Him better, I would do that.

If that's all I wanted in practical terms—some borrowed coping skills from a person who walked through the feminine realm like a warrior—why did I start by "believing" that Jews were collectively guilty of "killing Christ"? Was that not rather a large betrayal of deeply held values, for so slight a return? Well, no. They were linked processes—the effort to learn how to be cool from Suzanne and the belief about deicide—as I look back over the question from my present standpoint.

The "coolness" of Suzanne was partly effrontery. She had the nerve to defy the common sense of a situation by insisting that it *wasn't* the way it certainly looked. It was partly the effect of surprise that she worked with, her willed indifference to what was really happening on the ground. Sometimes she got above it. Sometimes she got below it—the reality of events. And sometimes she got ahead of it. But always she managed partly to dodge it, to take it glancingly, and to make her getaway. So there was in her "coolness" a refusal to be fully congruent with the place and the time where the real events in their linear sequence were happening. It was a refusal to be what I am calling "Jewish." It would have been too painful for her, possibly even too dangerous, to be "Jewish" in the sense that I mean.

When I decided to follow her in this refusal, it was because I could go no further, as I felt, in the Jewish effort. In my life, that effort seemed headed toward self-collapse. I inferred that Jews must have been wrong about God, and wrong also about history. *That very thought was an antihistorical act.* As soon as I thought it, I began straightway to be imprecise about history, and specifically about the event in history that marks off Judaism from Christianity: the crucifixion.

From a Jewish standpoint, certain long-dead individuals acting under particular circumstances would bear the responsibility for the death of Jesus. Unbiased historians of the period, Jewish or Gentile, would be free to attempt to reconstruct those circumstances and motivations, sketching the main actors, the political currents, and the sectarian controversies. Theirs would be an effort no different in its kind from the task of reconstructing what had led the Athenian jury to vote death for Socrates.

For believing Christians, however, the events leading up to the crucifixion could not be speculatively reconstructed as mere ancient courtroom drama. On their view, rather, great human collectivities were being drawn into the light, or else being pushed into the darkness, while Jesus hung on the cross. "Responsibility" for such an intrusion *into* history could never be fixed on the basis of mere empirical evidence. On that view, in this instance at least, the historical fails, as a category. Moral intelligence blanches. Whether or not there was a real crucifixion or a real resurrection, the whole Christian problematic of guilt and redemption is being pressed into this cross on Golgotha and is the real happening there. The very notion of collective guilt is *a part of the drama*, where "guilt" itself takes on another meaning than its ordinary one.

What I did by internalizing this Christian doctrine of Jewish collective guilt was begin to take leave of the plane of history altogether. I left it, the historical plane, out of profoundest impatience with it, an impatience that was the essence of my loss of faith. The "conversion" *was* just that loss of the Jewish faith—in the loss's specific theological (which is to say Christian) expression. So it was quite sincere, as sincere as any personal crisis can be. The death of Jesus had ceased to be taken by me as a finite event for which responsibility could be fixed in a court of law. And, from that unaccustomed theological point of departure, my judgment of other events and actions was to take on increasing imprecision.

(But why did I fix on *that action* to be "imprecise" about just then? Because that was the one you walked through when you walked out of Judaism over Golgotha to Christianity.)

Something over a year later, I was wintering with Suzanne in Portugal. Never had I imagined that anyone could have brought me to do such a strange thing. The decision, if it was that, came about by a series of small, incremental stages, each one pushing past a barrier in my own mind that I would have thought was guarding my exits most solidly.

At the outset of what had at first been billed by Suzanne as a summer idyll for the two of us—during which gnostic interlude she would be writing her perfect novel and I would be painting the idyllic scenes of the Portuguese coast—the two of us sat taking stock of our situation (our mayiyic and material situation, that is) at a marble-topped table in the vast, dark-paneled, mirrored interior of a café in Lisbon. On the Avenida da Liberdade. "We call it that," the last of our local drivers had said to us jestingly, "because it goes *down*." (He meant that freedom was going downhill under the dictatorship.)

Lisboa! Flowered capital of Portugal! It was the type of café that in the nineteenth century would have been right in the forefront of all that was thought of as "modern." A painter like Manet could have painted you into its grandness, amidst the bottles and their shining reflections, with your back to the long mirrored wall behind the bar, on which could be seen all the figures and objects in front of the bar.

Tyrannies have no discernible articulation, since their constraints are not open to public inspection. In Lisboa Salazar ruled uncontested then, in 1964, and it was as if the whole country had shrugged and not bothered to mark off the lines between its "modernity" and whatever else in the place was still looking premodern. Meanwhile, none of it, so far as I could see, was looking contemporary. Perhaps for that reason the country seemed to approach the traveler very intimately or artlessly, the way a child can, and to be free of mediating structures as it spread out before one: flat, monotone, seemingly without bones or neural circuits—just one long, unbroken, flutteringly primitive impulse. It was *almost* Portuguese, but not quite anything. There was nothing to be found there interposed between the straying seeker and the murmur of her private heart.

The brioches at the counter looked to me especially inviting. I thought that we might want to buy a couple, and, over them and the excellent Angolan coffee, try to figure out just where on the coast of Portugal this summer idyll of ours was supposed to begin. (It had better begin soon, my heart murmured silently, if my book of traveler's checks was to be taken for the limiting condition on the idyll that—most awkwardly for Suzanne's gnostic claims about the unreality of poverty—it still was. But that murmur of my silent, sequestered heart remained a private one.)

"You'll get the brioches from the counter," said Suzanne to me. "And, when it's time to pay, you'll give the signal to the waiter."

"Why me?" I asked her. "Not that I *mind* doing it, but . . . ?"

"Because," she enunciated distinctly, "it's safer for you."

Why? my heart murmured privately. Am I a boy?

"You see, Abigail," Suzanne explained to me with an excruciating effort to be patient, "race today is the worldwide symbol of sex."

It was? This was news to me.

I felt sorry for her. I knew that she would attract a slightly different sort of look in this café than I would, whether that look were additionally to be described as "sexual" or not. Yet I also thought that she had more feminine competence than I, in certain respects. She knew some secrets, such as how to remain undaunted in the midst of men while partly transcending the male-female game. From my point of view that *was* "gnosis," hidden knowledge, from which I might still profit in the vacation time that remained to the two of us. At any rate, we could not part just then, though I sometimes wanted to, with stifled urgency. It wouldn't look right (that was the thing uppermost in my mind) for me abruptly to cut short this journey with the Black female friend to the gnostic idyll. So I could only hope that, if I stayed with her and saw the trip through, it would not just be time and money shot to hell for me.

Nevertheless, safe here for once in this dark, cool, damp, crooked elbow of Iberia, at this long moment of the morning, it was left to me to try to imagine how these pudgy Portuguese waiters could "endanger" anyone. Or how these grey-tailored, languid, thin-legged *rentiers*, seated around us and having their pointed shoes shined over their morning papers and black coffee, could possibly endanger either of us. And apparently, it was to be left to me, too, to undertake the further neutralization of these soft and disengaged surroundings.

It was not the first time that she had put me in an awkward situation, from the erotic standpoint. As we had wended our way southward across Europe, black and white together, from Calais to the Pyrenees, and then from Santander to Burgos, on down to Valladolid and across the baking, dusty plains of central Spain to the borders of outlying Portugal, she had extracted verbal admissions and material concessions from our drivers on a scale that was wholly new to me. She gave them her strange brand of spirituality. And they gave her a lot.

Our drivers were unmarried young men. Almost without exception. And she would get them to tell her their stories, to put into words the whole framework of their lives. And would listen with pretended interest, sympathy, and agreement, till all at once she would puncture it!—that masculine ego in which was stored their sense of belonging, within their framework. And, since the masculine ego was a "limitation," this puncturing of it was, in principle, a Gnostic "healing"—as she would explain to me under her breath, while she went on conversing with them.

On their side, they would take time off from work and drive us some kilometers beyond their home bases. They would know hidden restaurants to take us to, on unprepossessing side streets, and would lean forward to hear more from her, over the succulent, successive courses that she was seasoning with so much gifted, unexpected flirting.

I had never seen the likes of it, this flirting, and I did not know just what to make of it. She had flirted with them just by being wholly transparent. Her self-assigned task was to "heal" them of all their limiting beliefs and to get them to come with us. (In gratitude, she hoped, they would continue to pick up the tab all the way to the Portuguese coast; or so I gathered, with no small sense of horror.) She was solemn as a fragile female child, in showing them our vulnerabilities. She was ruthless, in getting under their guard. And all the while she would appeal, in a pleading, childish, laughingly offhand and supplely feminine way, to their mercies—*outright*. If they came with us, they would get to be just as innocent as she was. That was the pitch. She was opening up a new era in male-female relations: beyond the masculine ego, beyond the unisex fear of a shrinking budget, beyond the multiracial taboos about race, beyond the female fear of rape in the night.

Since I could not help but notice in my private heart a much less kind suspicion about what was going on, I felt most painfully conflicted. For my "gnostic" turn had not overturned all my normal insights, after all. All it had done was cause me to retain such insights in suspension. While I was busy affirming that Spirit was infinite wealth and that male and female were divine ideas, my normal insights were still there all right—to trouble me, and to make me think that this whole thing was crazy. But I had put these insights out of play. I didn't act on them.

Instead, I was waiting: for this experiment—inverting the recognizable norms of my life—to be played out, for the summer to end, and for my life then to resume its regular course. While I'd been in London, I had about finished the reading for my dissertation and sent off a fairly eccentric first draft of the thing to my thesis advisor at Penn State. This *despite* Suzanne's sarcastic laughter about my continued attachment to that Ph.D. In the spring, there had even been some tentative job offers, which I had *discouraged* however, once they'd come, under Suzanne's careful tutelage and my own terror of being sent back to the woods of America. But that wasn't fatal, though it wasn't politic. I could still come home (to parents who would be worried, sure, but who would not throw me out before I'd secured working papers), and I could rewrite the dissertation there. Work would follow, I thought, in the normal course of my life. I could smell no bridges burning as yet, in the midst of that summer in Portugal.

Meanwhile, what was my much less kind suspicion about Suzanne's summer strategy? It was that people were paying for her borderline antics mainly because they saw I was there, silently to illustrate the "correct" liberal demarche of misplaced, sacrificial generosity. Whether they guessed or did not guess that I was paying for the trip, they saw me in every other way roped into it—as her French translator, social mediator, and facilitator.

I had the normal values. She had the far-out ones. I could interpret her to them, if need be. Or, at the very least, I could provide the model for the sort of conduct that she wanted from them too. And what I clearly had to do was cede to her the frontiers of flirtation. In a word, my financial and erotic substance was being used to fund hers.

But she was black! What did I expect, if we put aside gnosticism! We had moved through one white city after another. Cities of beautifully clad white women, of great-arched buildings with their sweeping, carved staircases and frowning stone portals. Cities blazing with enterprise, shining with the traffic that took white men to their projects.

She could not be enjoying this. She could not be moving right through it unfazed (gnosticism aside). What she must feel she needed was a vantage point from which to vault over the divides that would have handicapped her as a candidate for open and honorable long-term relationships (that led to marriage, which she unabashedly prized). So, what she'd worked out was a way to deny the reality of culture and history, of matter, and, a fortiori, of anyone's race-based aversions. She had redescribed her whole problem in history as an illusion. And history itself she had redescribed as an illusion. Which left her free to "heal" attractive young men of their budgetary, historical, cultural, and possibly sociobiological illusions, and to use me as her sorcerer's apprentice!

That was my much less kind suspicion, anyway. The one that I did not voice aloud and scarcely articulated even to myself.

If I halfway suspected this, why did I stay with her? For one thing, one counterexample does not refute a whole paradigm. It raises a question, of course. What I gave (in response to my heart's quiet protests) was an ad hoc explanation that put these uncomfortable details of our trip down to her racial predicament. (And, rightly or wrongly, she was always finding me extraordinarily obtuse about that predicament.) Whether or not she had complexes about race and dealt with them by taking advantage of me compensatorily, she was still my best expert on the gnostic hypothesis.

For all I knew, it might even belong to the gnostic experiment to get my cumbersome feminine ego and beliefs about money burned on Suzanne's pyre. Besides, that feminine ego had walked itself hors de combat in its long walk to London and Suzanne. I had no place to go back to, except in redoubled confusion and defeat. Whereas, if I stayed with her, I might gain either (at best) gnosis itself, an intuition of the Spirit's eternity at the price of renouncing history, or (at worst) a few tips on the Black world of cool. So I went on with her. It was a risk. I knew that. What I was risking was my erotic and personal authority in the world, risking it in the hopes of somehow regaining it. But, as Aristotle said about human nature: "All men by nature desire to know." In practice, long-term, I have had no greater desire.

After the brioches that morning, we made our way down to the harbor, where we crowded together onto the ferry and floated on its deck slowly out of Lisbon. By the time we were standing on the other shore, on the southbound road, and blinking in the brilliant sunlight, we were still without a clue as to our dream site for the summer. But here was a small red car pulling up next to us in the dust! Its driver, a young woman dressed in immaculate whites, had rolled down her window to ask where we were going. She spoke faultless English.

We told her that we did not know.

We did not know? Ah well, if we did not mind a place where nothing ever happened, she and her very young son were on their way to a small fishing village at a restful midpoint between Lisbon and the Algarve. They were staying with friends, but there were also modest accommodations for tourists—again if we did not mind a place where nothing ever happened.

A little place where nothing happened? Certainly I was alive to the possibilities, what with Suzanne's needing a little retreat in which to write, and I someplace to rest my more cumbersome painting equipment. We could perhaps afford to park the idyll there, take it on the cheap, and get it over with.

Sonho, which is where most of the dream that we two were

to dream together borrowed shape and substance, actually means "dream" in Portuguese.* It is to be found about two-thirds of the way down the ridgey torso of Portugal, on the side that lies exposed to the Atlantic. Sonho's was not the heavy sea that made for workday drownings in the north, but an unnaturally bright apron into which the fishermen dropped anchor and their nets and simply waited. From where they waited, they could see those steep stone shores, cliff balconies of Iberia, behind which sat, armed and unsmiling, its Benevolent Duennas. (Franco and Salazar, the dictators in Spain and Portugal respectively.)

Under its few contemporary signs and watering places, Sonho was one of those fishing villages, very old and whitewashed, that are to be found on the long coast of Alentejo. The whole village was shaped like a steep-edged, sand-filled horseshoe, its north side ending at the stepped waterfront where the fishing boats were assembled, its opposing extreme at the high, jagged, southern cliffs below which lay foaming ocean. So Sonho lived and murmured along the many winding paths that took it up and east from the Atlantic.

When we first arrived there, we did not settle in right away. Rather, the pattern was that we were kept moving whenever Suzanne felt that something untoward had occurred at the previous hotel or *pensão*. One time we even zigzagged back and forth between Sonho and Seville, returning to Spain because my fellow traveler had thought that we would be "safer" there. Or she would be. How anyone could think *that* about Franco Spain, I did not know. But I had felt disqualified from objecting, since the "dangers" she felt everywhere went mostly undetected by me, and since she had accused me repeatedly, for that reason, of not caring. When at length Seville proved no safer as a haven for women of color—significantly *less* safe, as even I had detected—we returned to Sonho. It was high summer by then, and all the tolerable rooms we had stayed in before were now rented.

Nevertheless, we had a new reason to try to stay now. During our first days in Sonho, just before we had left for Seville, Suzanne had found time to send off a postcard to the Basque driver who, of all our drivers, had been the most attractive and attentive to her. And now, the first day we were back from Seville, the clerk at the hotel had delivered a telegram to her that read, "Nous arrivons!"

"*'We* are coming,'" sniffed Suzanne. "Who does he think he is? Royalty?"

*Not its real name.

I did not care who he thought he was. By that time, I wanted nothing so much as to get out of there. But perhaps Jérez* could provide us with a lift. It was not that far from his home in the Basque country to the French border. For my traveler's checkbook was thinning out, from day to day. And so was my erotic and personal authority. I feared that the day was coming when I would see daylight through both.

So we looked for lodgings that day. The hotel had no vacancies, but we were accompanied by a well-disposed Portuguese lady tourist who had noticed us in the lobby inquiring about vacancies and had volunteered to pass a whole day assisting us. Her name was Mrs. Açores.†

By late afternoon, we had covered all but the empty side of the village, where the horseshoe ended in the steep southern cliffs. As we moved along that side of the landscape now, Suzanne exclaimed, "Look at that!" It was a two-story apartment house, with rounded corners in a "modern" style that looked faintly art deco. This building was light grey in color, and white curtains fluttered at its white-painted windowsills. It was neater and more aesthetic than what we had seen so far, and yet it looked handmade. Set far back from the strident attentions of the *praça* (the town square), the building faced into a sandy yard that stretched about two city blocks to the ruins of an old *castelo*, whose iron cannons overlooked the wide sea. And one of the windows of this grey house showed a pasted star! For rent, then.

At the head of the stair, the door to the upper story was opened by a remarkably pretty young woman with a symmetrically sensual face, pure of cosmetics and work lined. Brimming her high oval forehead was a halo of dark auburn hair, thickly braided and looped up in back. She had long, slender limbs shaped by honest toil, and she said—smiling and nodding and chattering ceaselessly in her musical singsong, Yes, yes, *pois*, *pois*, we could see the rooms. Yes, yes, that was her star.

Despite its conventional whitewashed interior walls and heavy Portuguese-provincial furnishings, five-and-dime-store ornaments, and plastic flowers, the apartment she showed us was sunny, cleanly and, again, "modern." It was an uneducated taste this time, but a clean taste, and merry. The two bedrooms held the usual ponderous armoires, large beds with satin spreads of nursery pink in one room and blue in the other, and tiny night tables on which were

*Not his real name.
†All the names of the Portuguese characters have been changed.

perched the usual teetering, doll-sized night lamps. But they held, too, a pleasing emptiness. The bathroom was almost something, with a bathtub over which a cold shower was affixed, a cracked mirror above the sink, and a toilet bowl that even had a rational seat lid.

Beyond the front parlor lay a kitchen. There was also a small storage room with a mere, thick-walled, narrow slit for a window, which brought in the sea air. It held just a cot on which the expected Spanish gentleman could sleep, and a night table. Our prospective landlady's head bobbed up and around now in the circle of her joyous and innocent curiosity.

If (as our translator told her now) Abigail wanted to paint while we were here, our prospective landlady said—with a speaking gesture of her hand—her auburn braid could be taken down in back. (So she knew that she was beautiful!) And, on the terrace, where the women roosting in the attic had hung out their washing, a painter like me could discover a commanding view of the sea and the boats at anchor. So Isabella showed me, when she took me up the narrow stairs to the rooftop, by the cramped, ramshackle attic where she and her family were quartered during the summer months.

Isabella, our prospective landlady, was just twenty-eight—my age. Her husband was a red-faced fisherman whose booted bulk we were later to slide past in the stairwell. He was illiterate. But she had a fourth-grade education and a diploma from the Singer Sewing Machine Company. She had married him at the age of eighteen. They had built the house jointly with the fisherman family downstairs and now owned it with them, jointly.

"Poor girl" was our translator's comment to us, as she gave us this autobiography that she had methodically extracted without Isabella's protest.

The rent would be a bit over what the hotel would have charged. But the hotel had no vacancies, and the bargain was better for three anyway, so it seemed that for the nonce Suzanne had overcome "the belief of poverty" for us.

"Não é caro." Isabella nodded, smiling at me and at Mrs. Açores.

Suzanne appeared to be staring distractedly through the sea window, as she had been during all these negotiations.

So she has won, I thought glumly. We stay here in Sonho for the present, I guess because a "spiritual idea" such as hers of a summer idyll cannot lack for material means, even though its means be of the most precarious kind. We had just enough money to get through the week, if Jérez drove us back across Spain.

I was worried. I wanted desperately to get out of the country by then. But dimly I loved Isabella, as one may be haunted by a certain image of arrested femininity, and I was willing to stay in her home. For a few more days.

"This," pronounced Mrs. Açores with satisfaction, "is a very nice, clean, *Portuguese* home."

Jérez did at length arrive with a Basque partner from his firm, and they stayed most of the week. A week from which Mrs. Açores was soon firmly—and behind her back scathingly—excluded. That good lady had had the misfortune to have cooked up a "typical Alentejo chowder" for us on the very night of the unscheduled arrival of the two Basques, who, quite naturally, joined us in consuming the chowder around a dining-room table that they supplied with white wine. But Suzanne's power with men, whatever its sources, required another setting. By morning I had found myself the target of dark accusations, to the effect that I had conspired with Mrs. Açores to conduct myself as an unconscious "white rival" for Jérez's attentions. And that this was a supremely Jewish thing to do, the family supper with Mrs. Açores. Because on her gnostic view there were no coincidences, Suzanne also blamed poor Mrs. Açores for the very timing of her anaphrodisiac chowder, which had supposedly transformed our unexpected male guests from Spanish suitors for Suzanne into "Jewish" sons for Mrs. Açores. Supposedly, I would have looked a more likely daughter-in-law than Suzanne, in that family setting.

As to the truth of all that, I could not tell, since accusations as to one's unconscious intentions and their subliminal effects are unfalsifiable. Notoriously. But just in case it was true, or anything like true, in the days that followed the accusation I tried to stay out of everybody's way. When Suzanne and her two Basques would skip out to the beach in the afternoon, I would wave them off cheerfully but stay home by myself to leaf through the Gnostic Manual and to ponder my unseen motivations. There Isabella would find me, reading alone at the dining-room table, as she scurried along the floor with a knee-high straw broom. And she would wonder aloud at my being there.

"Não gosta da praia?" she would teach me a little joyful Portuguese, like a red-headed goddess of hope. "You don't like this beach?"

In the cool evenings, all four of us would have supper together in the black field of the Esplanade, which was the big outdoor restaurant in the town. While I found Jérez's supple manners and puzzled, boyish responses to Suzanne more attractive than his Basque part-ner's rocklike stolidity, I tried to look mutely above it, and to stay out of it. Mostly I was quietly grateful to be getting one good meal a day now, for the Spaniards would pick up the tab for us as a matter of national honor.

Very early on the Thursday morning of that week of the Basques, I went to the plate-glass café that fronted the praça, but this time alone to have breakfast. I took one of the tables that were recessed behind the large pillars. Stirring my coffee, I squinted soberly at a small hand mirror that I'd taken out of my purse.

Let's see. I moved the mirror down. My breasts looked almost flat. Moving it to my eyes, I *saw* them. They were globular and staring. Circling the mirror slowly, I found tiny lines that were em-phatically not lines of character or experience. They came from nowhere, and they crisscrossed to end nowhere. My cropped hair (that Suzanne had drastically shortened for me when we were in London, to help me get rid of the "belief of sensuality" that she told me "white women" associate with their hair) now rose on end, as if in alarm. I tucked the mirror away, stood up, and paid the waiter.

Out in the bright sunlight, I found the main street of the town and followed it for some distance on foot till I came to a place just outside the limits of Sonho, where there was a fallen tree stump by the side of the road. I perched on it uncomfortably, feet off the ground, while I buried my face in my hands and tried by that dusty wayside to figure out whose fault this face was.

Was it my fault? Always in my consciousness of her there loomed this pre-gnostic awareness that she was far, far behind me in the great chariot race of invisible history, that she was hopelessly cruder than I was, that she was struggling, that she hadn't passed the first lap, that she would probably never catch up in this life-time. And this awareness was *in her case* perfectly justified, as from my present vantage point I can see fairly clearly. From the place in my pilgrimage that I occupied then, however, I confused this awareness with the forbidden impulse of bigotry—tiny, expunged almost to the vanishing point by so many hours of prayer and of Gnostic meditation, yet able seemingly to expand without warning, like a deformed grey beast that I owned, that I was liable for, that paced my horizon. Was every aimless crease in my face *my fault*, therefore?

I leafed slowly through the pocket-sized King James Bible that I carried with me in those days, trying hard to think. In the course of this Gnostic idyll, had she been leading me through any trials that I needed? Or toward any real renewal of my life's forces? I didn't see how. It seemed stale, her act. Dependent on other people's credulity, as the spider's web may be said to depend on the possible fly.

Looking back along the long threads of the summer's web, now it seemed clear to me that she had no ideal purpose. Not with the boys we had met on the road or in town, not with Mrs. Açores—how had all this helped *her*?—not on the night she had got up and left the café because Jérez had been sociably tossing my way a few questions about Kant. Not with me.

All she had wanted, in each of these situations of the summer, was to beat other contestants. It had been pragmatic. Each victory lasted until the next one was called for. What she had wanted was only to maintain an edge. And what she called "Gnostic Christianity"? It was the invisible racecourse, for the race she got people to run with her. A race she dropped out of when she perceived that it did not serve her objective, which was—still and always—to maintain an edge. The whole transparent web of the summer hung together if so construed, and nothing else could make sense of it.

As to my face, I had better take it back home while I could still show it there. When Jérez and Francisco went north at the end of this week, they could pack us both in the back seat, and that would be, literally and figuratively, the last trip I could afford to take with her. How had I let her take me so terribly far, anyway?

I glanced up at the outskirts of Sonho, sprawled across the escape route . . .

Apparently Suzanne had slept late that morning. When I got back, I found her still in bed. Buried under her blankets, she peered at me as, across her still-dark, shuttered room, I stood by the door. "Abigail," she murmured, "can you forgive me?"

"Not really." I glanced at her indifferently. She seemed no more a mystery to me. Just too much for me, but not a mystery any longer.

"I'm sorry that I made fun of you to Jérez last night."

Had she? "I'm not angry at that."

"Is it something more?" She gasped. "Have you worked it out?"

"Yes. I have."

"Then you have to tell me."

I leaned stonily against the door frame.

"As a friend, Abigail," she pleaded solemnly. "You have to do that for me. You have to tell me the er-ror."

So, quietly and without emphasis, I explained what I had just come to believe about her at the outskirts of town. I reported how strained and seared I had looked to myself at this juncture and told her that I wanted her out of my life.

She took it all lying down. "I feel very bad," she said meekly.

"I've spoiled your summer, Abigail, and Jérez's and Francisco's."
And she named a few other people, mostly young men, with whom
we'd had contact in Sonho that summer.

I nodded. And Mrs. Açore's, I thought. "You probably have," I
replied.

"Please, Abigail, tell me the rest."

What rest? Blue shadows seemed to line the unaired bedroom.
"I'll wait for you outside, if you want. We can talk by the castelo
ramparts."

I did not really know what else to say to her, I thought, scuff-
ing with a sandaled foot at the sandy dust that had curled up
from the beaches and blown into the yard. I had my own hang-
ups (as I viewed them) that I would be glad enough for her not to
know about.

I felt, as we walked together to the ramparts of the castelo, that
she was hanging on my every word now with a desperate unreal-
ism. But I did not want any hard feelings, if hard feelings could be
avoided. All of us would be going north soon.

So I eased up on the parapet to sit across from her sideways,
reminding her that she might do best not to march blindly out to
subdue the world when she had herself to subdue in the first instance, and suggesting that if she really wanted to vanquish this
error (of "trying to beat" other people), and if she kept it in full view
and faced it without flinching, it would be gone with God's help and
her own honest efforts, one day. She was not a pariah, I thought. She
had many remarkable qualities, as I said. And while I talked thus,
soothing bright sunlight played over the parapet and spanned the
beaches below. Until suddenly Suzanne looked up, alarmed, whispered to me, "I'll be right back!" and scampered out of my sight
toward Isabella's house.

I had the ramparts to myself now, the plateau I had sought all
summer long. During those rare few seconds of equipoise, I sighted
João (one of the young men in town whom she'd "befriended" am-
bivalently) coming up the cobbled walk unaccompanied. Suzanne
always called him a "gangboy," though he hadn't a gang. I hailed
him now, raising one hand. We held a gentle, nearly unintelligible
conversation in several languages, the gist of which was that the
Portuguese people still wait, or so João assured me, for the return
of Mad King Sebastião, the ill-fated Portuguese Quetzalcoatl, who
had wasted the coffers and chivalry of that unhappy land in his
quest for the king of the Moors.

A prooftext . . . for our summer idyll?

Chapter Sixteen

Framed

What Suzanne had sniffed on the wind was the sudden departure of our Spanish guests. It was not unreasonable for Francisco to have said to Jérez that enough was enough—this was no normal vacation—nor for Jérez to have gone along with his engineering partner, who was also the owner of the only vehicle that they had down here. But it certainly threw off all my anxious calculations.

By now I had on me a little less cash than it would take to get us both back to England in safety. We had stayed just one week too long. This was the hour to walk back, to the U.S. embassy in Lisbon perhaps, to my family with no perhaps about it, to ask for their disapproval at last, and their help. It was the last time when I could have done that, in anything resembling a normal condition.

After the Basques' unexpected exit from our lives, Suzanne and I had returned to the parapet of the castelo, to talk over our new situation. She had a proposal to put before me. Why not stay on? was what she suggested.

This town had some very good points, after all, was what she said now. Its young men were more "spiritually open," she said, not "jaded," as Americans were. Besides, we hadn't gotten the work done that we'd come here for: her novel and my painting. Because she had spoiled it, our project (the summer idyll) had not had a fair test.

You'll just spoil it again if I give it a "fair test" was what I replied, but in more tactful language.

But no, she disputed that point. I had to have faith that she would be healed, just as I'd told her she would. If I believed what I'd said to her, then I had to believe God would rectify things between her and me, between her and the world, and make her normal, emotionally. She would pull level with me, on the score of goodwill.

"We're out of money," I said, accurately, if non-Gnostically.

But I could apply to my parents for that, explaining to them that I wanted to see if I could become self-supporting as a painter, and asking them if they'd fund this provisionally, while I gave it a try. It would be like a bank loan, I could tell them. Five hundred dollars in two installments would allow us to stay here till Christmas. At least give it another try, she urged me, and get it right this time, this extension of the summer idyll. So went her proposal.

It was true that I had not exhausted the gnostic *hypothesis*. That is, I couldn't know whether she had betrayed it, or whether it just was that impossible kind of thing that existed on the ground of betrayal and always ran into that ground. So, I didn't know yet just what I'd been doing here, or where I'd been. I could have faced the extreme embarrassment of that collect call to New York if I'd been positioned to pick up the mental proceeds of this experiment and to bring those lessons home. As it was, a mistake whose secret I did not understand, and would never understand if I walked away now, did not provide enough evidence for me to steer by. I could not just return to my starting point in a crumpled heap. I would need to be roadworthy, if I was to be able to travel on.

So, neither inwardly nor outwardly did I have the return fare. Which meant my decision was really a foregone conclusion. That was the way that this story was going. It demanded to be figured out to its very depths. And I didn't have any better ideas. It was all flowing one way.

We took a week off in Lisbon to collect standby money on a small letter of credit that Suzanne carried, and to wait out the expiring summer somewhere. For meanwhile, back in Sonho, we had rented an entire house for the month of September, on the assumption that my family would respond to my dumbfounding letter in a "positive" way. Indeed, if they were to keep the lines of communication still strung between us, what choice did they have, at that point? They'd sensed for some time now that something must be going quite wrong. So that week, while we waited in Lisbon, the capital shaded the two of us, forcing us to cope with its city complexities and its blessed city indifference. That was a week when she was quite penitent with me. The only such week.

It was a cloudy, windy evening when we came back to Sonho, to discover that it had turned suddenly cooler there. Nonetheless, we settled into that coastal hamlet with all the determination that was due to our mutual enterprise. We were still waiting for word from my people, and our last dinheiro was scattering now on the storm winds of September. The hard Atlantic rains of the fall had already struck. *Chuva* is the Portuguese word for rain and, as the days went by, "Shoo-oo-vuh!" is what the townsfolk would cry after us disapprovingly. "Quando vai embora?" (when are you leaving?) would come the outcry, punctuating our speedy, raincoated appearances.

Suzanne thought it delightfully funny, their being so nonplussed at our staying there. Privately I thought Quando vai embora? was a very good question, and they must know why they asked it.

To her more puzzled and dazed fellow pilgrim, Suzanne remarked coolly, "They are just gonna have to be *taken* again."

First of all, she "took" our house, the larger part of a walled family compound across the roadway from Isabella's place, with adjoining little shacks into which the owner's extended family had retreated for the month of September. The spirit of its interior was contained in the framed, fading, sepia photographs of family forebears—photographs that Suzanne amused herself by identifying to me as of this or that African clan or stock—retouched with the negritude whitened out. Presumably, she had rather good social science credentials. I didn't, and, if she was right or not, I couldn't tell.

What I did know was that this was the kind of house in which I would have preferred merely to perch, as at a roadside campsite. But *she* moved to put her mark on its remotest corners, with flyswatters, drain openers, insecticides, air deodorants, sponges, and detergents, plus a stock of grocery staples to back up our daily marketing.

It seemed to me that she was taking possession, as if we were neither of us going to get away. Ever.

The townspeople let their old, dark, wool sweaters get soaked, as if these Atlantic rains were not the regular thing that they were, but a black-cloaked bandit who'd broken into their skies unexpectedly. They owned no rain gear, it seemed. Not even the *ricos* wore raincoats. Under the roaring sky sheets, the townspeople shrank in their doorways or cowered in their one "modern" café. They were soft, these mule-carted Portuguese, like one's grandmother, and fearful, like one's child. And I sympathized with them.

"Menina Abigail?" It was the postman, who had come round to the table in the modern café where we sat watching the downpour through the plate glass. He had come to deliver a registered letter for me, with my first check from home. And Suzanne was sent simply sky-high with glee, in consequence. "Whoopee! Two hundred and fifty dollars!" she sang out.

"Whoopee," I echoed weakly, trying hard not to picture the scene above Madison Avenue where a strange new determination must have been sensed behind what was, from me, a disquieting letter of application for these funds.

"Preta, preta! Ha-ha!" (Black, black! Ha-ha!), the small boys and girls of the village would yell in our wake every day.

They were not easy to see as pure manifestations of the Spirit, these children. Old women, in their tattered black dresses and shawls, would shrink back at their cruel mimicry. Even shop-keepers who knew us failed to call out a reprimand but rather hunched their shoulders behind their scratched counters, where the shrill, childish catcalls could be heard even so.

I wasn't sure just how to picture these children in terms of her Gnostic formulations, but Suzanne had no hesitation. She would pick out some one of her little tormenters and chase him until, backed into an open field or against the castelo, she would send a hard volley of smacks to his small boney head. I doubted that the children of Sonho had ever been beaten like that.

Once, when the mother of one such small offender had stormed to our door to protest, "So he called you 'black.' It's what you are, isn't it? I'm going with this to the precinct!" Suzanne had jeered back at her from our compound, "Take it to the police! Vôce é uma pobre! [You are one of the poor!] Go on! Just tell the police!"

I was amazed. She hit 'em with what she had, the little ones and the big ones. It was not exactly "uplifting," from what had been my point of view. But it packed a wallop. It got their attention. I could see that. It was a sermon in stone, and what it preached was, "I am not afraid of you."

Perhaps all sermons have to start there. I wasn't sure. But then, how could I be?

I don't remember whether Suzanne worked on her novel or not, in those days. But officially I was staying on in Sonho "to paint," as if the power of art were at work in our lives and could make even such occasions as these apropos.

I would have been thankful to retreat to still lifes, while I waited for gnostic light on the flowers and fruit, but Suzanne thought that my painting was also *in principle* a way of making the model's acquaintance. An antimodernist view of the matter, but I was no philosopher of art on that excursion, and I had no ready rejoinder in hand. Except to suppose that she, and not I, would be making the model's acquaintance. Which could be viewed as a prostitution of my efforts to paint.

On one level, I thought surreptitiously, well, she has to do that. She has to compensate for her racial predicament. And, on another level, well, she *might* "heal them," by her uncanny presence. And if she does, if she heals them by the Gnostic affirmations that she so deftly applies, that will make it all right. It will transmute the base metal of her frustrations, occasional rages, and seeming misuse of me in this instance into the gold of the Spirit. It's a *mixed* situation. But it's what we *have*, I thought.

So we gave over many hours to prowling the cobbled streets and the café, where we could accost my prospective models. Mostly they would not keep the appointments that they smilingly made with me. But when, from time to time, they did show up, darkly amused, secure in their peasant bodies and poverty and the obscurity that I could not touch, I would be pretty uncomfortable. What I lacked, figuratively speaking, was the painter's high stool, a place on which to perch from which to study them. Even a sketch must somehow move the world, and I had no such Archimedean place, if I wanted to move it. I had no perspective. As a result, I often seemed to myself to be falling into the model, whom I could hardly distinguish visually from the compound's white walls.

Isabella stopped by one time to look in on her former tenants, while I was painting our new landlady, a big female mountain who was (or so Suzanne whispered to me) "a mulatto, a tough babe—a *power* in the streets." This lady, who owned the whole compound, had shown up for her portrait on time, all right, but she sat for me now with such muffled *irony* that I thought it just a matter of time before she cuffed me and my tempera tubes to our dull wooden floor boards.

"The worse looking the sitter, the higher the price!" laughed Isabella uproariously when she saw who it was, clapping her on the back again and again.

On the day when our month in the compound was to expire, Suzanne climbed up her attic stair with me in tow to ask Isabella and her husband if they would take us on once again for the month of October. She was haunting, Isabella, veiled in a pale green, five-and-dime chiffon scarf, bright eyed in the sun and shadow that were playfully dappling their attic. She listened to us, then ducked into the only back room to hold a whispery conference with her recumbent husband. When she reappeared, it was with the fisherman's nod to rent to us for the upcoming month. This although they would all have to go on roosting in their cramped attic shed, which had not been built for the season of *chuva*. She hugged her arms expressively. "Frio, frio," she said to us, smiling. Cold, cold.

João, the young "gangboy," had sat for a portrait too, which he had never come back to let me complete. It was just as well, I had thought, since neither of us had enjoyed the experience. Suzanne had kept out of sight, clanging the pots and the pans and steel wool in the kitchen adjoining. But while she scrubbed, freedom songs had wafted out of the kitchen—"We shall overcome some day-ay-ay-ay-ay"*—and tears of helpless pity had stirred along the young man's downy cheeks, as if he understood her theme, while he sat totally still, caught in the vise of the painter's model.

Let me amend that. He sat *almost* totally still, while I continued to try to paint the full, clothed figure—but now more sketchily from the waist down.

By the time João had got ready to leave, Suzanne came forth in the body to denounce his lounging, leering fellow townsmen and to castigate the street rowdies till she had wrung from João, the excruciatingly sensitive "gangboy," one of only two legitimate sons of a widely known roving father, a private vow to "protect" her in the streets of Sonho. In spite of my own discomfort, I thought it was touching in a way, this little drama, and a sign of her striking naïveté—her purity, if you will—that she tried to impose the rigors of chivalry on these disorganized townsfolk. But I did not suppose that João tried very hard to keep the vow, wrung from him in this painful portrait sitting, since we virtually never saw him after that.

Finally, I had ten portraits completed. We had yet to sell one, so the "business" was bad, for which my parents had forebodingly furnished the capital. But Suzanne suggested that we find a carpenter to frame the ten portraits, and at least set the business in motion by hanging them on our own walls.

I didn't know much about business, but that tempera colors are water soluble I did know. The ever present chill humidity of Sonho in autumn was pouring through our unheated apartment. I wasn't sure that these pictures were worth either framing or selling, but I did not want them to rot in the damps of Sonho. They were worth at least that much to me, in the sense that they constituted my sole ostensible reason for being here. They were my only empirical evidence of good faith, in this project.

They were the honor of the business.

The carpenter we found was referred by the youthful shop-keeper's assistant from whom I bought artist's supplies in those

*"We Shall Overcome": Musical and lyrical adaptation by Zilphia Horton, Frank Hamilton, Guy Carawan, and Pete Seeger. Inspired by African American Gospel Singing, members of the Food and Tobacco Workers Union, Charleston, S.C., and the southern Civil Rights Movement. TRO—© Copyright 1960 (Renewed), 1963 (Renewed) Ludlow Music, Inc., New York, N.Y. Used by permission.

days. He was a half-brother of João's, one of the illegitimate da Madeiras. (He went by his mother's maiden name.) "The carpenter is my brother," he told us, taking in our little stupefied cries of astonishment at the inchoate traceries of his family lines in this gossipy village. It was a half-brother, of course, which meant in this case—besides João da Madeira—the only *other* legitimate son of the roving father. So it was Manoel, the shopkeeper's assistant, who conducted us to his da Madeira half-brother's large open shop on a back street and forthwith left us there, to perform our own introductions!

In the back of the open shop, moving silently among the enshadowed workmen, we saw a very tall, gangling, hangdog, and certainly poor young man, a sort of Portuguese hillbilly, who must be da Madeira the carpenter. Although he was married and clearly older than the two half-brothers whom we had met, he was probably younger than he appeared, for Sonho had a way of dropping a mask of age and decay over faces that, chronologically, should have staved it off for a decade at least. As Suzanne said, people "broke" early here.

On the strength of her social science credentials, Suzanne was later to claim Carlos da Madeira for another demi-African, of a pale, hillbilly type that was new to me, but that she had already fearlessly classified. Perhaps that was why she also felt free to favor him, and the whole shop, with a recital—childlike in its candor—of the insults and indignities we had become accustomed to fending off from the loungers and rowdies and little children of Sonho. "The men here," she said to him pointedly, "are not gentlemen."

"I am a zhentle-man," replied Carlos da Madeira, in the shy and implausible English that he had perhaps picked up at the movies.

"I hope so," she replied seriously.

Carlos da Madeira laughed, somewhat moved. He was willing to do our framing for us, and he had hopes of his own, whose fulfillment might flow from this project. Alone among all the brothers who were so oddly joined on his family tree, the carpenter's faraway hopes included America, hopes in prosecution of which he now went to the wholly unusual lengths of issuing us an invitation to dine at his house. Two days hence.

On behalf of the two of us, Suzanne accepted the invitation.

While the stew was still simmering over the fire and being patiently sniffed and stirred by his wife and his mother-in-law, Carlos da Madeira took his two guests on a short tour of his little home. The kitchen was the pièce de résistance, so we toured that the most, stepping around the two other women. He had designed it himself and built it all in wood, a pastiche of "modern," cantilevered outcroppings painted to imitate plastic, chrome, and enamel, such as a sensitive Portuguese youngster might have got pasted up in his head from old, technicolor, American film clips about suburbia, U.S.A., in the fifties. It was quite a mixture, and quite a sight: pop art surrealism, by which—through his weird kitchen shapes—Carlos controlled and impeded the movements of his wife in that narrow space.

He'd been in the military police. He'd commanded men in his time. He could box. There was tension and thwarted ambition in Carlos da Madeira, though it was not clear if he also had talent to speak of. He had boxing ribbons, he told us, giving his wife a playful shadow-box on the jaw by way of a heavy-handed demonstration. There had not been enough money to cover his and his brothers' education, which was the reason he'd ended up in the sawdust of the carpenter's shop. As with most such Portuguese sons, no one was allowed to go forward and outstrip the others. One thing Carlos da Madeira felt: Putting such a condition on coming to man's estate was *un-American.*

Meanwhile, Suzanne knew what many emancipated Americans try to ignore: that a fair number of the strollers in ancient and charming old world streets would drop out of those streets tomorrow if dropping out would give them a chance to possess the promise of America. She knew it and, perhaps emboldened by her doctrine that the divine gnosis implodes all barriers, she would discuss it with these people as if it were thoroughly feasible—their next move. As for Carlos da Madeira, and his wife and mother-in-law, he could realize his dream, she said. We could act as his "sponsors."

Sponsors? What was that? I wondered. Didn't it take a bit of money, whatever it was? Wouldn't we have to be back home and have jobs ourselves? Why did she hold out such a hope? (But of course, in the Gnostic perspective, which dispenses with the need for prosaic intelligence, all such hopes would be neatly fulfillable. One, two, three! One had only to turn them into affirmations and then give tongue to the affirmations with no trace of ambivalence.)

Since I'd not come to the point of renouncing the gnostic hypothesis as such, I could not utter the sigh of demurral that came to my throat. And Carlos da Madeira fixed on Suzanne all his sad dreamer's attention.

The evening at Carlos's house ended with two splendid promises. The one that perhaps could be kept was our host's dazzling one, which he made to me. It seemed that the owner of the modern café was a neighbor and friend of the da Madeiras. Carlos promised to get him to offer the café's pleasant, rust-colored walls as a gallery, where I could exhibit my paintings. And he promised to figure out for me how to hang them in the café.

And, after that? *Our* promise?

"America! America!" said the da Madeiras in chorus.

"America, America!" agreed Suzanne gaily, and I less gaily, as we turned into the cobbled streets and the dark.

By late November, with the weather darkening more each day, with Isabella still perched patiently with her family in their cold rooftop loft, Suzanne was murmuring about a new fear: that the townsfolk who gathered in bunches to gossip as we passed in the streets might be, actually . . . "up to something."

Up to *what*, for God's sake? I listened halfheartedly, concerned only that she calm down enough to let my paintings get hung in the café. That was all that I wanted now from the summer idyll. That was all I would have to show for it, plainly.

"I'm not at all sure that this town *deserves* a painting exhibit," said Suzanne. "Abigail, you're not listening to me! This town has not been Right in the way it has acted with us. It has not been Right a-t-all. Now, if what you're about is self-glorification, then why don't you just *go on* not listening!"

It was true that what I was "about" was narrowly honoring the promise I had made to my fond, anxious creditors. But, as I could quickly surmise, from the perspective of Gnostic redemption, all this (the promises to my family, the sacrifices of time and effort to the painting enterprise, and so forth, the months of exile with this somewhat fearsome companion), all this could have been just "a test" of my commitment to her race-based reading of the process of purification. After all, what was more important? A mere worldly promise? Or being "right" on those issues toward which I knew she was steering the conversation?

"And if Gnostic Christianity is what you're about," she went on, "then get into the Books! The trouble with you, Abigail, is that you don't know, deep down, what you want. And so you try to have it both ways. It won't work. It won't work a-t-all."

"Suzanne, we won't be here much longer. The town seems to me about like it always was, not better, not worse. What I'd like is to try to have the art show."

"Abigail, you're still not listening to me! I don't know what error is being stirred up in this town. THERE MIGHT BE A LYNCHING. And, if there is going to be one, I don't know what SIDE you'd be on."

I squinted at her, realizing with chagrin that if they strung her up, tarred and feathered her, I probably *would not even notice*, so absorbed had I got in the frightened self-monitoring of my own shrinking sensibility. Was this what my quest for the Absolute had come down to, at the last?

"Well, if it came to bloodshed, they would have to shed mine too," I muttered, embarrassed at the way that sounded—so theatrical—given the implausibility, to my sense of things, of such an eventuality.

At this slightly embarrassed concession, Suzanne seemed to exhale in the deepest relief.

What was *wrong* with her? I wondered. Was she really worried for cause? Had the tone of the heckling changed, and I somehow not noticed?

Finally, Isabella herself was called down from the attic. She listened to all the complaints about hectors, loiterers, rowdies, et cetera till we came to the questions on Suzanne's mind. How safe was the town? Could there be a lynching? She regarded the Black girl and the white one softly. "Sonho," she instructed us in the Portuguese we had learned from her, "is full of stupid, vulgar, coarse people. But, I have lived here all of my married life, and it is not dangerous. Sonho, não é perigosa. But, should it prove otherwise, I am always your friend. And my husband, he is your friend too. And this house is always safe. E esta casa esta sempre segura."

I raised my chin till it rested a moment on the translucent rungs of her ladder of personal kindness. And Suzanne? She seemed to listen to this in a quieter spirit. Even she might be letting this cool mist dim her white and black demons into passing cloud-trails of grey.

It was around this time that the last of our ten frames were supposed to be picked up at the shop of Carlos da Madeira. Carlos had been taking his skills to the end of his try square, apparently, for these last frames were cracked and ill-fitting. This was a man whose fancies seemed to overreach his achievements somewhat, and, sensing that, I would have been glad in this situation to accept what he'd given me. At least the ten portraits he had framed would be ready, if there was to be an art show at the modern café. And a thin remnant of the promise I had given my creditors could be kept, in a manner of speaking.

But, for Suzanne, as she insisted to me, the "idea" that the frames represented had been sullied by this level of carpentry. Well, perhaps she knew best. She seemed to have an artisan's sense of honor that was part of her family ethos and had never been rightly developed in me. (Or, if it had been, it reserved itself for occasions that had nothing in common with this one.) So, overriding my half-discerned resistance, she set me and herself the task of sanding the final six frames.

I had no complaint about doing the sanding with her. But a deeper alarm was stirring somewhere in me. I did not really like my paintings. I had not liked the manner in which the models for them had been rounded up, nor the double purpose—part painterly and part procurative of Suzanne's eerily naïve social life—that they'd been dragooned into serving. I did not think that the verbal contract we had with Carlos da Madeira was a fair one, since *he* was not doing all this for the money alone (especially not the art show phase of it), and we probably could not produce "America" for him.

I'd been going forward with all this on the strength of two promises: the one to my parents about the loan for the art business and the other one, to myself—to try Suzanne's path with its gnostic inversions of moral intelligence and hope that God could be scared out of hiding on her path, since He had not been, on mine.

Now all these promises had got worn down almost to transparency. But not quite. So I continued to go through the motions that belonged to these promises, and meanwhile I was waiting for the idyll to be over. Which it would be. In December.

As to where my life would be headed after December, either inwardly or outwardly, I had no idea. "Home," I supposed, whatever that word meant now. In the Jewish narrative, to which I thought vaguely that I'd be returning in all probability, sooner or later, it's best to come home with a reasonable story, if you have to "come home" in adulthood at all. If I had the art show, I would have at least that. A reasonable story. But, even in the best case, would it be deeply reasonable, or just shallowly plausible—a cover story?

So far as I could see, I didn't have the God of moral intelligence to play the game of Witness to my story with, any more. I had divorced Him, at least experimentally, or "hypothetically." And, out of respect for my hypothetical wishes, like any good Lover, He wasn't walking beside me at present. At least, He wasn't doing so within earshot. So, even if I were to return home with some kind of a story to account for the time I had spent here, the story would be episodic. Ad hoc. This was because the only absolutely *long* story was the one with Him in it. And somehow I still knew, even through all the fog that was swirling around in my head, that a plausible-sounding short story, or even a diverting little novella, is not the same as a "good story," any more than a disguise is equivalent to straightforward self-presentation.[1]

(All in all, I was getting pretty frightened. A crisis of faith was fast becoming a "real" crisis.)

We were still sanding the frames when Suzanne spoke up. An

"er-ror" like the one that the frames represented wasn't "handled," she said, until it had also been "called" (i.e., addressed) on the plane of motivations, where it still lived. Since this whole thing was my business, she said, I was the one who would have to go back to the carpenter's shop and "confront him."

Confront him about what, *nom de dieu?*

I wasn't sure who exactly owed whom an apology, but I found the carpenter hard at work in the back of his shop. Willingly, he allowed that his last frames had not been very good. Even more candidly, he confessed to not being a framer. He was, as he said now, a carpenter. He did not like to cut glass. He did not like to make backings for pictures. He just liked to be working in wood.

I nodded sympathetically, thinking that Carlos resembled nothing so much as a long piece of driftwood himself. "Okay, Carlos," I said to him sociably, "we'll come to an understanding. You'll do the job of hanging the pictures for the art show, and you'll frame any future paintings that we might have, but with more emphasis on what you like to do best: the wood. Only," I added, with a parting nod to my alleged mission of addressing the motives, "tell us the truth about what you prefer to be doing."

He smiled, baring his teeth awkwardly at this abstraction.

Suzanne received my report with no special show of emotion. Only, she said, if Carlos was not planning to bring himself into alignment with "the idea," then of course we could not use his services from now on. And, by the same token, he would have to know why.

"Go back, Abigail," said Suzanne, "and tell him."

"But Carlos is my only connection to the café and the art show."

"Well, Abigail, *you* decide what you want."

Tell him what, for God's sake? That I had something to tell him? That I did not know what it was? "Do you want to come too?"

We entered the dark shop and found Carlos at his usual bench. With Suzanne wedged in behind me, I began to tell Carlos that his terms of the morning were not right, because he had not faced "the idea."

Carlos bent and nodded in acquiescent expectancy. "If so, yes. Then what?"

"You're not *telling* him," Suzanne urged me.

I couldn't think of what else to say. I personally thought Carlos had a right to abandon "the idea." What sort of an idea was it, anyway? With an apologetic half shrug, I looked over to her.

"Carlos," Suzanne said finally, "those frames that you made for us were shit." She used the American word.

Carlos nodded. He had learned a sort of American. "Shit."

"*I* had to finish them." She pointed. "With my hands."

She had to if anyone had to, because I sure would have dropped the whole problem.

"Carlos, you are not a carpenter. You have no honor as a carpenter."

"Yeah, and what else," he said sarcastically, while the apprentices hooted, "Chickens! A pair of yard fowl!"

Then he was stumped momentarily as a black well of tears spilled over her lids while she looked up at him and said childishly, "And Carlos, you are *not* a gentleman."

That was when she walked out, and I followed, leaving that particular splint wedged between one of his joints and the bone. I felt it was very unfair to Carlos, almost a set-up from the beginning. But what did I know? Perhaps she set higher standards for others than I did. Maybe it was part of her feminine tribute to chivalry in an ideal world she could see and I couldn't, one that was free of all social limitations.

From the perspective of what I might have called moral intelligence, what had occurred was simply ghastly. But I had decided, some time back, to put on other spectacles. Was it time to take them off yet? Almost time. Almost time.

"From now on, Abigail," Suzanne said as we came through the door of our home and wheeled wide apart, "you take care of YUH BIZ'NESS."

"All right. I will," I said sinkingly, thinking that my only remaining business in Sonho was to want out, and nothing that we were still involved with here felt like my business.

"You see," she went on, looking very angry, "Carlos da Madeira is a hater."

He *was*? Then why had we meddled with him for so long, at her prompting? Or was the more appropriate question perhaps, Why had *I* never noticed that he was a hater? As it would also be a question for her, I guessed, whether I did or did not care about her and the dangers she underwent.

"He's going to want revenge, Abigail, and on me. Not on you. You did something very bad when you made me come along and do your talking for you. I've got an enemy now in this town. And Manoel will be overjoyed to spread malicious tales about me all over this town. He's never forgiven me for the night when I left the dance early because you were making me look bad. And João will hear of it! The belief of family is very strong with João."

"Well, look," I temporized, dazzled and lost in the sliding rocks that were crashing around me. (Manoel was of course the shopkeeper's assistant from the art store, the illegitimate half-brother, who had brought us to meet Carlos. We had gone to a dance with Manoel and João in mid-summer.) "At this point," I continued, "Manoel is really no loss. And João will surely believe your side." What side was that? I didn't know what I was talking about. I only knew she was furious, in consequence of a situation that, to the best of my knowledge and belief, she had rigged up herself to fall out this way. But I wasn't sure of the status of my knowledge and belief. I wasn't sure that she did not have the finer gnosis, and wasn't spinning headlong toward the Absolute, while I stood back where I caught the exhaust.

"Abigail," she said with bitter finality, "we will NEVER see young João again."

After the onslaught of the long, dark, fall weeks, it had needed one final downpour. Then, the mold and discoloration that, from the plaster, had been pressing into the backings of the paintings on our walls for some time now broke into visibility. A few mornings after that conversation with Suzanne about the various sons of Senhor da Madeira, I woke up to a framed assembly of ruins. Just like the real faces that Suzanne said "broke" early in Sonho, these painted faces too had "broken." Framed as they were, at such cost to me, and to the models, and to Carlos da Madeira, and to my backers back home, they had nonetheless become utterly worthless.

The tempera painting of Isabella, which had been my favorite, was waterlogged. "The picture is ruined now," I said to Suzanne.

"It is *not*," she insisted, denying the obvious.

"Oh, yes it is, for me, Suzanne. The colors were everything in that painting. They were very pure and light, and sort of exquisite. The *drawing* was banal. Now it's all a greyish blur."

She reflected a moment. "You're doing something very dishonest, Abigail."

"What?"

"You're trying to blame Carlos da Madeira for ruining your pictures. Your pictures are not ruined. A little damp would have gotten to them, no matter what. I see no change in the color, and I would catch that immediately."

But I could see it. Was I being "dishonest," in my seeing? What was a painter but someone who sees? And if I were not dishonest, and my pictures were really ruined? What then would I have been doing with her, down here in this lost place for two and one-half months, now that I really had nothing to show for it? "Waiting?" For what? For time to be up? For our allowance, through God's mercy, to be exhausted?

It would be, in a fortnight.

After breakfast that morning, she suggested that we two take a walk to the windswept, wintry beach. We often took walks at night, headlong walks, for we were bare legged and wore only thin summer suits and raincoats. But she had never suggested an idle stroll in the daytime.

This morning she left her sneakers on the damp sands and, walking barefoot, soon found a high, wet, black boulder to climb. I hung back in the shadow of the promontory and watched her pass before me along its flat back to the edge. There she stood, silhouetted, a tiny, dark, dazzling figure before the hissing sea wastes. Idly I envied her the apparent freedom of her isolation and light-footedness. I wondered if the townspeople could see her from the parapet of the castelo. Or would they only see her when she had finally taken wing and flown before the breakers?

Later, when we had climbed the stone stairway and were in the crowded praça once again, a murmur went up. It was young João, the same that we were—because of my to me uncognizable flaws— "never" going to see again. I looked over the milling town square at him and smiled in relief.

Well, I thought. There he is after all! She can be happy now! And, on those sovereign waves of malice by which sweat and fellow feeling are passed back and forth between armpits and unshaven jowls in Sonho, the loiterers were still bobbing and surfing. "João," went their murmuring now. "They go for João, the American girls!"

João had a certain kind of virility, almost an emblematic kind, that verged on skittishness, as if he could not quite stand the emblem. We wandered to his side of the praça now, and I stood by while they talked, feeling in some small degree vindicated.

The two of them were exchanging a few brief words, face to face. "Till tomorrow." With a remote half smile, he was nodding at her.

Oh, Lord. It was a promise from him to serve as *my* model again! Oh, when would I be done with this? There was no more art show. There were no more paintings. She had not even asked me if I felt like completing the painting of João. It was the *last one* I could feel like completing. What did she want of me? The art works were exhausted.

Another day went by, the very day on which we expected our skittish young model. Who never showed.

All during that afternoon, while we waited for João, Suzanne moved tensely about the apartment, expressing her doubts about

João, his intrinsic worth, the purity of his feeling for her, his chivalry, his stability.

In fact, João was a high-strung boy, his father's most fragile product, liable to get migraine headaches and disappear in his baby bed for days that, as far as the town knew, could have been spent underground. He surfaced rarely. No one could count on him. He could not put his elusive masculine bent in the service of a lady. No doubt about that. He was not *cavalheiresco*. All that was true. But all afternoon I did what I could to prop up the image of João in Suzanne's twitching mind and to assure her of his pure love and fidelity, as one lifts the red cape round the bull in the bullring, till by nightfall it had become clear that he was not coming, and equally clear that I was not really surprised.

"You *sensed* that he wouldn't come, Abigail," she said, ever on the alert. "Why didn't you *tell* me? Why didn't you *warn* me? We could've done WORK on it in the Books all day today. Instead of which, all afternoon, I've been *encouraged* to believe in young João's love for me!"

What was I supposed to say? In the normal course of things, it would have been fairly unlikely that a boy like that would have wanted an open association with a foreign woman who was older than he, an American, and a *preta* besides. I thought that he rather liked her. But I didn't think he could buck all those tides, or indeed any tides. Not in this town. But I wasn't going to tell her that, first because of the *preta* business, which could hurt her feelings, and second because in her Gnostic perspective (which I had been doing my damnedest to adopt), all these psychohistorical determinants would be viewed, quite simply, as "error."

As always, the gnostic commitments of my thinking were not wholly coherent. There were cracks in them. I had thought I could simply transcend those complexities, and tell her soothingly that João loved her, since "Love" of some kind could be safely assumed in the Gnostic religion. But perhaps that was fatuous. Also, I was conscious of having had the additional motive of containing her ever threatening rage. But I hoped that I had not had the unconscious motive of trying to quench her natural fire—her spirit. Searching among the mysterious tides of these inner motives, trying to see them more clearly under the pressures brought to bear by her accusation, my eyes widened now as a new insight struck me.

"What is it?" she said, sitting watchfully.

"It just hit me that I saw contempt in João's eyes when he looked at you while we walked into the praça." Contempt, or at least something funny, as he'd stepped down from his level landing, his face a little askew in the mirror of the grinning faces around him.

Her small face constricted. "That's the worst thing I fear from men."

I nodded. I was supposed to confess to *something*, wasn't I?

"And knowing that"—she got up—"you led me on all afternoon. ABIGAIL," she roared from that wet, black bedrock beneath all my sinking feelings, "WHY?"

"Suzanne, if you knew how it frightens me, you wouldn't yell at me like that."

"But why?" she asked, pacifyingly. "What *in you* gives rise to such fear?" And then she said it, or perhaps we both did. "Why, you must hate me."

I nodded, almost imperceptibly, with the faintest smile of embarrassment.

Now she stared at me wildly. "Why, you've hated me since London!"

I had to nod. I had, in a way.

"But"—she gagged and shuddered, choking—"why? I've given you NOTHING BUT GOOD." She was turning to stare, no longer at me, but perhaps at some Message she alone could see streaking our damp Babylonian Walls.

"It's very hard to love you, Suzanne," I explained accurately. "You *threaten* so much, about what you would do if you found out the truth about people . . ."

"That's not a reason." She stood frontal and rigid, right in the axle on which the wheel of her anger revolved. "Why, you've strung me along since London! You were NEVER serious about Gnostic Christianity! Were you, Abigail?"

"No." I had tried earnestly to be. I had mentally searched out and diligently dueled with every errant thought that betrayed a Jewish background and its sense of the sheer weight of history, and had prayed hourly over the dueling field. So far, it had not worked. I had got only as far as Confused. I had not got to Gnostic.

She shook her head now in wonderment, like Little Red Riding Hood over the wolf, who, despite his lace nightcap and matching nightgown, is not really Grandma. "And to think that I actually loved you! I thought that I was the luckiest person in the world, to have found a friend! Why, in the name of Gnostic Christianity, didn't you *tell* me?"

"Because," I offered reasonably, "I was always scared that you'd run out and leave me alone in Iberia"—something she'd frequently threatened to do, in point of fact—"so I would have to get home by myself." In sum, I hadn't wanted this risky and doubtful adventure to end in a given catastrophe. Of personal and intergroup relations, no less. And she'd known that. And it had strengthened her hand with me. Which in turn had confused me still further, as we'd gone along here.

She thought that one over. "That's a cheap thing to say," she decided. And she swiveled what looked like a very surprised little head toward me. "You don't *like* me, do you?"

"No," I had to agree. "I'm afraid of you."

Not exactly giving the lie to my fear, she reached for the coffee-pot with a violent suddenness. "GE-EHT-OUT-UV-MYE-SIGHT!"

I obeyed.

But a moment later, she was behind me, in my bedroom. "Why, I've been living for months in the same house with racial prejudice, haven't I?"

The average American would sooner jump off the George Washington Bridge than say yes to that one. "No," I said stoutly.

"Nigger-Suzanne, nigger-Suzanne! That's what you've been saying to yourself, all this time! Why don't you come out and *say* it?"

I grinned, in *sincere* denial, for once. I had never put her proper name and the bigoted epithet together in my mind. It was bad style. Impossible style, in fact. What did she take me for? "Suzanne," I broke in here, with the hopes of explaining myself. "I don't just 'hate' you. My 'hatred' is the side of me that I've been trying to get rid of. It's the 'error,' as you often say. But beyond that, I really do love you, too. It's just not that simple." (It's called ambivalence. And I would have been crazy not to feel it, considering how she was riding me.)

"Nah, Abigail. You can't hide in the Books any more. THE ER-ROR IS YOU. And you're not really sorry yet, are you? You-Jews-think-you-can-get-away-with-everything-and-nothing-is-ever-really-seri-ous-don't-you?"

Numbness was taking over the upper reaches of my feeling, and underneath lay somewhere untouched the well-appointed heir apparent whom nothing could ever deeply malign, or hurt, or get to. I was all right. I was Jewish. Nothing had ever been consequential, fully. I had been protected. Was that wrong? Should I feel guilty about that? Maybe. For where was equity, since *she* had not enjoyed the same sense?

"You think about me: 'nigger,'" Suzanne was saying, very close to my face. "Well, lis-sen, Jieeoo. I gave you a *real* religion. You learned that you didn't have tah hate."

(Interesting, wasn't it, how we were still worrying about my prejudices? For a fact, I didn't hate. She, manifestly, did.)

She was insecure, I was thinking in that room in Portugal, back then. That's why she was talking that way about Jews. For historicocultural reasons, I was not so insecure. So I could take it. Probably. It wasn't her fault. I was sorry that I hadn't helped her lose her insecurity. That probably was my fault. I was very sorry.

(And very scared. How would we get home? What would I tell them, at home? And where was the coffeepot, at present? Cooling off, I hoped.)

"I took you into Gnostic Christianity," Suzanne was going on now, "and you used it, not tah heal yourself, but tah hide yourself behind! I've seen a lot of your type of so-called believer in the Gnostic Meeting Halls, Abigail. You could *easily* fit in among them."

I could? Good. Then I would be safe. They would be kind to me.

"But I wanna tell you this. You will neh-vah make it in Gnostic Christianity—in this world *or* the next!"

How could she *say* such a cruel thing to me? I could feel my heart lurch with the impact of it. It was *spiritual malice*. I hadn't known it was even possible. I would have thought it a contradiction in terms.

Suddenly she reached upward, as if through an invisible skylight. "GOD!" she cried. "GA-AH-OD! GAHAHA—." This last invocation faded into a scream which instantly dimmed all the sounds in the house, as our neighbors, already astir upstairs and down, now tensed behind their cold walls.

"Shshsh," I said, with clear conviction for once. "The neighbors! For God's sake, Suzanne, take it easy. Calm *down*. I'm not *worth* it." (A costly concession, as things would turn out.)

"Gu-uh-uh-uh-d-d-d." She had fallen to her knees now. "Why-y-y? Why did you LEAVE me?"

How can she place herself like that, so naïvely and directly under God's imagined intentions? How can she *care* about herself so, to the point where she can expostulate so directly with the Absolute? I wondered, half admiringly. Just like a child, with its tall mother.

(I had a sinking feeling that what I was witnessing was not quite the same thing as childlike faith, and that *I* was being assigned to play the tall mother in this case, but I did not let that sinking feeling become fully conscious, then and there.)

She swiveled her head around with an expression of sheer hatred. "You've seen me ON THE FLOOR!"

I understood the implication, even while I suppressed the thought that she herself had placed that stupefying sight before me.

"I can't even remember your NAME now," she complained. "Is it Adelaide, or Agatha? Who are you?"

Well, I wasn't Adelaide or Agatha. That was not *nice*. Still, I admired the purity of her disappointment, in a way. Many people did not carry that much passion inside them.

(But now, could we go home, please? This summer's idyll was not working out.)

"Come back here, Abigail. I have to understand this."

What was there to understand?

"You ran, when I picked up the coffeepot. You thought I was going to throw it at you. I threw it at the wall. Why should you think I would do such a thing to you, unless *you'd* hoped to do it to me?"

But didn't you tell me about some person in your family doing exactly that? What could be more natural, given your attitudes, I mean, than for you to want to make my face coffee colored too, especially when you are in such a violent rage? (But this flash of thought was so quick that it scarcely found its way into my silent, ongoing monologue.)

"What do you mean?" I said to her. "*I* would throw a coffeepot at you?"

"No. That's not your method. What you would do is let an 'accident' happen to me, through your carelessness. You'd let the boiling grounds slip. Same result. You're not *just* a hater, Abigail. You're not just prejudiced. The fact is—" she paused and looked at me with fascination, as if at a painted face that had just "broken" under the damps of Sonho—"you're a murderer! That's right, isn't it, Abigail?"

"I don't know. I don't think so." It *was* one hypothesis, I supposed. Who knew what lurked in the silent deeps of the psyche? I was not, on her hypothesis, a good person whose paths in life had so often seemed blocked. I was, rather, a bad person whom God was perpetually placing in quarantine. The reason I am outside the mainstream is because the mainstream is good and I am not. That's it. It was that simple, on her hypothesis. (Had I still been self-committedly Jewish, I would have been able to say to myself, No: *This is silly. You have suffered, that's all. In human history, one can suffer, being innocent.* Except that I wasn't Jewish, any more. I didn't know, any more, save only that I was far too tired and numb to argue about it.)

Finally, very late, with Suzanne still promising kindly to help me get spooned, piece by dismembered piece, through her private keyhole to heaven, we were both permitted by her to retire. "If only you had said to me, 'Suzanne, I have these very strong Beliefs of hatred and murder, and would you help me work through them,' *think* what a stronger position you would have been in, Abigail!

How much more quickly you could have hoped to get your healing! You just can't drive out er-ror with a lie, Abigail."

About the last point, she was certainly correct. But you can drive an error in deeper, with an abusive lie repeated often enough. My real "error" lay, of course, in considering even for a moment this last "hypothesis," one that was absolutely destructive to me, alien and quite false as well. But I was too tired and emptied out at that point to shrug it off.

So it happened that when, on the night of her first sounding of what Suzanne considered to be my lower depths, I went at long last to my room to get ready for bed, I glanced down at my hands. Astounded, I raised them, turning them over and back again. From what I could see, the skin on my hands had turned drastically *whiter*, so that the veins stood out deep blue against what looked to be flesh white as marble, and the fingers seemed to have twisted and curved at the joints involuntarily. They weren't the same color they'd been before. They did not form the same shape. They didn't look like my hands any more! They looked sinister, like the hands of a strangler.

I glanced in the mirror curiously, to see if there were any other repercussions to match my bleached, bloodless, bent hands—and there was indeed my changed face. It showed a bright flush from forehead to chin. The cheeks had swelled up to the point where the shadows beneath the cheek bones were erased. The jawline had melted into what looked like jowls. And I seemed shorter physically, my shoulders having moved up to crowd round my neck like a dowager's. *Christ!* I thought. I look just like Nixon! What is this? What's happened to me? Am I really guilty? This isn't the face of suffering. It *looks* like the face of guilt.

It was a moment in hell. A purely American moment. For hell, for Americans, is just that threatened possibility of the inversion of grace, the reverse of that action of self-renewal that is our American dream. And that reversal of activization is the real fire next time, of which the destruction of the cities we walk among is but the enlarged reflection. So, by that passage, I became an American. I'm naturalized now. There's nowhere I don't fit in.

When I woke in the morning, the sudden swelling had *not*, as suddenly, gone but was still there. We two took occasion to visit upstairs for a moment, where Isabella was bent quietly over her sewing. She looked somewhat different too, for no neighbor could have missed our raised voices. Flushed and faintly swollen, like a purple plum, but the swelling still kept within the bounds of her naïvely perfect bone structure, she looked to me to be in a state of deep-questioning shock. And the wooden roof still answered, rattling above her.

Her question was, I think, Could America—the free world—simply disintegrate around her? She missed nothing. She noted the storm-dusted, physical integrality of Suzanne this morning, and wordlessly she noted my precipitation into Suzanne's screaming vortex that was costing me my physical outlines. And her impulse, surreptitious or nearly unenacted, was to reach forward and pat my hand.

It is no small gesture, ever.

Chapter Seventeen

Policía Internacional

The whole process of alienation of my identity was not as yet quite complete. There were several more stages through which it still had to go, and I to plummet. There were to be more rigged encounters, and more damning interpretations concocted to describe my missteps through these preposterous situations, situations I had neither chosen, nor desired, nor understood.

Just a week or so after that terrible long day and evening, João had simply reappeared, without apology or the pretext of a painting this time, but bringing along a distinctly unsavory-looking older man whom he introduced to us as his "cousin." What followed were several visits by the two men, which occurred a few evenings in succession.

Since, on João's side, this was courtship behavior, I felt relieved for Suzanne's sake. It salvaged her wounded pride, I thought, and made all my soothing protestations of that long afternoon (about João's "love" for her) sound more plausible, in retrospect anyway. It was bold of João to come courting this way. Bolder than I might have given him credit for.

So relieved did I feel at the prospect of this partial exoneration that I did not think I could turn down the fetid and thankless assignment Suzanne had straightway given to *me*, of keeping João's so-called cousin out of her way while she'd be working on something incomprehensible to me that she was all set to call João's "healing." Without going into the details, later transmitted to me, of what that healing involved, let me merely say that, in her Gnostic view, flesh and blood, black and white, male genitals and female hands were all parts of the greater illusion of materiality, illusion of which João had to be healed. His largest delusion, she told me, was that he was "white."

This unwelcome assignment of keeping the cousin out of the way was one that I did not know how, harmlessly, to fulfill. For example, the cousin asked me not to sketch him, and asked in such a peremptory way as to give me the distinct impression that he might be *wanted* for something. You know, the way you are "wanted" in the post office. To call my conversational efforts with the cousin "labored" or "unsuccessful" would be to compliment them. Had I point-blank refused everything he was trying to get by force or cajolery, it seemed clear enough that he would have told João he was marching out, João would have followed his sinister chaperon forthwith, and Suzanne's accusations against me, which were still burning through my nervous system, would have sprung up full flame from their ashes.

What I finally figured, giving up as it were on all the alternatives that I could narrowly picture, was that I could keep João's chaperon in the Gnostic picture only by acquiescing, in some degree, in his unwanted advances. Materiality, after all, was alleged to be an illusion. By the third evening, Suzanne had led us out on a walk in the dark. She and João were having some indistinct private interlude at the castelo ramparts. The stranger and I stood on a landing below, where I was letting him wrap my raincoat in the anaesthesia of his unwanted hug. The walk then continued, led on by Suzanne and her João. Would it never be over? It went down to the cold rainy pier at the waterfront.

Suzanne and João had found a seat there at the front of the pier. So the cousin and I walked out to the pier's edge together. Where he directed me to perform, with my hands, one of those crassly sexual services demanded in countries where girls cannot go the whole way and that, when Suzanne did it with João, would get called a "healing." It sure didn't feel like a healing to me, but I hoped that Suzanne could appreciate what sense of erotic self-esteem I was sacrificing for the sake of giving her time alone with her youthful, not-really-white, Gnostic beau.

What an acrid, unpleasant memory it still is when I look back on it.

Since it was clear that even this grim expedient would be of limited usefulness once it was over, I thought I had done enough (or anyway all I could stand to do) to keep the raincoated cousin out of her way. I could have turned home alone, but I wasn't sure that such a gesture would not be disruptive of Suzanne's scenario. Yet there was only so long that I could be part of this Portuguese double date. What else did she want? Could we not call it a night, perhaps?

Hoping to learn that we could, I returned to the end of the pier that held Suzanne and João. With the cousin still behind me. At which point, Suzanne stood up suddenly, asked me for the house keys, and left—a dark streak in the Portuguese night.

João looked to be on the verge of a breakdown. "What is it? Why did she leave like that, without saying a word?" he asked me in terror.

"I don't know, João. It may be she is angry with *me*. But go find out! You talk to her! Go after her!"

"Yes," chimed in the cousin, in heavy sympathy. "Go after her, boy! Hurry!"

But she turned João away at the top of the ramp with what looked like some very sharp words and a striking gesture, and the boy came back to us, quite upset and demoralized. And I, utterly out of compass by now, returned slowly, on the arm of the so-called cousin who was not one, to Isabella's grey house and our apartment, where Suzanne's lights were now blazing over the town.

What followed this last of the evenings of Portuguese double dating, evenings that had filled me with deepest dread, deepest confusion, and deepest self-scorn, were more nights of hellish interrogation, enveloping me in gutter language, and punctuated by physical blows that I could not dream of returning, so responsible had I come to feel for her fury.

"Abigail," she said to me on the first of those successive nights, "when João came up to me at the waterfront ramp, that boy was in a killing mood. We wrestled up there! Physically!" she answered my unspoken question. "You *assumed* that would happen, didn't you? The only thing that you didn't count on was that God would protect me, so that I could get safely home and expose the er-ror. But you know, when I passed the three of you—you and João and João's so-called cousin—with your heads together down beneath the waterfront ramp, *I did not stop for a second*. You looked like a gang of conspirators!"

She caught her breath. "Now, what did you *say* to João?"

"Nothing! I just said, 'João—go after her!' "

"Go AFTER her? Those are murderer's words. You sent that boy up to kill me, Abigail!"

"Oh, Suzanne." I stumbled, missing a foothold, into the stupefy-

ingly inadequate motions of wry *denial.* "Why would I want to 'kill'
you? I wanted him to talk it out with you because I thought that the
evening was my fault—that you left so suddenly, I mean. It was the
same way that I once said to Jérez, after you left the café without
explanation, 'Please, go after her, Jérez.' "

(That had been right after I had replied to a question from the
Basque about Kant. Immanuel Kant. Not someone whom Suzanne
had read, as I gathered. Since, when she had decamped from the
café on that summer evening, she had favored me with a look of
sheer loathing, I hadn't thought that I was the one best qualified to
do what she'd told me, in a previous sharp lecture, was the friend
thing, and go after her myself, till I "found out what was wrong."
Besides, I'd had a pretty good idea what was wrong in that case,
and I well knew just how contraindicated any healing applications
from *me* would be. It had been on the same general view of her
motivations that I had figured João to have been the best medicine
for her inscrutable ailments on the winter night now in question.)

Wide-eyed, she looked back at me now in the kitchen. "And
Jérez never gave me such a fright as when he came up to me by
the ramparts that evening. That time you worked with Mrs. Açores,
didn't you? You—a bitching, jealous, *sexually experienced* older
woman—plotting with Mrs. Açores, who was probably an Aging
Jewish Lesbian. IT WAS YOU THAT TIME, AND IT WAS YOU THIS TIME!
Only, this time, you had an experienced murderer to work with
when you put that confused, anguished boy up to it!"

With regard to the particulars of her accusation, that I'd put
João up to throwing her from the waterfront ramp, or strangling
her, or killing her some other way, they were so bizarre and so
wholly unwarranted that they tended to freeze the neurons where
the counterarguments are said to be stored. Not that this was a
topic that I'd had much practice discussing! But I had had training in argument. So the right words could have been found in the
neurons and put together in the right combination somehow.

Not in this situation, however. Here, in her kitchen, where she
sat perched high above me on the rim of the sink, where I sat
huddled beneath her in the dark, in the chill, bare legged, where
the inquisition would be punctuated by physical blows from her
side, *here* I could almost feel the neurons refusing to fire.

Nevertheless, I was shaking my head now and trying to think.
It had been a fact of those evenings with João and his so-called
cousin that I'd dearly wanted this passage through hell with her to
be *over.* But from there to "murder"? And "murder" by conspiracy?
Whom would I get to act as my coconspirators? And where, in my-

self, would I find such an incomprehensible motive? I shook my head with an effort. It was one thing to accuse me of unconscious hostility, or unconscious prejudice. But . . . this was getting unreal.

"No, Suzanne. 'Murder' was the furthest thought from my head. There may have been some confusion maybe . . . some darkness . . ."

"Abigail, I *know* the mind of a murderer. He doesn't think, 'At 9:00 I will get the gun. At 9:30 I will load it. At 10:15 I will go see my victim, et cetera, et cetera, et cetera. He thinks about all kinds of high-flown abstractions, or about what he's wearing, or about every which thing, *except* what he's setting out to do. You know, if er-ror called itself by its own name, er-ror would be the same thing as truth!"

But how then could motivation ever be established? And how could a normal person ever know what he or she had intended to do? I certainly could not look down on the waterfront of humanity, as she claimed that she could, and "know" the minds of people who (presumably) did not know their own minds. Did that very opacity of mind mean that she could be *right*? Or was my vindication so elusive to the tools I had at hand that it would be better to forget it for this season and cast my crumbs of integrity on her dark, luminescent waters?

"Do you know what happened up by the castelo, before we all walked to the waterfront?"

"No, what?"

"João was wrestling with me, at the edge of the ramparts, and I had my back to the drop. That's when I called out your name and said, 'Abigail! Help me!' "

I hadn't heard her. I'd been some distance below, with the cousin. Sounds had been muffled, by night, by distance, by disquiet.

"And do you know what João said to me at that moment? He cried out, 'I love you, ABIGAIL!' "

As he was pushing her over the ramparts? Then I must have been there, mentally, or at least somehow providing the sanction in João's young mind. And if I was providing the sanction, then why not the force, since thoughts were effective forces (or so, anyway, she had trained me to affirm). He must have picked up on my thoughts. And how could I deny that I had thought, "I want *out*!" Oh, yes. Out.

As, in my benumbed state, I very slowly put together this enthymematic argument, one premise next to the other, with only a few left out that she could insert in the argument later, I felt a tug at my cheeks and my mouth. It was as if the "hypothesis" of her Gnostic religion, which I had put on like an actor's mask in London, had meanwhile taken up residence inside my head, from whence it could reach out now to grip, tug at, and replace my original face. For my face was the face that my story had worn. And my story had become unrecognizable, subjectively.

She stared with a hellishly distant absorption as my mouth began to work and to twist, shuddering, and I took my head in both hands to quiet it, pressing it from each side and saying, "My God."

"No, Abigail. Don't think about yourself, as usual. Think about João! Think about what that *poor* lad must be going through! What he will go through, for the rest of his life. You know, people don't move after they try to block me." She caught my demurral on the fly, almost before I did. "No it's very true." Staccato. "I have seen it happen repeatedly. That's why I always try to warn people. I tried to warn Carlos da Madeira, and the little kids in this town. And I tried to warn you, not to come up against me."

So, in the days that followed, such were my confessed "crimes," for which unlimited expiation would now be demanded. The first way that she found for me to expiate was to let her dictate all my outgoing letters and to read all my incoming mail. So the first way had to do with communication. The second way was about work and money. "We are staying in Sonho," went her second sentence, to run concurrently, "until every last one of your traveler's checks has been spent. You are going to work for *me*, from now on. You are not leaving until you've paid me back for everything that you've done to me."

These sacrifices were not terribly hard to wring from me in my present reduced state. Each day saw new additions to the crowd of witnessing accusations with which she surrounded me. They stalked our recent summer idyll like grey sentries filing into the fragmented days, gone by in the dust. They stripped the lost years of childhood. They pillaged the brief passage of my life that I had traversed with Pheidias. There was no detail of our family's history too delicate or interwoven with a saving context to have escaped her surreal "exposures," in which fact and fiction were hopelessly intermixed. I began to feel that if I stayed with her, in this hidden place, and fled from my family forever, I'd be *protecting* them from her exposures and likewise protecting everyone who had ever known me.

Since I felt responsible for her fury, there was no walking away from it. It was she who had to give me leave to depart. And that, of course, she would never do.

It was as if the whole world were in a state of fury with me, and I had to stand there till the fury had exhausted itself. But it never seemed to do that. There was always a little more, a new batch in the morning. It fed on what, for any other emotion, would have been self-exhaustion.

Once, when I walked with her through the praça to the post office, she having had a package in tow that she wanted to mail, she observed aloud to the darting, ducking townspeople, "You called me 'black.' But I beat you."

It was at that moment that I saw, speechless with indignation, that there is no rest at the bottom of humiliation. (Anyone who thinks there is should take note.)

The deadline for leaving with a bourgeois standard of living intact had come and gone, and now we were hungry much of the time. Daily, Suzanne would lead foraging expeditions to the *praia*. We usually got there just ahead of the cold, smashing tide, and I would slip and stumble, trying to keep up with her there. She followed what seemed to be her unerring intuitions, dodging the homecoming waves, running lightly over the wet, sharp rocks, and finding the hardy clam beds tucked under the muck of the oil-slicked, wintry beach.

Over the (as I came to regard it) *inexcusable* whiteness of my feet and legs was spreading a crimson network of abrasions. Coming to meet these, threading their way up from my hands and my arms, was another such fine, crimson network, acquired from scrubbing the household laundry over the cold, stone tub in the kitchen. And there were other bruises that I had, purple and swollen, from our stone floor, which would be given me to wash with an old, frayed rag. But it was never enough. It didn't atone. Suzanne could still detect what she termed "resentment" under the very helmet of penitential intentions with which I armored my face.

One day Isabella brought down a "Letter to an Unknown Landlady." It was from my mother, penned in her long and elegant hand, in rather fervent French, and it was adjuring Isabella to give whatever information she could as to my whereabouts.

Frankly, Isabella did not see how she could very well ignore a mother's plea of that kind, which I obligingly translated for her.

Frankly, I did not see how she could either, and I hoped that she wouldn't, but that was before Suzanne had rendered her verdict.

Certainly she could ignore a mother's plea, said Suzanne. That is, she could if she wanted to keep us as tenants. An ordinary mother would have been a horse of a different color. But the mother of Abigail . . . (and here she painted a picture that was sheer calumny and that I will not dignify by reproducing here, not even for the record, so-called).

I do not know how persuasive Isabella found these arguments, as seconded by my docile, faintly smiling, bobbings of the head, but she was sufficiently "persuaded" to have left the letter with Suzanne, when she retreated to her attic.

It was this episode that convinced Suzanne that more drastic measures would have to be taken, and my most subliminal thoughts and gestures controlled and repressed, if I was to be kept from waving a whole rescue party over this way while her back was turned. I was to stop any more such letters from arriving in Sonho, to forestall any visits from friends or relatives, and to block any inquiries coming to me from third parties, however remote. She did not care how I got that difficult assignment done, she said.

She would judge by the results.

There was nothing for it, or so I felt, but to write the kind of letter that would keep them all away, a letter violent enough to cut off all direct inquiries for several months, though nothing—not even the most appalling letter from me—could have done that job indefinitely. (We *were* a Jewish family, after all.)

"And another thing, Abigail," Suzanne added in the same connection. "You are going to write a letter to *my* mother, with a Full Confession of everything that you've done to me. And you're going to sign it. I'm not taking any chances on your parents and their jew-lawyer getting here and me having to fight it out all alone."

"I'm not signing anything." As long as nothing was *signed*, this whole thing might remain, in the view of the record keepers, a mere bad dream.

"Oh, yes, you will. I'm gonna make you."

I shook my head again, this time with finality. "You can beat me till you're blue in the face," I said interestingly. "You cannot make me sign an incriminating paper, Suzanne."

"You don't know me, Abigail." From her now familiar perch, on the high, high kitchen sink counter, her blue-jeaned knees up in sharp peaks, and her sandaled, small-boned, brown heels flat on the counter top, she grinned down at me in icy triumph. "I'll break your glasses."

The violence that I would have had to make use of to stop her was so thoroughly foreign to my nature, and above all to my nature in this situation that I did not understand, that I was, to all intents and purposes, without defenses here. If she wanted to do it, I knew she could. And how could I read a train schedule without them? Or pack? Or get safely to the railroad station? And, if I just went "outside" this house—to the wharves, or the praça, or the *guarda* (the local precinct)—for help, with what words could I frame an appeal?

Unless one is simply an animal or can function like one, one cannot take a single step in this world without the words for it. I had no words, any more. She had taken the words out of my mouth. That's all.[1]

"It's only fair for you to write that confession, Abigail," Suzanne went on in more cajoling accents. "Because it's true. You did try to murder me. And I have to have that protection. Because I am engaged here in the work of Gnostic Christian healing. And every malicious slander, in the human, is ready to strike at that work. And my mother is not vindictive. She is a Gnostic. She knows er-ror can be healed. She's not likely to use it *unfairly* against you."

My sole option wore a "kind" face, and I put it on therefore. With the letter in her hand now, she could wave me down a road with no turning. So it was that we entered into her long, cold "spring of healing."

We would spend the cold days like hedgehogs waiting for the weather to turn, under frozen sheets, sleeping off nights of interrogation that—even if they chanced to turn up no misfit thoughts in me—still filled me with speechless dread. Suzanne never seemed to get tired of rooting under the deepest motives that I could offer for my past misdeeds, real or imagined, or of withholding any but her most provisional of absolutions.

If it was purity that I had persistently sought in my life, then I was still, I supposed, living that life *now* . . .

We were subsisting on the remnant of my traveler's checks, on the money that I had kept in Barclay's Bank in London for my return voyage (and a very clever, British-sounding letter Suzanne had composed over my signature to get it, too), on some money that Suzanne had written to Chauncey to "borrow," and on the sum of one hundred dollars that my sister—inspired to try a separate approach—had forwarded in return for some Gnostic brochures and renewal of contact with me.

By May of that year, my sister wrote me again, with the news that she would be landing in Lisbon. Her friends in the literary marketplaces, where she worked, had arranged for a European errand or two, letters attesting to which she had had photostated and sent on to Sonho, to meet the scrutiny of whichever one of the two of us might turn out to be the boss and the paranoid one.

Aside from a letter from the U.S. consulate to the effect that their man had spoken with me by the town telephone and that I had seemed well and competent at the time (with Suzanne praying beside me in the booth I had parried his call with practiced, if somewhat overcooked, gentility), our parents had not heard from me or about me since the end of November. And what they *had* heard, at the end of November, had not been reassuring. So my sister's errand was to get me back, if she could; and, if she could not, at least to find out all she could.

As may well be imagined, that interview was not an enjoyable one. It took place in our little hotel room in Lisbon and the modern café on the Avenida da Liberdade. Suzanne had wanted three things from my sister, wanted them badly enough to have steered herself and me all the way up to Lisbon for the rendezvous: She had wanted my sister, first, to publish her novel; second, to begin to adopt Suzanne's Gnostic mind set. And she wanted one other thing.

When my sister saw that her own first objective was unrealizable, she got about her remaining options in Lisbon: beginning discussion with some rather concerned and humane American personnel at the consulate and elsewhere, and getting off a long and informative letter to our parents back at home. "They still want something from me," she wrote in that letter. "I am not sure what it is."

What it was, was money.

"No," said my sister, most reasonably as it happens. "You want my 'healing,' and you want my money. You can't have my money." Nor did she promise much about Suzanne's manuscript, which she pronounced "not ready," in her (quite accurate) judgment. And she was noncommittal on the score of the Gnostic doctrines.

All in all, I would have to call it a laudable effort. It was truthful, shrewd, and carried through with sisterly feeling.

The next initiatives proceeded from my father and mother together. They had come to London for a conference. (On parapsychology, in fact, where my father read a paper decrying it.) They sent me an airline ticket and an invitation. I sent back a Gnostic brochure, a letter signed "cordially" (at Suzanne's dictation), and their ticket. They came down to Lisbon with my sister and sent me repeated telegrams, urging me to meet them there, or to call them.

I did nothing. I was under Suzanne's heavy guard and orders. At least, I thought, she won't destroy them, since they *have* stayed away. Before they emplaned for the States, they came to think of me as rather deadweight, and to explore with the embassy the possibilities for my being lifted out of there by main force. For the present, however, there was only a mutual agreement to keep in touch on all hands.

Throughout most of the following impoverished summer, Suzanne still supposed that we could become self-supporting in Portugal. Her diverse enterprises—to sell paintings by mail, mine *and hers* now, to sell fudge in the shops, to sell fragments of English to the children of tourists—had not yet paid our rent, but they had just about paid for our shopping excursions in Sonho. Isabella and Alberto were worriedly renting to us "on credit" by now, but in the evenings Isabella would donate some fish to us from the daily haul.

Summer came and went. Then Thanksgiving. We received a notification from the town hall that we were to present ourselves there. Our oft-renewed visas would not be reissued to us, we were told.

Ah-hah! I thought privately, at once resigned to the prospect of getting mustered out because the war had been declared over by powers that even *she* could not control.

Meanwhile, Suzanne was doing her Gnostic affirmations, as I could by now recognize from watching her, while she read the notice impassively. "Isto não é nada," she reassured the rather seedy young clerks who were perched in their cages. "Nos ficamos. [We are staying.] Não é preciso vistos."

Their young, civil servants' heads bobbed as they repeated, nodding to each other, "Visas are not necessary!"

Letters followed, from her or at her dictation, to the director at the Gnostic Headquarters, the ambassador at the U.S. embassy, the head of the widely feared PIDE (Policía Internacional e Defesa do Estado), and the dictator, Salazar, himself. The letters explained that the country could hardly dispense with our "healings." By the time they had all gone out, our visas had indeed expired, and we were in Portugal without papers.

Around Christmas, there was also a separate visit by my mother, to Sonho itself. It began with a war of words with Suzanne, a war that I watched, largely in silence, and that my mother seemed to me to be losing. But she was not one for losing.

Understanding the hopelessness of effecting a separation between my mind and will and Suzanne's, she began to take substitute measures in secret. First, she built a reliable contact with Isabella and her husband, climbing their attic stair and speaking a patchwork Romance language of their common devising. Out of that came a correspondent, the French-speaking village schoolteacher, through whom Isabella could keep her informed of future days. "Whatever they cost you," she promised Isabella, "I will pay."

"Do not worry," Isabella had replied in kind. "I will feed them. And, if they leave, I will tell you where they went."

As long as she stayed in the village, my mother made friends with the local shopkeepers, who reported to her that they themselves did not like Suzanne. She saw the mayor, who assured her that he would do his best, as someone who was also a father, to see that we got deported during the time of her visit, so that we could still be jostled in her jointly protective direction.

(As I see from the letters she wrote home and wrote me afterwards, she was trying to get through a wall whose minute construction even *she* couldn't fathom or penetrate. She didn't guess how afraid I was and thought me accessible to persuasion—a volunteer, not a captive. She saw that I was not myself—in gesture, in voice, in the eyes—and that I was "emaciated." But she thought that the smiles and expressions of contentment were my own. She thought I was merely "dominated." She didn't know that I was terrorized. Or demoralized beyond recapture. She didn't know the history. And it wasn't in her to have guessed it.)

The extraordinary courage with which she faced me, as realistically as she knew how to, and faced the situation with full realism, even buying us yards of wool for Isabella to make up into skirts, is what comes home to me now as I go through her letters. The last one that she wrote home from Sonho was the darkest. In it she said: "And I don't know whether she will ever come back to her normal self. That is: I don't know at present. Just as life brought on this calamity, it can remove it. We must hold on to each other and go on, in work and strength. I'm consoled that she's alive. For where there is life, there is hope. *Our great love* may have the force of a miracle. So far as I can judge, its work cannot be immediate."

After she left the village of Sonho, she walked in tears down a Lisbon street, there meeting the wife of a high-ranking Israeli diplomat, and cried to her, not to be comforted (like Rachel, my mother's biblical namesake), for one of the children.[2] At the end, the U.S. consul promised to keep her informed and to do what he could to prevent us from being left, penniless and without papers of any kind, on a pathless edge of the Spanish border. (That was still Franco Spain.)

Thus she let the environs of Iberia that we occupied resonate with a mother's anxiety and a family's resources.

After she'd gone, the mayor asked to see us.

"I promise you," said Suzanne to him, "that you will see the power of God here in Sonho."

"I hope so," the mayor riposted to her, unsmiling.

At about that time, Suzanne began to compose letters, barbarous epistles with crazy spacing and raw, alien language, that demanded money in exchange for the "healings" of their recipients. If I reread any of those letters today, some of which went out over my signature, I am as appalled as I would be if I were to look directly at the face of Medusa. To read them is to feel one's sensibilities turned to stone. Nor is it possible to answer with precision the question of whether I did or didn't write some of them. "I" did. She didn't dictate every word. But I had been wholly invaded, wholly taken over, frozen, benumbed, deactivated as a personality. Sometimes the letters were cosigned. And at other times they bore her signature alone. When they went out to friends of mine, or to people in my world, they would bear along their coldly fictional tides of malice some microcrumb of recognizable fact, witness to my shadowy presence somewhere behind this appalling tangle.

One such letter she sent to my mother, primly signing it "Miss Suzanne Pines."

"I was so happy," my father would one day say to me, "when I got that letter. Because I knew I *had* the little beast. Right in the trap. I had it copied, for worldwide distribution."

It is evident

went his letter of May 6, 1967, to the U.S. consul in Lisbon, going out the same day that her letter arrived and enclosing a photostated copy,

> that my daughter is in the hands of a dangerously insane person.
>
> I urgently and respectfully request that the authorities be immediately alerted to give my daughter every possible protection against the possibility of violence, until she can be returned to the United States.
>
> The [Pines] letter is, I believe, an attempt, however insane, at extortion. I am turning the letter over to our attorney.

The embassy replied with its consent (informal, to be sure) to intervene. And a request went out to the local precinct to have me placed under "informal arrest."

"I sense that we're on the verge of a real breakthrough," my brainwasher was saying to me, concurrently, in (happily unconscious) synchronicity. And, with her own perfectly uncanny sense of timing, she promptly sent me up to the guarda to apply for drivers' licenses for us both, in stages, the first stage being the application for the learners' permits.

(I still wished I could see myself as "God" apparently saw me. How the heck, I shrugged privately, could I learn to *drive* if I could not see the road? Although Suzanne had received the inner command to dispose of our glasses some weeks before, the "breakthrough" to letter-perfect eyesight still had not been made. And, in the market, where she would also send me out unaccompanied to "buy" groceries on credit, I had to be eyeball to eyeball with a lemon if I wanted to distinguish it from my own hand.)[3]

So, on that afternoon in May of 1967, I set off nervously for the precinct, ducking under the arch of the smaller, wedge-shaped praça, now emptied of its biweekly produce and stalls, and feeling my way with my feet up the steps to the guarda, stone steps that were subjoined to one outside wall of the castelo's ruins. A sleepy guard, sprawled picturesquely on the stone stairway, stood up as I passed and scrambled to the door above me, to intercept my impatient raps with his own.

After an interval, a uniformed cop unlatched both the inside screen door and the outside wood one and bowed me in. "How would I go about getting a permit for learning to drive?" I asked him, in the tones of exaggerated gentility that I had assumed recently.

He disappeared through a door on the far end of what looked like the recreation room—from the Ping-Pong table just dimly discerned I could imagine that nights at the guarda must be long and dull—and was back a few minutes later. Would I please step this way?

Trying not to make any unwonted sound in this dark place, I followed him to a rear office, which looked private, where his lieutenant, uniformed in more heavily braided cap and green-banded jacket pockets, was seated. At a broad, dark, gleaming desk. "Yes?" said the lieutenant.

I leaned my fingertips forwardly on his desk top and stated my errand.

"I see. Very good." The lieutenant began leafing through stuff that might be the requisite folders and forms. Had we ever acquired, at any time, a police record? he wanted to know. Routinely.

I laughed, with a suggestion of broad good cheer that the lieutenant did not seem to share. Another policeman seemed to be waiting at attention by the lieutenant's side, and meanwhile some brother officers were crowding in.

They are crowding in to see me, the poor dears, I thought, rounding my shoulders a little, so that my dark-blue, wash-and-dry T-shirt from Marks and Spencer's would fall forward of my brassiereless and undernourished front. (To Suzanne it had been revealed recently that underwear was only for those whose thoughts were impure.)

"To get a learner's permit is not difficult," said the lieutenant. "You will merely have to sign a few papers, which will in turn enable us to send a requisition through to Setubal. And of course you know there are letters of reference that we will ask you to supply?"

Since the Gnostic rules of the road assured us that all our needs would be met in abundance, I thought it superfluous to tell the lieutenant that we had no way, humanly speaking, to get a letter of reference.

I half turned, ready to go.

"Menina." The braided lieutenant was speaking again. "You have borrowed, as I have heard, a typewriter from the gas man. And he has been asking for it. Why have you never returned it?"

Uh oh. "Oh, that typewriter was not borrowed. It was a gift. From the gas man. For us."

Authoritatively. "I want to see it now. Bring it here."

"But why should I? That typewriter is ours. I don't ask you for your uniform." I smiled at him unflinchingly.

A heavy official grin creased a few faces. The lieutenant appeared to be shaking off something. "You do not understand, menina. I have the right to commandeer anything in this town that I want, right now. If I wanted to, I could send an officer to your front door, and I assure you that that officer would get the typewriter."

"No, you could not. Not if he came to take what was *ours*."

Quietly the lieutenant reached for the black phone beside him and dialed. "Hello, Antonio," he said. "Would you come to the guarda right away." He hung up. The gas man had given no argument.

Behind me, the heretofore formless shuffle of policemen had shaped itself into a lineup of about nine, standing in the at-ease position, booted heel to heel, between me and the exit.

This was alarming.

Speaking of officers who might be sent to one's door, a jowly cop, who had once resolved in my favor a deadlock over my buying on "credit" at the butcher shop, spoke up now. Why, he wanted to know, had we refused to open our door to him on a night last week when, with a representative from Setubal, he had banged on it for so long, vainly?

"Because God did not tell us to," I smiled at him nacreously.

"And why," chimed in the frowning lieutenant, as he tapped with waiting fingers on his broad desk, "did you send those letters to persons in Sonho?"

It is unwise to bore a cop, I thought, and the real explanation for our letters was a little obscure even for me at that time. I was thumbing through my pocket edition of the Gnostic Manual, looking for some remarks that might fly here, when a near voice from the grey line suggested a few: "The bakery lady told one of our men that she'd heard that the letters were for the *good* of people . . ."

I smiled in relief and turned to the young speaker. "Look," I said to him confidentially, "no one—who was not crazy—would *choose* to live in this hole for two years, right?"

Grins.

It was strictly Suzanne's routine. But I'd seen her work it on people. So I went on with it, having long ago lost my *own* words. "Now, we have lots of money, and our families have great importance in America. So if we buy here on credit, it is because God tells us to—because we have healed many people here in Sonho— and God wants people to pay for their healings, and in that way become more pure. You see, God is Life. And those who are obedient to God"—here I raised the red leather book above the lieutenant's head—"will go higher. Whereas those who do not obey"—I lowered one hand beneath the book—"will die, because they do not follow Life." I shrugged at the simplicity of it.

All this stage business, including the shrug, I'd watched Suzanne produce for the benefit of the bakery lady.

"This is simple loucura," muttered the lieutenant, looking down, and using the Portuguese word for craziness.

Feeling the attention of my audience flagging, I swung back hard. "It is very easy to laugh," I said, "but it is even more easy to die. Since we have been in Sonho, there have been lots more deaths than usual, is that not so?"

They reflected uncertainly. Cops are powerful, to be sure. But they are not all-powerful.

"That is the work of God in driving out er-ror." I checked into the book again.

"That bobbing in and out of the book is beginning to irritate me," complained the braided lieutenant.

Oh, I thought, if *only* I could leave! But, in the paragraphs I flipped open to, God seemed to be adamant. No breaking and running. Besides, at nine to one, I wasn't likely to make it. Still, panic was loud.

The braided lieutenant lit up a cigarette.

"You should not smoke," I parried quickly. "It is not good."

I reached for the full ashtray on his desk. The lieutenant stood up in alarm. "Where can I empty this?" I said, grimacing.

A full ashtray had always been something of which I could disapprove with conviction. Even before I'd met Suzanne.

In haste, he signaled an adjutant to take the *cinzeiro* out of my hand and empty it for me.

But, by now, I had gotten some limited mobility inside his office. Moral advantage, and one took a step. One step at a time, and one could walk. Perhaps.

In comic, stumbling, male concern, the gas man was now walking into their midst.

"Explain to them, Antonio, what you told Suzanne, that you gave her the typewriter!" I called out instantly, giving way to some want of faith in the Gnostic divinity's total control of the situation.

"*Gave* it!" he exploded. "Não! I didn't give it to anybody. I *lent* it to these meninas. For a few days. And for weeks I can't get it back from them!"

The cops shuffled from foot to foot on the lineup, in what looked to me like grinning recognition that their lieutenant had ambushed me.

"You are a liar, Antonio! You told Suzanne that she could have it, at your last meeting with her." (So Suzanne had told me, anyway, though I guessed that his acquiescence might have been partly unspoken.)

"*What* meeting with Suzanne? Não—I never—"

"*Yes*—the meeting where you tried to embrace her!"

"Ohhhh—não."

"Yes! She came back from you with her hair all rumpled, and I asked her, 'What happened, Suzanne?' and she told me!" (She certainly had told me.)

"These are fantasies," muttered the lieutenant irately.

I didn't like the sound of that word. It was one you applied the world over to frustrated females.

"*No*. These are not fantasies. The typewriter is ours if Antonio says it is, or if he does not say it is. It is ours in any case because God gave it to us!"

At last I was no longer hiding behind Human Opinion and its views. Perhaps God (Suzanne's God) would be more forthcoming now and come up with a rescue.

"Look," said the braided lieutenant, with all his insinuating pride of command, "you are in Portugal, you know! This is not the

United States." (He had certainly been once or twice to the Cinema Explorador.) "Here I do what *I* want."

Once again, it looked as if "God" were forcing the issue. Equal at least to his arrogance (or to the fear behind it), I jabbed with my middle finger at his beribboned chest repeatedly, saying in the gangboy style I had watched Suzanne imitate in her brother, "Lis-sen to me now!" ("Lis-sen muh-thuh fuck-uh" was how it had gone in the original, and in 1967 those were not household words. Not where I came from.) "None of you here knows what power is!" I went on, borrowing more and more liberally from Suzanne's coffer of rhetorical devices. "Antonio thinks this policeman has it—or that one." I pointed jovially to each, while they smiled eagerly back at their teacher. "So *he* thinks, with each additional policeman, five, seven, nine, you have more power! And *you* think"—here I pivoted to jab the lieutenant again—"that your superiors have power. But none of you is right. Pow-er is di-vine prin-ci-ple"—I punctuated each syllable with a jab—"here and in A-mer-i-ca!"

The lieutenant paused briefly. Outbragged.

"And you, Antonio," I said reproachfully. "God will punish your ingratitude."

"My *ingratitude*," he stammered indignantly to the policemen. "I gave them a heater, in exchange for a painting!" A faint gesture declared the painting's value to the gas man. "For months they owe me for the back gas. I lent them, for a few days, my typewriter, that I need."

"We have worked, for days, for your healings . . . of scrofula . . ."

"Scrofula!" He grimaced.

"And is it nothing that today you walk like a man, whereas before you weaved and bobbed"—I did an imitation—"like a serpent?"

There was a semblance of shocked silence, into which I quickly swung with, "If you are obedient, Antonio, you won't have to die."

"I won't have to die!" He laughed, with true, Jewish laughter. "So I'll die later."

"No. You'll never die."

"I'll never die?"

Consternation in the cops' assembly.

A conclave of cops gathered round the gas man. The line shortly reformed.

I checked the, by now, enigmatic book. And looked up. I had had it.

"God says I may go now," I said, with spectacularly demure, feminine pride. And walked, head aloft, straight toward the dead center of the locked grey line—which broke, a foot from me, into two lines, through which I passed unscathed. And kept on going. And crossed the rec room. And could not see how to open the screen door. And heard the lieutenant's voice behind me. And heard a rapid tread of boots coming up. And did not look round.

A young officer was at my side. He unlatched the screen door and ushered me blinking into the daylight, with a graceful smile of unforgettable chivalry—how brief!—that belonged to no world that ever was.

But how did I get from the long, dark nights of "confession" to the delusion that "we" (under Suzanne's terrifyingly implacable leadership) were effecting "healings" by buying on "credit," or by sending out letters of the kind indicated; or to the delusion that those who were "healed" in that way had also entered into an apocalyptic, deathless condition? Easy. The "confession" itself was a delusion. Once I'd surrendered to delusion in that all-important respect of my moral identity, other delusions could be let in—to keep the original delusion company, as it were.

This happened by steps and stages. What steps? What stages? These need not be chronicled exhaustively, it seems to me. They had their own weird inner logic, all "following" from the original *suspension of my understanding* that I was being horribly, wackily, and unfairly abused. I had been made to confess to something I had not done and then made to "atone" for what I hadn't done by going along with conduct that had rendered me unrecognizable to myself, and to society. I'd been converted into a social outlaw. And each step and stage of this process bound me closer to a battering, terrorizing brainwasher, as it was intended to do.

Was I unusually weak, or weak-minded? *I don't think so.* That's the funny thing. (I could point out some parallels between my reactions then, and the reactions of a larger society to similar pressures now. I won't, but I could.) What then is the difference, if any, between the way I was then and the way I am now? The difference is that, now, I try harder not to play cards with people who cheat at cards. Whether they cheat from the left, or from the center, or from the right. And there are certain games that define themselves to me now at the outset as cheating games. So (if I spot them in time), I won't play with anyone at those games.

What is the point of all this? The point is this: *One can suffer, being innocent.* And I was suffering very harshly. "But"—so the objections will run, from the reductionists of varied persuasions and the hyper-Augustinians of every type and degree—"weren't you 'enjoying it' all *unconsciously*? Wasn't it bringing out your hidden

talents—talents as a con artist, talents as a street person, talents
as a hustler? Look at that scene in the guarda! It's rich, girl. Rich.
Don't tell me you weren't secretly in your element there."

I was not secretly in my element there. I was very frightened. I
was nearly helpless. I was maneuvering on no basis, with nothing
to guide me, no place to go, nothing to look back on, no dignity and
no self-respect. I was living from hand to mouth and speaking out
of desperate cunning lines that were not my own. What I said was
bluff, and I knew it. It was false, and, if I didn't quite "know" it,
that was because I no longer knew how to "know" anything with
conviction. It would be a tremendous mistake to confuse the com-
edy of the scene in the guarda as recalled from the platform of the
narrator that I now am, with the experience of actually living that
scene. The pleasures of living as I live now infinitely surpass the
panic and desperation of my life then. I was suffering. And (as anyone will recall who takes the trouble to remember what happened,
in sequence), I was innocent.

Once again, and all together now, hyper-Augustinians of the left
and the right and the center: *One can suffer, being innocent.*

It was the first day of June, 1967. Suzanne and I had wandered
to the sheer edge of town, the southern cliffs, to look down at the
pounding tides that scoured the bottoms of these palisades.

It was an uncomfortable moment for me, for I knew from experience that I would learn something terrible about my conduct
toward her in a past life, once we got home. We turned to go.

"Suzanne," I said as we walked down the sandy road, "I feel as
if I don't want to go on living any more."

"That's good," she parried indifferently, probably knowing I
wouldn't do it. "So, why don't you jump off the cliffs? You can lead
the parade. Give everyone else in town the right idea."

In a long, single-file column of the condemned, she had seen
that the villagers were supposed to drop from these southern cliffs,
drop out of the present millennium, falling one by one to the rock-
cut Atlantic below while the sky glowed in that green of apocalyptic
extremity that seemed more and more to streak it with each passing day.

"Suzanne"—I waved my arms in an awkward way as I walked
beside her, for when I missed my cue in the great script of the
apocalypse, there were no other cues that I could hear now, "I can't
even hear God's *voice* any more!"

"Abigail," she looked at me impatiently. "You have to realize that
you and I are just not that important. Even when you can't hear

God's voice, you can still do God's Work." Regretfully, she shook her head. "That's Human Personality you're still involved in. What you must learn to see is that all that really matters in the slightest is God's Plan, the bee-eauty of *His* Plan."

I strained my imagination to take in the beauty of the plan but could do no better than to picture the dark seas, rocking in the earth's cradle.

By the time we were headed home, coming up by the fork in the road beside the castelo, I saw Suzanne hesitating, evidently getting her afternoon plans on her private line. Then she preceded me on the homeward fork, though what God said to her in those last few seconds I never knew. Perhaps she had been advised to let my ambivalence, which seemed so incorrigible, *appear*, in some outward form. For, as we neared Isabella's house, we spied the dark-suited, grim, and unmistakable figure of an agent of the PIDE standing a few paces forward of our front door.

Oh, dear, I thought. The treacherous undertow of the unexpunged Beliefs from my old life must have brought him to the surface. He was right between us and the door. Where could we go? It was too late to back out now.

Chapter Eighteen

Beginning Again

Far from backing out, we picked up speed instead, went by the man, and were just about to unlock our upstairs door when a male voice from the landing beneath us called out, "Policía Internacional!"

"Donde?" was Suzanne's genteelly ingratiating inquiry.

"De Lisboa."

"Oh, *do* come in!" she gushed, with her engaging overeagerness.

Oh, dear. What a time for him to show up! And my thoughts so stagnant and swamped.

After he'd written the consul, and acting through the family attorney, my father had retained an able, well-connected Lisbon lawyer. Still, his "worldwide distribution" of activated concern was making its way over sea and air at its own not-to-be-hurried pace. All of the strategies that were suggested and outlined by the Lisbon lawyer were slow, arduous to execute, prohibitively costly, and cloudy, legally.

In the end, not much could be hoped for without cooperation in some form from the Policía Internacional e Defesa do Estado, the PIDE. That they knew how to make people disappear was incontestable. Could they also perhaps recover someone? And might the State Department be moved to intervene from Washington, as a "matter between governments"?

Minor agreements would be lined up and then lapse. Bureaucratic goodwill and lethargy would collide in the same office. New

York psychiatrists would take fees to think it all over, ponder the letters, and then refuse to endorse high-level efforts at intervention. So they had to proceed, those efforts, without psychiatric endorsement.

But it was all so slow. The directrice of the Commonwealth House in London at length expressed her very great concern, wrote Suzanne's mother, and even tried to contact Suzanne's Gnostic Christian counselor, who was then discovered to have died some months before. Friends of my mother, in Paris and Switzerland, wrote eloquently, letters full of somber and practical reflections. Friends of mine, some of whom I had not seen in years, were calling home transcontinentally to voice anxiety across the shrinking spaces. To go through these letters now, as I have just been doing, is to walk through a vast wave of love. And to see how slowly, very slowly, the vast army of the bourgeoisie was gathering the clanking chain mail of its superior resources.

But the bourgeoisie, like God, is very slow.

Meanwhile, the mistress of our house was ushering this new and distinguished caller into our denuded living room and urging him, with a preposterously polite gesture, to take a chair. He started to, but, as he perceived the meninas continuing to stand, the gentlemanly agent was soon on his feet again. So we three remained standing around the table, which had been pushed all the way to the window today, and, from where Suzanne and I were standing, we could take in the familiar ramparts of the castelo, and the Atlantic in the westerly light.

The agent who faced us was of medium height, as I could see, neither thickset nor tapered in the waist, with the ochre-complected, thin-lipped, soft face of the Portuguese bourgeois. He had black hair, combed smoothly off the brow. It was a completely indoor face, with a decided hint of aggression submerged beneath the features. Would the meninas be so kind as to show him their *passaportes*, please?

"Oh, we threw those away!" was Suzanne's thrilling retort.

"Threw them away? But how," the agent looked up in astonishment, "do the meninas, as foreigners, expect to stay in a country without *passaportes*?"

"Oh, that's simple. God told us we'll never need them. Soon, you won't need yours either."

It was a disloyal thought, my present one, that she wasn't telling the literal truth here. She had intended to burn our passports, lest anyone try to deport us before we had moved the Gnostic "breakthrough" to a threshhold beyond "the Belief of the Nation State."

But the fact was, we had not gotten around to it yet, and I knew that our passports were stacked together in the narrow drawer of her night table.

"Soon, I won't need mine?" The agent seemed dumbfounded. "Why, if I traveled abroad without the requisite documents, I would soon be . . ." He made a pessimistic gesture.

"Look," Suzanne broke in impatiently. "What is your name?"

"My name? Why, uh"—with a slight bow—"Sebastião Ribeira."

"We shall call you Sebastião," she answered hospitably, while he looked shy. "I am Suzanne and"—smiling, pointing—"this is Abigail." And there was a happy exchange of bows and nods all round the table. "Listen, Sebastião," she went right to the point now. "I know you are not a fool. You know who we are. The whole PIDE knows us. Now the PIDE wants to know what the message of God is. And God says: He chose you to be sent here, to take His instructions back to Silva Pais who is *chefe* of your organization in Lisbon. You see, I knew you would be here today."

I eyed her doubtfully, while he said the last words over again once more with hesitation. "You knew I would be here today . . ."

"In fact," she continued, smiling, "we have seen your men around Sonho for weeks now."

We had?

"And you know that we knew *why*."

We did?

Sebastião Ribeira grinned, shook his head, and then looked attentively at her, as Suzanne briefly explained what the PIDE had been doing here. What they'd been doing, of course, was *leaning* on the merchants who had failed to cooperate with us! Now Suzanne gave him the ramifications of her plan, for immediate relay to the *chefe* of the PIDE, Silva Pais. There were other ways, further up the line of the economy, that credit could be withheld from the shops that had withheld it from us. Shops *also* ran on credit. We wanted that credit withheld, Suzanne told him. Those shops had to close.

The sense of apocalyptic doom had subsided, but I still felt faintly sick, standing here beside her. What in the world could be troubling me now? Really, it seemed to me that I must be incorrigible. Why could I still *not see* that the particular shops denying us credit deserved to go out of business, or that this agent from the notorious PIDE would do well to destroy his passport? After all that Suzanne and I had been through and risked together, whence these unruly hopes that Sebastião Ribeira would brush her off, instead of proceeding to question her, as he seemed to be doing now, with a sort of enthralled levelheadedness?

"But," said Sebastião realistically, "here is a practical question. Suppose the shopkeepers still demand to be paid? Or your landlord, for example." His eyebrows signaled the pressures he could have told us about from the attic. "That man's been complaining to us for months! Suppose we did what you said. What could we tell him?"

Suzanne smiled puckishly. "Are you the type of man who cries at funerals?"

· "I? No—I don't cry." He giggled, for the emotional dissolve of the Portuguese on those occasions was all too well known.

"Good, because soon, Sebastião, there will be a lot of funerals here."

I smiled agreeably, privately picturing my own case as the object of such a soothing, safely sociable, and conventional rite.

"You see," she continued emphatically, "God says that the man upstairs is a dead man. The same goes for a lot of people in this town who still seem to be walking around. So *let* Alberto complain. It is of no importance. He will not be complaining much longer. Believe me." She nodded her head in her friendliest way.

The agent of the Policía Internacional nodded slowly too, being a man who had heard the authentic language of power before. I thought it brave of him to go on as he did, naïvely probing to extract her real views.

"But what," he inquired of her relentlessly, "does buying on credit have to do with religion? That's what I cannot understand."

With her fine feel for the last protocols of history, Suzanne obligingly sketched it out for him, her head bobbing sociably as she spoke, her forehead almost asparkle in the late-afternoon light, her long neck twisting to include him in—and twisting just as far in the other direction to gesture me out—her whole enigmatic form twisting to refuse to be the body that she was, in the particular, concrete time and place that it was. It was a panoramic view of the secrets of the kingdom that she gave him instead, a kingdom cut back to its minimal number of moving parts.

It was also, as I could not help thinking, a far cry from the candid confessions of two young women delinquent as to credit and visas, remiss as to every other human obligation, and under investigation by the secret police of a foreign dictatorship. Would nothing, on earth or in heaven, stop us?

Suzanne had unfolded a Michelin map of Iberia on the table, to help illustrate her point that what would happen here in Portugal today would happen in those adjacent places tomorrow, and in the whole world soon enough. Noticing how we squinted over it, the agent asked tactfully, "Do the meninas wear glasses?"

"Oh, we threw those out too," she said blithely. "God said that they were not necessary. Already our eyesight is *much* better than it was before!"

I nodded glassily.

"We also threw out our watches." She pointed to our bare wrists. "Now God tells us the time, and we get so much more done!"

He laughed, bowed, and removed his prescription sunshades into the dark case obtruding from his jacket pocket.

I watched, stupefied.

"You were with me," Suzanne pointed out tenderly, "often, in the cycles. When I was George Washington, we fought many campaigns together."

I forced a comradely smile too, while he said, with his honest uncertainty, "I don't know, as to that . . . I have no recollection." I hadn't either, but it was probably just as well. God only knew what I'd done at Valley Forge.

"In fact," Suzanne continued smoothly, "you recognized me from the moment you walked in the door. Only you were saying to yourself, 'What in the world is she doing as a *woman* this time?' "

This seemed to break him up with admissive laughter, laughter in which I tried manfully to join.

With the openness of the true adept, Sebastião persisted in expressing all of his last few remaining doubts. "But," said he to her, "if I obey the orders of God from inside the PIDE, I would probably lose my situation, and"—he shrugged awkwardly—"it would become necessary to find another, and I don't see . . ."

"Oh, yes." She came swiftly back to the point (of the apocalypse). "You probably will. In any case, God says you will soon be working for us. So, have no fear. So will your superiors, unless they want to embark . . . for the other place."

The general laughter ran its course around our table.

"For two years," she admonished the agent gently, "I and Abigail have stayed here alone, working, sacrificing, preparing ourselves to receive this revelation. It was not easy. Often we were cold. Sometimes we were hungry. For months we had no one that we could talk to! We gave up alcohol, coffee, tea, all bad language. We had no money to buy clothes." She brushed her skirt modestly. "I have one suit."

He bowed, smiling. "It is very pretty."

And what about *my* suit, I thought irreverently.

"So, Sebastião, remember, you have nothing to lose."

Hadn't she said that to me, once, long ago? I thought rebelliously.

"Besides, as for buying on credit, God says—the police do that *all the time!*"

Sebastião exploded with suppressed laughter. It looked like she had really hit a home run that time. Now he was shaking his head and checking the wristwatch that he still wore. "I must get back to Lisbon by the five o'clock train so, regretfully, I will have to leave now. But before I go, tell me, what message shall I carry back to Silva Pais?"

"Tell him," Suzanne returned on the instant, "OBEDIENCE OR DEATH."

" 'Ta bem," repeated Sebastião, with a soldierly nod and a twinkle.

After Sebastião had gone, Suzanne suggested to me that we take a turn about the town square. She was clearly cheered up. We stopped in at the modern café, whose proprietor was not glad to see us. However, we did not order anything today. We merely took a table. And they were not prepared to carry us out in full view of the June clientele, on that pleasant, early-summer afternoon.

Five o'clock came and went.

In Lisbon, the interpreter was translating aloud some of the documents, from a file about twelve inches thick, in the office of the subprefect of the PIDE. The file contained our letters. It itemized what we had bought on credit. It recorded all we had said. And to whom. And where. And when. The subprefect listened, almost impassively, to the recitation and the translation. There was (as my mother was later to recall) a faint suggestion of complacency and corpulence shading his otherwise indistinct, ward heeler's features. It was a face that could on occasion be cruel. At present, it was polite and even courtly, as he explained through the interpreter that a high-ranking agent was already in Sonho. He then outlined the plan.

My mother, in a short speech in French, expressed her abiding appreciation of the humane attitude that the PIDE had taken toward a family in distress. As she began to speak, the U.S. consul lifted his eyebrows and nodded at her, with a brief, enigmatic glance of approval.

The subprefect replied directly to her in French. He was a bachelor, he said amiably, but he had nephews and nieces. He understood and he sympathized with family feeling.

Not long afterward, when the consul, the Portuguese lawyer, and the parents who had been carried back to Lisbon by the aforementioned family feeling turned on the corner in front of the PIDE to shake hands, the Portuguese lawyer pronounced it "a major triumph!"

At that very hour, in the modern café in Sonho where we were still sitting idly, Suzanne had decided once again to give me the benefit of the doubt and suspend her ever pending condemnations. "The only thing that I can't stand is disloyalty, and even there—"

Even there stood Sebastião Ribeira, with one of the taller cops from the guarda. "I missed my train," he fibbed sadly.

"It is clear," Suzanne whispered to me in English, "that he's been conferring with the cops in the guarda about us. And they've told him to cooperate, or the whole guarda will break his ass."

"Boa tarde!" Suzanne greeted him and the big cop genially.

Sebastião Ribeira, meanwhile, had been bobbing and bowing like a prissy schoolboy, till his great, grey-uniformed chaperon left him there. Then, alone at last, the agent pulled out the empty chair at our table, took his seat next to Suzanne, and sociably ordered lemonades for all three of us, which the waiter was now in haste to bring.

Out of the corner of my eye I observed that the June patrons—townspeople and tourists from all parts of Portugal—were getting up with great promptitude and emptying the café. Here was this grand coalition of all powers coming together, temporal and spiritual, and no doubt that was just what they could not bear to sit helplessly by and watch. Suzanne and Sebastião were joking about it, between sips from their long straws as, in a gracious and desultory way, they accommodated their conversation to these many signs, big or tiny, of the inexorable Gnostic "breakthrough." And I chimed in as best I could, all the while wishing that I could summer alone in the Alps or, better yet, that an avalanche would fall on the New Jerusalem.

"I am forced to stay over in Sonho tonight, and it is very depressing to dine alone," Sebastião was saying now. "Would the meninas do me the honor of dining with me, at my *pensão* this evening?"

Suzanne accepted at once for us both, with real feminine grace, which may be the sentiment that such things are due one. It was a sentiment that I could by no manner of means conjure at that point.

Dinner was a convivial and homelike affair. Later, Suzanne took Sebastião and me down our old, and to me still hateful, walk to the pier. The intelligence agent was feeling his way in the dark, without glasses, and murmuring over and over how grateful he was, what good fortune it was, to have met two such agreeable, sympathetic meninas, and to be rescued in this way from the grim solitude of a hotel room in a strange town, and to be strolling with these meninas on this picturesque moonlit path—such an agreeable contrast to the doldrums of his usual Lisbon life!

Aside from his evident willingness to go the whole way with the "breakthrough," Sebastião was now the very picture of a staid Portuguese bourgeois, faintly old-maidish and very much the gentleman, although a gentleman under orders.

As we were bidding each other goodnight at the fork of the road, he promised to come to see us once more, and treat us to breakfast one last time, before he'd be catching his morning train. He would be by at nine, he promised.

It was later than that before he showed up the next day. (There is a different feel to midmorning, and also we could tell by where the sun was.) When we let him in, he looked preoccupied and not inclined to infuse our greetings with the latecomer's usual, expected, polite apologies, though he did murmur something in that general line.

What followed was a typically genial social hour, at the sheer edge of nothingness. I had nothing to say, nothing to object, and nothing to suggest or imply. There was nothing I owned, nothing I could look forward to, and nothing that I could fall back on.

After breakfast, we got up, at Sebastião's suggestion, to stroll slowly around the labyrinthine back alleys of Sonho, bleached as they were in the morning sunlight, till we wended our way back to the castelo's ramparts, proceeding oh, so slowly, toe and heel, toe and heel, for he was such a slow, well-mannered, bourgeois *flâneur*, taking the morning off from work.

Far below the castelo's ramparts the sea stretched, green and beautiful, where we chatted penultimately by the stone turrets about the future extending before us, and the daylight seemed to grow nakeder.

It was time at last for Sebastião to walk us back to our house and to say his goodbyes. "Let us," he suggested suddenly, "take one more turn up the hill." And so we dragged on a bit farther along this sandy roadway, which cut past the town hall and the mayor's office. It was the road that abutted the southern wall of sea cliffs, where the dream of this village's life was supposed to be ended.

A young man loomed in our path and was drawing Sebastião aside, with official unsociability. Although he was dressed in a light-grey suit that looked to be several cuts cheaper than Sebastião's, the tone that he used to delay our escort was abrupt and authoritarian. "These meninas," he said audibly, "will be required in Lisbon."

"Must it be now?" objected our courtly Sebastião.

"Agora!" the young man repeated.

"On the orders of whom?" insisted Sebastião, who outranked this young man.

"On the orders of Silva Pais!" said the agent. At which Sebastião argued no more.

I glanced back toward the house, our round-cornered grey house that suddenly showed no curious face at the curtains and gave off no sound. Instinctively, I must have reached toward the air behind us, as if to grasp for our few things. In half a second, soundlessly, an immense, grey, shining limousine had drawn up between us and the road. A woman with a giant face was standing behind me. She was speaking very loudly. She was edging up against the passenger doors. She had such fearsome proportions! How could I ever look up at her? How had they moved so quickly? Had Sebastião by any chance complied with them ahead of time?

"Our things," remarked Suzanne.

"Estão dentro!" came a booming, second female voice. In the capacious rear of the van it looked now as if another large woman were sprawled, who was pointing to a cluster of objects beside her—my much-traveled, moldy hatbox, Suzanne's satchel, and our album of paintings! During *breakfast*, all that work had been done? And how many eyes were now watching, behind the fluttering curtains?

"Well, let's go," shrugged Sebastião, still standing beside us, in his dark suit.

I looked uncertainly at my spiritual guide.

Suzanne, smiling with martyred poise, brushed at her suit collar, as if to smooth into place her imaginary fur wrap, now slightly mouse gnawed. Like an iron-willed chaperon, she bent her head and arranged the seating, sliding between me at one window and Sebastião, whom she gestured to sit at the other. "Where are we going?" she asked him, when we were all three inside.

"To Silva Pais, directly!"

"Okay," she agreed, adding in reproof, as the limousine backed hastily to the castelo and rolled up the eastern side of town, toward the Lisbon-Alentejo highway, "but with the plan of returning—no?"

"Oh, yes," our good Sebastião assured her. "Probably this evening. A meeting with Silva Pais was inevitable, sooner or later. Only I did not think that it would come *now*. For me, this car is a convenience, since otherwise I would have had to take the train. And for you, of course, it is a lift, save that the circumstances are not the most agreeable."

No, not the most agreeable. The opaque partition between us and the driver had rolled up mechanically, and the opaque side windows behind their inner steel mesh were up likewise. It was, unmistakably, the car to take you on your last ride. Only green-cheeked Sebastião still looked familiar, clasping and unclasping his hands nervously. The massive, mascaraed matrons who were sprawled behind us in the seatless rear of the van—decidedly not the most

agreeable. But beside me there was still Suzanne seated, and on
her inspired alchemy depended our last chances for transforming
this massive steel trap into her promised royal coach and four.

We were many kilometers out of Sonho before we stopped at a
roadside restaurant, where Sebastião got out. Perhaps he was telephoning Silva Pais? Or telephoning someone else for instructions?
He was not his own man, after all. Suzanne leaned forward to open
the windows.

"Não abra! Não abra!" the matrons chorused.

"I will do some mental work to make them sorry," she said to me
meaningfully, and also to Sebastião when he came back with some
beer and cold sandwiches for the women. Immediately, he ordered
the partition and side windows rolled down.

"Quem manda aqui sou eu," said Sebastião, assuring us that he
was the one in command here.

We both smiled in relief, though it felt odd to be meeting the
astonished eyes of an elderly Portuguese gentleman, who looked
like a well dressed *flâneur*, visible through the steel mesh as we
waited in traffic. I saw that the need for concealment could work
both ways.

Suzanne ignored the bystanders and toyed with a long-stemmed
red rose she had carried becomingly since breakfast that morning. "Do not worry," she said to Sebastião, newest among all her
charges. "I've been preparing for this meeting with Silva Pais for
the past two years. Don't think of it as a test between human wills.
God says either the breakthrough will take place here in Portugal,
or else there will be nothing here any more."

As she patted his twisting fingers, Sebastião nodded at her and
appeared to take heart. He began to translate her words to the
matrons, who listened with curiosity, brightly repeating each sentence two or three times. "God has chosen Portugal!" they echoed
the main theme. "As the country that is highest, in the whole world
of Spirit!"

It was apparent to Suzanne, and she passed this information
along to me, that the matrons were coming no longer to think of
us as women of the streets. And, she noticed, despite the beer, that
they were on the way to conceiving of *themselves* as something
more than charwomen. So things were moving right along, in a
good direction.

During that long, long ride to Lisbon, Suzanne kept prodding
me to "look up," in the Gnostic Manual that was still clutched in my
hands, the past lives of all the personnel of the PIDE who were so
fatefully gathered together in this van. I scanned my imagination

and the pages to which I opened and did my level best, speeding these "discoveries" to all corners of the vehicle, flipping the pages as fast as I could in this wheeling, sultry, grey limousine that had the smell of so many old, implacable miseries on its metal shanks. "Suzanne," I gasped at length, closing the book. "I'm feeling carsick. I can't turn the pages any more."

She looked at me, briefly quizzical. "What's this Belief? God says you're already cured."

I didn't think so. She had just told Sebastião that we "fought sometimes," and that as a friend I was "only so-so." And there were more narrow, relentless turns of the road to swerve round as we neared the heights of Setubal.

"What are you waiting for? Find out who Teresa's husband is supposed to be!"

"It's Mendès-France," I said, vomiting into my threadbare, shredded handbag. No one appeared to notice. So I had to be grateful for that.

I could see tears sparkling on Suzanne's brown cheeks. "God has just told me," she said in English, smiling at me, "that with this last sacrifice all my debts are now paid in full. Ten billion dollars' worth! Only just think, Abigail!"

So I translated her good news into Portuguese for them all, and, in the general hat tossing and congratulations that followed, I gave her a little pat on the knee, to soothe her.

Now the limousine swerved off the main highway and pursued a ribbon of road that led by a roundabout route toward a dusty, gated compound that looked military. We approached the cross-wired, sentried gate, which lifted immediately, and we drove through. What was this? I wondered. The Portuguese Pentagon? A prison?

We drew up, on Sebastião's side of the limousine, against a massive stone building. Dusty grey. Some khaki-clad sentries were standing about informally. Sebastião got out, entered the building, returned to the car momentarily, and said we could go in now. "Suzanne, first."

Suzanne bowed in polite acknowledgment of the honor and slipped noiselessly through the limousine door.

A sentry immediately placed himself in front of the window, and that was the last I saw of her.

Waiting alone in the back seat I tried, flipping once more through the Gnostic Manual, to figure out what was going on now. If Suzanne was not around, and the Book couldn't tell me, I didn't see how I could *ever* find out. Was Suzanne being banqueted by

Silva Pais like a visiting head of state, while her doubtful sidekick
was about to be shunted off to some dark prison cell in the base-
ment of the very same building? What was it that Suzanne had said
to me earlier, by way of admonishment? Even if I was not fit to
represent "the breakthrough," I could still try to serve it. For instance, in song. We'd been doing that just this morning, while we'd
waited for Sebastião.

Hesitantly, I joined my voice to the now-silent ranks of the saved
remnant, rehearsing the chorus that had sounded so apt in the
morning:

> "Passing through, Passing through,
> "Sometimes happy, Sometimes blue,
> "Glad that I ran into you,
> "Tell the people that you saw me passing through."

Odd how bell-like and clear the notes are, I mused, pleased by the
bright sound of them. I could see the driver lean sharply back in
his seat to hear better. No doubt it was nicer than Fado. More tune-
ful. "That's enough, now," I could sense God was saying. "Back to
the Book."

Was I wrong? The worn pages were giving no clues. Was
Suzanne *not* being received like a head of state? Was she being
stripped now instead for the Zyklon B showers? It was perhaps a
ten-minute wait before the tan tunic finally moved, and I was told
that I too could enter.

Nearsightedly, I followed the back of a uniform through a
marble-floored anteroom to a larger reception room, which had
a sort of registrar's cage, partly barred and partly enclosed by a
shoulder-high wooden counter. There was our good old Sebastião
and some others, standing beside a long marble table. Teresa and
Maria, the matrons, were standing there too and seemed to be
looking at me sympathetically.

"It seems"—Sebastião stepped up to me with his full military
smartness—"that Silva Pais is not here. You will be obliged to remain here overnight, in order to be able to see him in the morning."

"All right." I was not surprised, though I knew that the wait
might extend through the morning, the whole day in fact, and more
days to come. "Will I be able to room with Suzanne?" (Will I be able
to languish with her, unforgiven, until the end of time? In loyalty, I
should at least *ask* for that privilege.)

"I don't think . . . that you have rooms together. But I don't
know. Possibly, not far apart . . ." With a worried, abstracted air, he

went off to the wooden counter, to confer there with some other colleagues.

I returned to my song, and to the stanza that seemed apropos:

> I shivered with Washington
> One night at Valley Forge.
> "Why do these men
> "Suffer like they do?"

There was an old man who seemed to belong to the anteroom. He was dressed in a baggy suit, and he now nodded understandingly. "Pois, pois," he said, picking up my hatbox. "A jail is not a hotel. Evidently, it cannot be as comfortable. It is a jail."

As I passed Sebastião, still conferring with his friends by the portal, I reached out, with the thought of cheering him up, to shake his hand. But, among all his people, his habitual look of distaste seemed to have grown embarrassed, as he nonetheless took my hand politely.

Moving then through the portal, I followed behind the old man, taking especial care not to lose my footing on the imposing marble staircase that conducted us to the upper story.

> He said, "Men will suffer, fight,
> "Even die for what is right."

"Shshsh. Don't sing. You may not sing here. Pois. It is a jail, you see."

> "Even though they know
> "They're only passing through."*

The old man shrugged and shook his head.

My guide unlocked a set of windowed doors at the top of the stairs, and we proceeded down the marbled length of a corridor. *Where were my glasses?* I thought, wondering at the same time how I could be so disloyal to the breakthrough, even to the last. But it had been different back in Sonho! There, my old perforated sneakers had known the back of every stone in the village, blind. It was all very well to try to cope with a prison in the manner of an apostle, but suppose that you couldn't *see*? What then?

At the juncture of the second set of opaquely windowed French

*From *Mormon Pioneer Song Book*, © 1980 Theodore Presser Company. Used by permission of the publisher.

doors, a prison warden was waiting to meet us. I lifted my hatbox
from the old man's hand and followed her. It was a moment or two
before I realized that I had forgotten to say a polite goodbye to the
old man. Tsk! But it was too late now. How impolitic of me! First
impressions were *so* important, in a prison!

The warden preceded me down the gleaming corridor without
comment, and she left me at an open door, where an unassuming,
shabbily dressed young woman was waiting for me. She was perhaps a kitchen maid. She did not assume that I spoke Portuguese
but showed me by bare-armed gestures where I could use the toilet
over which she was keeping her shabby vigil. If I did not mind that
the booth had a door that could not be closed.

"Obrigada," I said definitively. I preferred to wait it out. If I had
to wait till kingdom come.

After some hesitant moments, the girl waved me on, with that
downward Portuguese gesture, into another chamber.

There was no one in this cell. I faced the door, back to the barred
window, waiting.

It was the warden who reentered, coming very close to me now
and speaking in the thickish, extremely soft accents of an ingratiating, female, Portuguese prison official. She was here, as she said,
to search me.

I took a step backward.

Would the menina be so good as to undress?

"Why? *I* don't want to be seen in the nude," I smiled.

"Yes . . . it is disagreeable. No one could like it. But it is necessary,
in a prison, I have to know . . ."

"Whether I've got guns hidden about me anywhere," I finished
it for her. "That's it, isn't it?" I smiled again, in sheer disbelief.

"Pois," she agreed, cajolingly, deprecatingly.

"Believe me"—I shook my head emphatically—"I've got no
guns. But I *really* cannot do that." (I had never in my whole life
been more sincere.)

"I very much hope that the menina will not be unreasonable. It
would be much more disagreeable . . . if I had to call several men to
come here . . . and hold the menina. The menina could be forced . . ."

"But of course you understand that I could not be forced to do
anything that was *unprincipled.* Principle is in command of this
place. As principle is in command of you and me."

Her cajoling nod had become a shade nonplussed.

"Now"—I struck on, while the iron was hot—"I am not afraid of
you." And I smiled again.

"Pois." She showed me a docile shrug. "There is nothing to be
afraid of." She shook her head to convince me.

"Pois. And you are not afraid of me. But we are both afraid of God."

If I would hold still now, she would just run her hands up and down?

"Fully clothed?"

"Pois."

"Oh. I had not at first understood you. Fully clothed, that would be quite all right." (Suzanne might not think that this was 100 percent all right. The warden's hands had no business to be sliding over skinny hips and breasts. But, on the other hand, this is a jail. As the old man said. This is not a hotel. Let us not try to push our luck.)

"You don't wear a bra or pants?" she questioned me curiously.

"No. God told us, when your thoughts are pure, underwear is not needed."

She disappeared without comment, and presently she was standing again at the door of my cell. Would the *menina* just step this way?

I moved to pick up my hatbox and soaked handbag.

"No—just with nothing."

With nothing? For how long? I snatched up my red-leather Manual and passed by her ushering hands. She was waving me into a sunlit cell. It was a bit larger than any that I had yet seen and lined with a sink and flush toilet behind a partition. In the front part, there was a cot, a small table, and a chair that I could see. The cell looked quite decent and clean. It was horizoned by a barred window that was wide and large and gave on some distant ramparts. There, shouldering bayonettes, sentries were pacing picturesquely, and beyond them I could take in, however dimly, the rolling, blue, Portuguese countryside.

"It is agreeable here, is it not?" said the warden to me. "Not a bad room. It is really not bad. Almost like a little hotel. Unfortunately, there is no hot water today. And, you were not expected, so we can find just a portion of soup for your lunch. Pois. But otherwise, you will be comfortable."

I nodded agreement, beginning to feel white, concentric circles of relief rippling out from the place where I stood, for the first time in three years—a place locked and barred against Suzanne. Thank God she's not here! I can do mental work, to pry all the disloyalty out of my thinking . . .

I will have *time* . . .

The morning brought me to my feet, rather chastened. God had demanded that I forego sleep to upspade any hidden errors, and what my digging had hit on in the night was a wholesale will to betray the breakthrough. That finding made sense to me. It would have taken something that big to get us trapped in this jail. But how long would my punishment last now? And Suzanne's, who deserved none of it? Would anything open the door for Paul and Silas? And did Suzanne know everything about me already, with her long-distance laser intuitions?

I had got myself bathed, dressed, and breakfasted, by the time the matron reappeared.

"You are supposed to leave now," she said. "We have your things waiting for you downstairs."

I smiled gratefully. Some wheels were working. But what wheels?

As the feminine kitchen crew collected at my door for adieux, I bestowed on one gentle, misshapen girl from the crew my particular blessings.

"Ahhn," breathed the women appreciatively. "She is religiosa."

Then I trooped past the women and steered myself singlefootedly down the grand marble stairs, with the warden in front of me. In the same reception room where I had last seen him, Sebastião Ribeira was standing and looking sober.

"You will have to leave now."

"Where is Suzanne?" I accused him, vaguely and automatically, not choosing to guess what he meant. "When can I see *her*?"

"I don't know," he replied. "Probably . . . in America."

Then I sent him a grim stare of comprehension and turned abruptly away, maybe to hide the ambiguous lurch of my feelings.

Waiting at the front door for our limousine to arrive, I caught sight of our matron, Teresa, who would be riding with us today. She gave me a kindly look.

"Sebastião," I said, as he strolled up again casually, "God says to tell you that you are a traitor!"

Looking green, he bit his lips thinly and replied, with restrained wrath, "That is not true! I am not in the least to blame for all this!"

I walked away from him to peer through the glass doors impatiently. Suzanne . . . where was she? What would she *think* if she knew how easily I could get reconciled to going home? Could she tell, even now? Perhaps so, since she had already proved that she could scan my dreams *while* I was dreaming them, waking me up when on occasion I would dream disloyal dreams! Would she be on the next flight, then? Her people would be in the United States somewhere. Would they be looking for me? If the world was not going to end, by some chance, then what in the world had happened to me?

Had I been less intellectually assembled, as a human construction, I might have let all those questions settle themselves, in time and by chance. But, constructed the way I was, I thought that the most coherent course would be to act *as if* the apocalypse were an ongoing script, despite this sudden and rude collapse of most of its props.

The script had served me for so long, after all. It had convinced Suzanne to stop hitting and threatening me, to let me sleep sometimes, to stop accusing me—well, not quite that, but still—and last night the matron had not taken off my clothes! How about *that* for a miracle? And the grey line of officers at the guarda—look how they had parted for me! And look how Sebastião had taken in Suzanne's battle plan! Why, even now, he was angry that I'd accused him of betraying it! Wasn't all that an indication of how I should plan my conduct from here on, a good tip for the future? And, if it was not, if the play was played out, it still remained true that I no longer knew how to act or what else to say. The world that other people lived in wasn't constructed, even by those who belonged to it, out of nothing. I *too* had to use what I now had, to get by.

The limousine had arrived. Sebastião and Teresa took a seat on each side of me, and we coasted downroad, piloted by a driver from the PIDE. (It was just a big car, not like the other.) Seated there in the middle, I was checking my book to see if I could somehow tone down the dreadful reproof I had given Sebastião, when Teresa handed me my black handbag. Dry and clean.

"It was all soaked," she said sadly, looking at me. "I washed it."

"Obrigada, Teresa. I never meant you to."

(Tears come to my eyes when I think of it, that small act of kindness.)

Sebastião was just getting nasty and personal about my page-flipping, when I tracked down the saving passages that I'd been looking for. "God says the reason you could not get in to see Silva Pais, was because God did not want you to."

"God did not want me to see Silva Pais?"

"No." I was glad to have hit on this truth for resentful Sebastião. And it proved that God was still talking to me.

"I don't yet know what God wants," I replied, still thumbing. "If He doesn't want me to be on that plane, then there won't be a takeoff."

"Pois," nodded Teresa, with her ponderous thoughtfulness. "Com Deus, tudo é possível."

With God all is possible, but it was looking less and less likely. At the entrance to the airfield, our car stopped short for a moment, permitting a portly man in a dark suit to slide in next to the driver. The new man took me in jovially. "Ah, fine," he laughed to Sebastião.

There ahead was the plane. It was already loaded for takeoff. We all got out.

The U.S. consul was not on the airfield. But I learned later that he had been watching from inside the terminal. And Suzanne was still in the jail, which was why he had come. The subprefect had promised my parents that care would be taken to separate us, as it was. So it is possible that Suzanne would be in that Portuguese jail to this day, or in some other one, had the U.S. consul not made that trip to the airport in Lisbon, to ask my father if he would make one more phone call to his high-level friend, once he got home. The consul wanted the State Department to come up with a "loan" to cover the safe return, under escort, of my brainwasher.* My parents were very kind people, as kind as the consul no doubt, but it is unlikely, under the circumstances, that they would have thought of it had he not asked.

That done, the consul had said his cordial goodbyes to my mother, had shaken hands warmly with my father, and, directly after we were all three airborne, had gone dutifully off to the jail to see Suzanne in her cell.

Me they hospitalized. They had to, once we were back at Kennedy. I don't see what else they could have done, with the resources then available to them. In the mind of the public of that time, "brainwashing" was bound up with repatriated Americans, coming out of their years in the prisons of communist China, who had confessed to crimes that, clearly, they could not have committed. Or else it concerned released POWs, held by the Chinese or the North Koreans, and the intensive indoctrination to which they'd been subjected. Or else it emerged out of Arthur Koestler's *Darkness at Noon*, shedding light on the shocking "confessions" of treason made by row upon row of old bolsheviks in the Vyshinsky trials of the thirties, those great purge trials of the USSR. Or else it was evident in the appalling "confession" of Cardinal Jozsef Mindszenty of Hungary, made at his trial in 1949—and who knew what vile physical tortures had been inflicted on that man? And there was the process portrayed in George Orwell's *Nineteen Eighty-Four*, of a step-by-step deconstruction of moral identity, put in the context of a science fiction dystopia. Now, *that* was brainwashing!

*The "loan" was provided, though the high-level friend had had to wrap up the business with me rather quickly and give his attention to Israel's Six-Day War, which was starting just then.

What was widely believed at that time was that "brainwashing," or "mind control," or "coercive persuasion" required the following elements: a physical capture, a threat of imminent death, totalitarian state power, and total isolation of the prisoner or else his or her complete submersion in a group whose members had themselves already been brainwashed. The destructive cults that emerged in the seventies had not yet brought into public awareness the fact that the process takes place in the mind and can therefore take place without all that paraphernalia.[1] It's like staging a play without a full stage set. If the script is intact and the actor can act, then the play can go on with just a few minimal props, and the rest can be supplied by the imagination.

It was not that in June of 1967, when I was returned to the United States, there existed no good research on the subject of mind control. On the contrary. There were studies dating back to the 1950s, authored by psychiatrists working under military auspices. Such of that early work as I have read is humane, respectful of the patients, and intelligent, in that it tends *not* to take "personal identity" to be a mere myth, or to suppose brainwashing to be the mere substitution of one myth for another.

Instead of all that, I found in these studies a sober and historically informed concern to discover the means (the *crooked* and *unfair* means) by which a person's moral identity can be alienated and the person robbed of his story. By the same token, such early studies as I have read are not made top-heavy by too much reductive theoretical machinery, nor are they made excessively light-headed by what have since become our current, philosophically fashionable, anomic, Germano-Franco-Dionysian revels in the head.[2]

But for all that, back in 1967 what the general public knew of brainwashing was that the Chinese communists had done it, and so had the Russian communists, each doing it to somewhat different ends. So it was thought to need government power implementing policy on a fairly grand scale. And some people thought it never happened, that it must be an artifact of the Cold War propaganda exchanges. Nor was the average American practicing psychiatrist notably better informed, at that inconvenient juncture of my life. In consequence, what the staff at the hospital did with me was administer drugs, although none of the studies of brainwashing and its cure that I have read since recommend doing that. It was rather like kicking the television set to get it going again.

So, when I woke up one morning and stretched, in my hospital bed in New York, it was without comprehension that I saw my chin start to drop downward and, with it, my neck to twist clockwise. Making some effort, I shut my lower lip against the bow of my mouth and turned counterclockwise. Only to find that my neck had just tilted as steeply, in the other direction.

Good grief! What was God doing to me? What did this represent, in the Gnostic sign language? Quickly I reached for the red-leather Book. It must mean . . . what I fear. That God cannot stand my ambivalence! That I would be forced to *choose*. But what choice did I have, after all the innumerable, wonderful healings that I had witnessed in person—healings of my resistance to buying on credit, for instance, or of my sin of trying to murder Suzanne in this life, and of repeatedly murdering her in past lives! In my head, I was rattling off all the "miracles" I could remember. You see, God. I've made my choice, God. I'm undivided, now.

But the symptoms, though they wavered in intensity, hung on.

All during the hours that followed, as these symptoms of mine surfaced and then resubmerged, I travailed alone with the Book, under the handicap of a nearsighted squint, trying to make my thoughts proof against *second thoughts*. For this convulsive attack had struck me as a sign of real madness, of frenzy such as they would have chained to the wall at La Salpêtrière in an earlier era. I must be mad! I thought.

Would my cure lie in a still-more-abject submission to the coming apocalypse? But what more could I try? I looked—rather, rummaged—through the Gnostic Manual once again, though its purview seemed to be narrowing daily. Lately, it had climbed to a real pitch of dull repetition. If it was not harking back to the Pharisees and the crucifixion (which I took to be a reminder of what I had done to Suzanne), it was repeating some mindless truism. How long will you forget me, Lord?

But while I searched on, a revisionist point of view suggested itself. Why *couldn't* I have it both ways? Would so much harm be done in the interim if I lived like a regular human being for a little while, until the return of Suzanne and her troops? Couldn't I juggle the whole set of options more *lightly*?

With that thought, the convulsions relaxed, and I retook control of my muscles. "Gnostic Christianity really works," I said aloud, to no one in particular—there being no one on the ward just then— and closed the Book feeling satisfied.

But, by the next morning, I awoke to misgivings. I could not hold the pose. I was not one to live masked. And, I suspected, God wanted a wholesale desertion of the false world for the true.

As suddenly as I thought this, the muscles in the back of my neck clawed together, as if they were nailing my scalp to the wall right behind me. And now my jaw hung, once again, irretrievably limp. What to do? Twisting this way and that, I only managed to fall into one rictus or another. There was no getting away. For where, or to whom, outside of God's own world plan, could I turn?

From the door, a girl patient asked me if I'd like to join her in a game of Ping-Pong.

Face averted, I thanked her and said that I needed to rest. And she left.

It was visitor's day, a Thursday, and looking up not long after that, I saw that my mother had walked into the empty ward. As it happened, she was alone on that day.

"Mother," I said to her urgently, "I think that I'm *really* going mad. My jaw keeps pulling down against my will—just like a crazy person's. I don't know what to do!"[3]

"Probably, you are taking the first step *out* of the illness. Have you told the staff?"

"No. It's just *me*. I don't see what they can do."

"I'll tell them." And she must have done so, later. But they didn't check in, till the next day.

"Mother, may I lay my head on your lap?" I stretched out on her blue-flowered, silk-clad knees, resting my exploding head there.

A soft voice traced a blue line above me. "You know, Abigail, what happened to you, you *think* is unique. But in reality, all that happened to you in Sonho has been studied and classified. It fits into a category. It is familiar to experts in the field."

"But I've proved God's power!"

Sometimes, my mother could be quite philosophical. "A system can have internal logic and still be unreal. That's one of the features of illnesses."

A category? The apocalypse in a category? "Mother, I think if I had to retrace the whole way I've come, I'd have no claim to a shred of integrity. I'd just want to die."

With immense, feminine tiredness, she replied as follows: "All people want to die at times. I have wanted to die, often, during the past three years. You don't die for wanting to."

If the promises Suzanne had made were not true, with regard to the apocalypse anyway, then I was mortal, just like the rest of the people. Oh my God, I realized, I *am* going to die. I won't just live on, endlessly. I *will* die. And suddenly time stretched before me unsupported. There was a boredom in it that seemed to wash over me now. A boredom called sanity. "I've been So Happy, mother," I protested now, weirdly. "I've never been bored, in the Gnostic religion!" Was it all meaningless? What was one to do?

"You'll find a saner happiness. A happiness that's involved with people. You think you have gone too far, and that you cannot come back. *But you can cross over—on waves of our love. And you will be safe.*"

"I don't know, Mother. I don't know." And my jaw was still wrapping its desperate dislocations, like fictional messages, round my face.

Visiting hour was over. And what an hour!

Now I stood up and paced the room. Where was I to go? Backwards? The passage that I opened to in the well-thumbed red book spoke only of the gropings of a blind, crippled man in a cave. A man with a face like a gargoyle. No help there. Now I walked quickly out to the nurse's station.

"I'm sorry," I said embarrassedly to a placid blond nurse. "There seems to be something wrong with me. I can't seem to control the muscles in my face and my neck—the whole upper part of my body—at all. I think that I'm going insane."

She checked my card. It was undoubtedly a result, she told me, not frequent but sometimes occurring, of the highly concentrated dosage of the stuff they had given me two weeks ago. There was an antidote. It would take some time to prepare. But I could wait in the violent ward, where there would be privacy.

Thither she led me now. I waited a long time, as it seemed, for her to return with the antidote and, while I waited, suffered these ever enlarging incursions of my own muscles, like an intruding double, overwhelming their helpless host.

"Are you all right, dearie?" asked a "violent" patient, in tones of anxious concern. And she came up, fellow sufferer, to my chair to press an empathic hand against the by now wild muscles of my back and shoulders.

Then the doctor at last, taking me to a private room and his nurse, and they had an intravenous shot, and I could surrender my body to strengthless sleep.

Do those people *have* to break you, to help you?

It was near to the dinner hour when I woke up and came into the common corridor once again. My reflexes were normal now. But I would have to stay in close touch with the staff, as I recognized, until the effect of that excess dosage had worn off completely. I would not want to go through *that* again, ever, for any price.

Then I leaned against the corridor wall, some few steps back of the dinner line, to think.

PSYCHE

AND

SOMA.

There was no other explanation. The body *must* be subject to manipulation independent of the mind. Therefore, it follows that life must be *complex*. Therefore, there must be at least two sorts of factors governing me. Despite what the Gnostic Christians have said, there isn't just Spirit. And there must be, necessarily, more to life than ideas. And, necessarily, more and better ideas than the ones I've been twisting myself out of shape to believe in, these past three years.

Let me get this straight now. Wait a minute. I will have to seek some other level of accommodation. What it all means is that these people won't feed me forever.

But, what about my erstwhile, beloved leader? What about Suzanne? Could *all* that have been wrong? Could it be that she *never* healed me—never purified me? That all those "healings" were just self-deception? But that would have to mean that, as such, they were not called for. In which case, for the most basic one, it would mean that I never tried to kill her.

Well, how could I have tried? I wasn't near her!

But that means that she was an insane girl, my enemy, who unjustly—terrifyingly unjustly—accused me and then beat me down till I believed it!

So

my

buried,

my

underlying,

my

originary suspicions

were right.

Of *course* they were. What *else* could they have been? Why else had they been ineradicable?

I walked up to join the dinner line.

That was all. There was no more light than that in the cave, and no more fanfare in the turning around of the soul. Just an intellectual reassessment. Nothing more dramatic. Nothing *could* have been more dramatic. Done under duress, admittedly. But this response to duress was not forced on me.

"We can't keep her here," they said, when they looked in on me in the morning. "We need the beds."

New York was to look just beautiful to me through my new glasses, although the traffic would give me a scare. It was beautiful, for there were now no better memories against which its defects could look garish. Only much worse memories. As it had not been when I'd come back from Paris just eight years before, it was all there now, to be got and spent.

One time, when I sat in the luncheonette in my old neighborhood and looked through its glass doors at the sunny streets of that urban day in July, streets paved with their particles of dusty silver, I thought with a swell of exhilaration, I'm free! She can't *find* me in New York! It's too big. It's the big city. I'm really free!

Actually, it was not to be quite so simple as that. As witness the inaugural sentence with which I began this effort of recollection in the fall of 1967, while I was also writing my dissertation for Penn State. It went like this:

> There is an illness called sanity.
> Sometimes, after you've been through everything,
> you walk the streets alone and you wonder
> how you can hook in again,
> how you can rejoin the body of the world—
> how you can run your stint.

It was to be a task. I would begin to recover my story in the early drafts of this memoir narrative, and to test dialectically, in my life and in thought, a succession of hypothetical principles for the interpretation of these recollections.

But I was at least free, with God's help, to pursue the recovery of my historical intelligence.

And it's a romance, that.

Epilogue

What sort of a story have we just lived through together? As told here, two major episodes allow for the playing out of the premises with which the narrator begins. The first occurs in Paris, where the narrator has a Fulbright project to discover "Definitions of Man through Aesthetic Experience." The project is actually a specification of her life project, which is to play the part of the individual within the Jewish-historical vocation of seeking justice and mercy immanently, in the cultural and historical contexts of our real lives.

At that period in Paris, what many intellectuals there believed in was utopian history, an "unreal city in the future," to attain which force and deception were believed justified. What was "Greek" about these views (aside from realpolitik's ubiquitousness in Thucydides) was that this was more or less where philosophy itself, that anciently Greek gift, had partly but influentially come to *at that time and place*. What was "Jewish" about the narrator was her belief that one had to confront and engage with the views and assumptions current in one's cultural context and not merely stay above or outside the battle. The most direct engagement is of course the erotic one, where the "aesthetic" or sensed dimension represents both the lure and the problem. (Force and deception will not be props enough to support the project of justice in history— *or* erotic relations within that project.) So, seen as a kind of true, contemporary fable, Part 1, where the narrator and her lover meet and part, may be described as a fusion and clash between what the theologians—referring to the parabolically pure types—call "the Jew" and "the Greek."

The crippling silences that follow, in the interlude that marks Part 2 of the story, serve to underscore the lack of any obvious *way* to continue one's historical project in the aftermath of that collision of values in Paris. (It may be that everyone "knew" what no one said. There was still no *hodos*, or method. There was still no way.) Accordingly, the narrator tries, logically enough, to invert entirely the historical project, under the tutelage of a young African American woman who has reasons of her own to want to see the whole world of culture and history treated as unreal. That the gnostic attempt to escape the historical project only paves the way for more terrible injustices is the lesson of Part 3. The story's conclusion returns the narrator to the historical framework, with its struggles and partial lights on the darkling plain where we all still are.

Is it a "happy" ending? Yes, in part, in the sense that the understanding of the path already trodden provides a "way" to go forward into the future. To show that the denial of history reduces to absurdity is a proof that the historical way is the right way. And, as reductio ad absurdum is a philosophical method of proof, there is a marriage of "Jew" and "Greek"—of the historical and the philosophical projects—after all. However, it is a "happy" ending from which suffering and heartbreak are, naturally, not excluded.

That said, meanwhile the hyper-Augustinian in us all must be already at work, rummaging through this material and trying to figure out *what the narrator left out* that would erase the effect of the whole tape, or what I (to resume the first person) did after that, or what I have yet to do, that will nullify this narrative.

Cynicism is a fearful thing, especially when self-directed. All the same, it is not an argument.

The real question comes down to this, however: Can one *accept* one's historical existence?

As to Jews, they *must* do so, since it is constitutive of their existence as such. There is no other interesting thing for them to do or to be. All the *other* interesting things that they do, and are, can be but commentaries on this core reality. To live that core reality consciously is to get themselves (with all parts of their pasts and their projects) involved in the human conversation. It is also to get others, with their pasts and their interpretations thereof, to join it too—*the* human conversation, the one about justice and mercy, the world narrative. It's very hard, of course, this Jewish assignment.

But there is no real choice. The very effort to choose elsewhere is what brings it home to one.

Since one wants to have this assignment "brought home to one," one will choose elsewhere. And the assignment will be brought home to one. It's very pretty . . . this covenant . . . and very eternal. I should know.

Can one accept one's historical existence?

Suzanne clearly could not. Since she couldn't win on that level, as she saw it, and she wasn't willing to come in second, she had no obvious way to cope except to catapult herself out of the historical world entirely, inverting every one of its values and road signs. Which is what she did, using that upside-down gnostic world to gain delusional advantage in what would turn out to be, after all, a race to the imagined finish line of world history.

To destroy another person is, as Sartre has shown and Hegel showed before him, rather a loser's game, but it is hardly a noncompetitive game! So let no one, in the face of this story, go on with the claim that one escapes Hegel's "life and death struggle" or "master/slave relation" *just* by running to ground one's historical sense of a linear progress through time.

There is only one way that one can partly escape from the great guilt of destructive human relations: by forbearing to engage in them, insofar as that is possible. At least, forbearing sufficiently to allow for the maintenance or (if need be) reinstitution of the social contract. Absent which "history," in the authorized sense, cannot even *begin*.

The invisible thread of the human narrative through time is not precisely a matter of record. For what is on the record will always be contestable, fragile—almost, it would seem, reversible at every point. No conceivable series of first-person recollections, court decisions, human inventions, improvements, or refinements would neatly illustrate the progress of justice and mercy through time. Yet it may be glimpsed only in real time. Or rather, real time is a function of *it*. So dialectical progress can never be found wholly real, as a continuous line through time, but should not be abandoned to the realm of the ideal either. One is not supposed to cut the cord between its empirical reality and its transcendental ideality. Rather, one has to try to live, as far as possible, so that the two realms coincide. And it's a fine line. One has to walk it, that's all.

But readers like a happy ending—at least if they are like me they do. And a happy ending is found in the realization of one's defining purposes in life. So then: What about my purposes, as they were set forth at the beginning of these pages? What about my struggle to find God, to realize the Absolute in the context of actual history? Did I ever do that? Did I find God?

Well, yes. So far, yes. I have *found* the struggle and the finding to be one and the same. So, yes.

Notes

Preface

1. The claim might prompt a question: Can a "good story" take the turn that this one does, toward the *catastrophic*? The answer is yes.

2. Benedict de Spinoza (1632–1677) was the great Dutch, Marrano, seventeenth-century champion of modern science, rationalist and philosopher of God, excommunicated by the Jews of Amsterdam and regarded as an atheist by European Christendom. He was one of those who helped to construct the conceptual supports for the modern, secular life and may have been the very first to have lived such a life.

Chapter One: Beginningwise

1. The discontinuities alluded to by contemporary French philosophers are, I suspect, mostly between a failed Marxism with its lost and regretted utopian prospects, and the rest of human history. Since these *are* philosophers, they take hints and suggestions from other philosophers in buttressing their disappointment. So there is a contribution taken from Heidegger's critique of the Subject of experience as "a fable," and many ingenious moves to replace the Subject with other locutions (that would get the same work done at less personal risk). And there is also recourse to Freud, with

his convenient assurances that we never—on principle, never—say precisely what we mean. But these other tributary philosophic streams seem less important in accounting for this phase than the demise of the Marxist hopes, since they don't leave one quite so puzzled as to what *to do* next. But anyway, even in France (where at least they know the grand tradition in philosophy, its intellectual linkages and its importance for history), we are now more or less at the moment of discontinuities. Some people there are intelligently disquieted and ironical over this moment. But it is still such a moment.

2. An inspired exception is Emmanuel Lévinas. There are others. The foregoing are broad generalizations that depict some recent trends, not every worker in the vineyards. Against the view that still prevails—amongst even the reviving friends of narrative—that "pluralism" *between* narratives is and ought to be indissoluble, I have offered arguments in "Virtues and Relativism" in *A Good Look at Evil* (Philadelphia: Temple University Press, 1987), pp. 39-47.

3. The stated or unstated biblical foundations of some of the major edifices in Western philosophy of history are uncovered in Karl Löwith's careful analyses of the cases of Marx, Hegel, Proudhon, Comte, Condorcet, Voltaire, Vico—and, of course, Augustine and Bossuet, among others (see *Meaning in History* [Chicago: University of Chicago Press, 1949]). Kant would be another clear example, as would Husserl. As Alasdair MacIntyre has noted, the concept of a philosophy of history is a religious one.

4. This precise characterization of Saint Paul I owe to Elmer Sprague. When Francis Fukuyama mistakenly assigns to this notion of a progressive, universal history a *Christian* origin, he is close to being right, if we forget that Christianity itself had a Jewish origin. The biblical originators of the notion of universal history retained an interpretation of what they had started that was older than Christianity's, distinct from it, and at least as enduring. See Fukuyama, *The End of History and the Last Man* (New York: Free Press, 1992), p. 56.

5. "I have no philosophy of history." Maurice Merleau-Ponty, *Humanism and Terror: An Essay on the Communist Problem*, tr. and with notes by John O'Neill (Boston: Beacon, 1969), p. xlvi; *Humanisme et terreur: Essai sur le problème communiste* (Paris: Gallimard, 1947), p. xlii.

6. So Jacques Derrida speaks of "ruptures and heterogeneities" ("Eating Well: An Interview," in *Who Comes after the Subject*, ed. Eduardo Cadava, Peter Connor, and Jean-Luc Nancy [New York:

Routledge, Chapman, and Hall, 1991], pp. 116–117). He goes on: "We know less than ever where to cut—either at birth or at death. And this also means that we never know, and never have known, how to *cut up* a subject. Today less than ever." "On sait moins que jamais où couper—et à la naissance et à la mort. Et cela veut dire aussi qu'on ne sait jamais, on n'a jamais su comment *découper* un sujet. Moins que jamais aujourd'hui." See " 'Il faut bien manger' ou le calcul du sujet," Entretien (avec Jean-Luc Nancy), in *Cahiers Confrontation*, no. 20 (Winter, 1989): p. 112. And Jean-François Lyotard puts it like this: "Simplifying to the extreme, I define *postmodern* as incredulity toward metanarratives." See *The Postmodern Condition: A Report on Knowledge*, tr. Geoff Bennington and Brian Massumi (Minneapolis: University of Minnesota Press, 1984), p. xxiv. *"En simplifiant à l'extrême, on tient pour 'postmoderne' l'incrédulité à l'égard des métarécits."* See *La Condition postmoderne: Rapport sur le savoir* (Paris: Les Editions de Minuit, 1979), p. 7.

7. "Akiba," said another rabbi, a contemporary of his, "the grass will be green over your head before the messiah comes." It was the second century A.D. or C.E. Rabbi Akiba had just endorsed a certain messiah claimant whom the Romans later destroyed. This was said to Akiba some time before the "Bar Kochba" revolt was put down. It was said, as we can well imagine, with weariness, with a smile, and in the practiced mode of someone who lives historically, and cannot live any other way. But the identity of the messiah was, evidently, not a matter for excommunicatory blows, unless, for collateral reasons, the Jewish people had stood in danger of schism. And wrong though he must have been about the messiah in that case, Akiba is still revered in Jewry.

8. Reductionists will have many objections to make. The overriding premise of psychological reductionism is that people, whether alone or in groups, never really act for *reasons*, only for *causes* (biochemical, stimulus-response neurological, class, race, gender, or other). The "reduction" of the order of reasons to the order of causes is what that aspect of reductionism is all about, and we look at it more directly in the next chapter, as well as from time to time in some particular context thereafter.

9. Readers of a reductionist turn of mind will be inclined to make the following demurrals: (1) It (the covenant between God and Israel) never happened; (2) the alleged covenanters (the ancient Israelites) were very cruel; (3) all that the tribe of Israel wanted or represented was its own biological continuation. These demurrals are (as is usual with reductionism) imprecise. It is not here being claimed that any particular ancient event happened.

I have no informed opinion on that subject. What is rather being claimed is that *what is biblically alleged to have happened* (the covenantal event) is just the sort of happening that has to be postulated for "history" (the search for justice and mercy within an imaginatively comprehensible metanarrative) to make sense. With regard to the second point, reductionist objections on the score of "cruelty" cite the biblical instances where the Israelites seem virtually to be trying to be *un*fair, as well as God's role in the whole effort. Witness the divine command to exterminate the Amalekites, or certain inhabitants of the land at the time of the conquest. Such passages did remain troublesome for the rabbis, whose commentaries treated them as local, exceptional, and *the contrary of exemplary* for future conduct. Explanations were given, such as that the adversaries in these cases had been contagiously unregenerate. It was also explained why no such command could ever be applied again. (In the case of the Amalekites, the reason given was that the command had not been followed and, since that time, the peoples of the world had become "mixed," so that it no longer could be followed.) In sum, the "cruel" stories were viewed as contained episodes, which, like the sacrifice of Isaac, became models of how in future one was *not* to be allowed to behave, even in conditions of warfare. In better conditions, when neighboring rulers accepted offers of peace, treaties could be signed in token of good relations. With non-Israelites who were not a threat, all licit fraternization was permitted, constant injunctions to be solicitous of the stranger in the land were given, and these were buttressed by a structure of legal protections. (I am grateful to Samuel Klagsbrun and Milton Schubin for sharing with me their understanding of the rabbinic responses on these points.) Finally, with regard to the third of the reductionist objections, about "tribalism," Judaism has never held that being non-Jewish necessarily put one in a bad position with respect to God. But if one thinks otherwise, and sincerely believes that Jews are in an enviable position, one is free to join them and enjoy their imagined advantages. Jews are not a race. One can convert to Judaism. Jews are a people, with a given historical sense of itself and vocation. A convert is one who enters that people as a full member, and assumes both its past and its vocation.

10. John Rawls, *A Theory of Justice* (Cambridge: Harvard University Press, 1971). Against Rawls's view, Michael Walzer writes: "Even if they are committed to impartiality, the question most likely to arise in the minds of members of a political community is not, What would rational individuals choose under universalizing conditions of such-and-such a sort? But rather, What would individuals

like us choose, who are situated as we are, who share a culture and are determined to go on sharing it? And this is a question that is readily transformed into, What choices have we already made in the course of our common life? What understandings do we (really) share?" Walzer, *Spheres of Justice: A Defense of Pluralism and Equality* (New York: Basic, 1983), p. 5.

11. I am indebted to the argument of Michael Wyschogrod in *The Body of Faith: Judaism as Corporeal Election* (New York: Seabury, 1983) for its depiction of this inbuilt necessity.

12. As will be obvious to anyone who has read it, this interpretation of the covenant was suggested to me by Henry M. Rosenthal's *Consolations of Philosophy: Hobbes's Secret; Spinoza's Way* (Philadelphia: Temple University Press, 1989). Jewish Scripture is not the topic of that book except glancingly, however.

13. Ibid., p. 84.

Chapter Two: Paris without End

1. Evidently this is not an argument, but the conclusion of one. For the argument from which this conclusion has followed, see my article, "Getting Past Marx and Freud," *Clio* 15, no. 1 (Fall 1985): pp. 61–82.

2. The point is that "the unconscious" is first of all a *concept*, which has its cultural context. It is not a raw, unanticipated finding. The genealogy of influence, from Schopenhauer to Freud via Darwin and von Hartmann, with the role of Nietzsche in shaping the contemporary concept of the unconscious, has been charted briefly in Frank J. Sullaway, *Freud, Biologist of the Mind: Beyond the Psychoanalytic Legend* (New York: Basic, 1979), especially p. 253 and note. For the ongoing character of Nietzsche's debt to Schopenhauer (a frequently controverted point), see the strong case that is made by Julian Young in *Nietzsche's Philosophy of Art* (New York: Cambridge University Press, 1992). The Nietzsche-Freud relation, as it affected European high culture generally in the period just before and after the First World War, is described, with many references, in Steven E. Aschheim, *The Nietzsche Legacy in Germany: 1890–1990* (Berkeley and Los Angeles: University of California Press, 1992), chap. 3, "The Not-So-Discrete-Nietzscheanism of the Avant-garde," pp. 51–84.

3. For an account of the struggle between the "hyper-Augustinians" and the thinkers of the eighteenth-century Enlightenment, see Charles Taylor, *Sources of the Self: The Making of the Modern Identity* (Cambridge: Harvard University Press, 1989), pp. 246–50.

Those psychotherapists in U.S. medical circles who first followed Freud were themselves schooled in or at least culturally attuned to the dark view of human nature. "It is a tribute to American puritanism that it should have been a straight-laced group of New England Brahmins who took up Freud's ideas in America; they knew at first hand what Freud was struggling against." So writes Paul Roazen in *Freud and his Followers* (New York: Knopf, 1975), p. 374. Roazen is perhaps naïve here, since it is just such people (Calvinists' cultural descendants) who would have found Freud's dark view most congenial.

4. On the failure of the empirical claims, especially as regards the Oedipus complex, see James Q. Wilson, *The Moral Sense* (New York: Free Press, 1993), pp. 103-14, 142-43. On the implications of these findings for the Freudian *system*, see my "Getting Past Marx and Freud," pp. 66-68.

5. Some of these interesting contrasts, between the Jewish and the Catholic views of romantic love, have been delineated with precise and refined strokes by Emmanuel Lévinas in "Le judaïsme et le féminin," reprinted in *Difficile liberté* (Paris: Albin Michel, 1976), pp. 51-62, especially pp. 59-60. It has been translated by Edith Wyschogrod as "Judaism and the Feminine Element" (*Judaism* 18, no. 1 [Winter, 1969]: pp. 30-38, especially pp. 36-37).

Chapter Three: Green Age

1. The reference here—had coquetry been minded to give it— would have gone to Léo Bronstein, philosopher of art, who was my father's best friend and something like a godfather to me. I think that his remark about Christianity, made to my father, must have been part of a long question rather than, as in my version, a short answer. See, for example, more recently, Léo Bronstein, *Romantic Homage to Greece and Spain: My Fable. Their Art* (New Brunswick, N.J.: Transaction, 1993), p. 104 (published posthumously).

2. Maurice Merleau-Ponty, "La guerre a eu lieu," in *Sens et non-sens* (Paris: Nagel, 1948), pp. 245-69; "The War Has Taken Place," in *Sense and Non-sense*, tr. Hubert L. Dreyfus and Patricia Allen Dreyfus (Evanston, Ill.: Northwestern University Press, 1964), pp. 139-52.

3. In a recent article, Tom Rockmore writes: "Until the French student revolution in the late 1960s, nearly every French intellectual of any significance had at one time either been a member of the French Communist Party, interested in Marxism, or at least

knowledgeable about it." See "Aspects of French Hegelianism," *Owl of Minerva* 24, no. 2 (Spring, 1993): p. 196.

Chapter Four: Purity and Impurity

1. They are the idealists and the materialists in Plato's metaphor. See *The Sophist* 246. In that dialogue, because—notoriously—materialists were as hard to talk to then as they are now, Plato has Socrates construct a *modified* materialist, with whom an instructive argument can be conducted.

Chapter Seven: La Méthode éternelle

1. Simone de Beauvoir, *Le Deuxième sexe*, book 2, *L'Expérience vécue* (Paris: Gallimard, 1949), pp. 154-55. *The Second Sex*, book 2, *Woman's Life Today*, ed. H. M. Parshley (New York: Knopf, 1953), p. 390.

Chapter Eight: Of the Impossible Position of the Jews

1. See Henry M. Rosenthal, *The Consolations of Philosophy: Hobbes's Secret; Spinoza's Way* (Philadelphia: Temple University Press, 1989), pp. 179-94.

2. To say that the "hand of God" remains on the contract document is to say that the time frame of the contract can impose itself over all the relativities of calendar and perspective that vary from culture to culture. The contract is an absolute, and for that reason applies to—and makes thinkable—a universal history. So *injustices* can be discerned within and between all these varying cultures, and the corrective envisaged, or at least hoped for, that embraces all cultures. Factually, the human race exists in all its ethnic, geographic, and religious strata and compartments. But, by their very nature, justice and injustice do not so exist. They are global. So most of those—Annalistes, Structuralists, and post-Structuralists—who refuse the "novelizing" attractions of narrative history do so because those attractions are thought to disguise the underlying mechanisms of a repressive *politique*. Their very refusal of narrativity, therefore, has to be justified by that global struggle for liberation from injustice, which they pretend must be invisible and incommunicable.

Thus, for prime example of the breakdown of any universal-historical narrative, Lyotard has cited "Auschwitz." (In *Le Post-*

moderne expliqué aux enfants [Paris: Galilée, 1988], pp. 37-38.) But no. The core story in the metastory is that of the Jews, who did not become a mere footnote to the Thousand-Year Reich's chronicle of its ferocious misdeeds. Things did *not* turn out as those people had hoped. Rather, the killers lost the war, and (though they don't like it) Auschwitz became but one more chapter in Jewish history. As long as there *are* Jews, no one can truly say, "I have no philosophy of history"—although Auschwitz may have been one more such *attempt* to say that. And, against the view, popular among some intellectuals, that Auschwitz too represents a hopelessly ambiguous moral domain, see Abigail L. Rosenthal, "Banality and Originality" in *A Good Look at Evil* (Philadelphia: Temple University Press, 1987).

3. See Hava Lazarus-Yafeh, *Intertwined Worlds: Medieval Islam and Bible Criticism* (Princeton: Princeton University Press, 1992). The gist of Islamic biblical criticism, as reported there, is that the Hebrew Bible is a corrupted text whose lost original sense has been recaptured in the Qur'an. The latter Arabic text, though much later chronologically, would be uncorrupted revelation.

4. To avoid misunderstanding, it should be made clear that, since the Second World War, there have been some official retractions on this one. And, all honor to those who have helped to bring them about.

5. For an account of some of the theologico-political obstacles that have surrounded the archeological dig at the most contested site, see Meir Ben-Dov, *In the Shadow of the Temple: The Discovery of Ancient Jerusalem*, tr. Ina Friedman (Jerusalem: Keter, 1985), pp. 19-27.

6. See Léo Bronstein, *Romantic Homage to Greece and Spain: My Fable. Their Art* (New Brunswick, N.J.: Transaction, 1993), pp. 29, 34, and, on "fearless nostalgia," 66. (Jessica, in Shakespeare's *Merchant of Venice*, is of course the example alluded to in my discussion.)

Chapter Nine: Of Silence in General

1. Choderlos de Laclos, *Les Liaisons dangereuses* (Paris: Pauvert, 1959), letter #141.

2. Erotic love merits definition here as one of the primary channels through which the individual's relation to world history may be grounded, and through which it may gain irreplaceable positioning in time. Just as the covenant between God and the Jews insures that the relation between God and humanity becomes concretely "historical" and not abstract, so erotic specificity makes the

human trajectory through time concrete and not abstract. Therefore, if it takes cognizance of this implicitly contained significance,
it has the potential to be the most difficult of all conscious relations.
Next to it, textbook philosophy is relatively easy. But this difficulty
is an approachable difficulty. It is *not intrinsically* the difficulty of
an impasse, nor—except that we have all been born too soon—the
hardship of tragedy. There is also a lurking question, in the heart of
anyone who is of a romanticizing or idealizing temperament: Does
God design certain people for one another, as the rabbinic legend
has it? Of course, I don't know the answer. But possibly He does. In
any event, I can't think why He *wouldn't*, since He's not averse to
designs.

3. One of the recurrent themes of feminists, and of French
feminists notably, is extreme wariness with regard to "history," with
its linearity and progress motifs, because these motifs have been
orchestrated by patriarchal power. But no. It's a mistake, and a misunderstanding. History is the realm of the struggle for justice, and
it is linear *because* of that. If one cannot establish what happened in
sequence, one cannot find out whether it really was fair or unfair.
Feminists point to the unfairness of men who sacralize the unequal
advantages that they have gained in the course of history. But if
anyone, from a historical tradition, wants to make what is *unfair*
into something sacred, then he stands open to correction—indeed
he practically invites it—from within the "historical" standpoint.
Such is the imperative of what we here call "history." It is when one
has *not* the historical consciousness that all these multiple slights,
hurts, and usurpations will occasion little more than a smile and
a shrug.

4. The times to which these lines particularly applied differ
somewhat from the present time, at least in some parts of the world
of men and women. Indeed, some contemporary Western men have
ample reason to feel *victimized*, in a sense that runs concurrently
with, and may even be causally related to, the enjoyment of "power"
referred to in this narrative. First and immemorially, they continue locked in competitive relations with other men, the outcome
of which is linked—at least linked psychologically—to their erotic
success. (The self-will of the male member is, as Montaigne has
ruefully noted, not the same, for good or ill, as the personal will of
the man to whom it belongs.) Additionally, feminist reproaches now
threaten in advance the prospective glory even of the competitive
victors. Furthermore, affirmative-action programs are presently
redrawing the battle lines so that legitimate male winners may be
deprived of their winnings by bureaucratic intervention. And it re-

mains a fact that conscientiously "feminist" men who cede power imprudently may be despised for it after all.

The end result is that male power today feels, to many who "enjoy" it, like a bitter joke. And yet the bitter joke is still *about* male power and its thralldom, for all who are concerned. No doubt, as I have written elsewhere, "we all deserve each other."

5. This is Hegel's term for a way of approaching a situation that precludes getting a purchase on it. It prevents closure.

6. De Laclos, *Les Liaisons dangereuses*, the last letter.

Chapter Ten: *¡Venceremos!*

1. For these somewhat tardy recommendations I am indebted to Douglas Dubler, with whom I recently raised the question. More precisely, Dubler remarked to me that in similar circumstances he might have consulted with foreign mercenaries who knew the area and its hazards.

2. Any endorsements by me of books on political subjects would have to be provisional, but a full-length biography that supplies what looks to me like a gap-free chronology and very extensive documentation is Georgie Anna Geyer's *Guerrilla Prince: The Untold Story of Fidel Castro* (Boston: Little, Brown, 1991). On Castro's own account of his end of the Cuban missile crisis, see John Newhouse's article, "A Reporter at Large: Socialism or Death," in the *New Yorker*, April 27, 1992, pp. 52–83.

Chapter Eleven: Of Women and Philosophy

1. William Carlos Williams, *In the American Grain* (1925; reprint, New York: New Directions, 1956), p. 128.

2. "North America will be comparable with Europe only after the immeasurable space which that country presents to its inhabitants shall have been occupied, and the members of the political body shall have begun to be pressed back on each other." Thus Georg Wilhelm Friedrich Hegel, in *The Philosophy of History*, tr. J. Sibree (New York: Dover, 1956), p. 86. ("Mit Europa könnte Nordamerika erst verglichen werden, wenn der unermessliche Raum, den dieser Staat darbietet, ausgefüllt und die bürgerliche Gesellschaft in sich zurückgedrängt ware." Hegel, *Vorlesungen über die Philosophie der Geschichte*, with a foreword by Eduard Gans and Karl Hegel, *Samtliche Werke*, vol. 11, ed. Herman Glockner [Stuttgart: Fr. Frommann, 1961], pp. 128–29.) The Felix Meiner edition relegates this sentence and its context to an appendix.

3. As to poor man's Heidegger, the lines of influence have worked at least as powerfully the other way, apparently. Heidegger got a good part of it from Nietzsche, who had got a fair share from Emerson. For documentation, see George J. Stack, *Nietzsche and Emerson: An Elective Affinity* (Athens: University of Ohio Press, 1992).

4. The visit of André Philip remains unclear in my mind with respect to its dates. It may have taken place before the Warren report was issued, or else just after, which would place it right before I went to England on an entry permit stamped September 25, 1964.

Chapter Fifteen: Thought Reform

1. A scholarly, and philosophically informed, introduction to the panorama of ancient gnosticism, with striking comparisons to contemporary existentialism, is provided by Hans Jonas in *The Gnostic Religion: The Message of The Alien God and the Beginnings of Christianity* (Boston: Beacon, 1958; enlarged second edition, 1963). The apparent overlap between ancient texts now variously classified as "gnostic" and "hermetic" is acknowledged in Frances Yates's *Giordano Bruno and the Hermetic Tradition* (Chicago: University of Chicago Press, 1964). The politics of ancient Christian gnosticism, with its feminist strain, is reconstructed from clues in the Nag Hammadi texts in Elaine Pagels's *The Gnostic Gospels* (New York: Random House, 1979). And, despite its cheerful obtuseness about rabbinic Judaism's tenets and spirit, Giovanni Filoramo's *History of Gnosticism*, tr. Anthony Alcock (Cambridge, Mass.: Basil Blackwell, 1990), provides an engaging overview and update on the entire subject.

Chapter Sixteen: Framed

1. A more searching (if more carefully secular) look at the concept of a good story, and its counterfeits, can be found in Abigail L. Rosenthal, *A Good Look at Evil* (Philadelphia: Temple University Press, 1987), pp. 3–24.

Chapter Seventeen: Policía Internacional

1. Actually, that's not quite all. The process has something occult about it, though one doesn't like to talk in those terms. I am not a determinist. I love liberty. I respect human dignity. I revere the moral order. But it was a fact that she had taken me over. Her

consciousness had invaded mine and taken it prisoner. That is what I endured. That is what I remember.

2. In the communications of that season, there is also to be seen a decent concern for the welfare of my tormenter.

3. The shopkeepers had my mother's assurances too that they would be repaid if they kept careful accounts. Which they did, and they were.

Chapter Eighteen: Beginning Again

1. This is perhaps the place to express my gratitude to Robert Jay Lifton for his splendid op-ed piece, "On the Hearst Trial," which appeared in the *New York Times*, April 16, 1976. It was both a revelation and a deep relief to me to see the stages of the process I had been through so succinctly, clearly, and compassionately detailed in that article. It was the first time that I understood under what *category* my experience was to be classified.

2. The following are some titles from that period that I have found helpful: Robert Jay Lifton, *Thought Reform and the Psychology of Totalism: A Study of "Brainwashing" in China* (New York: Norton, 1961); Edgar H. Schein with Inge Schneier and Curtis H. Barker, *Coercive Persuasion: A Socio-Psychological Analysis of the "Brainwashing" of American Civilian Prisoners by the Chinese Communists* (New York: Norton, 1961); O. John Rogge, *Why Men Confess* (New York: Nelson, 1959).

3. What I must have had in mind here, as I reconstruct it now, is that the term "madness" involves those to whom it's applied in immediate loss of social power. While I doubt that I would have agreed with Michel Foucault that that's *all* there is to these distinctions, I understood that a person who looks like a gargoyle has lost social power. I understood that, and I was quite right, as far as that went.